QL ASSEMBLY LANGUAGE PROGRAMMING

QL Assembly Language Programming

Colin Opie

McGRAW-HILL Book Company (UK) Limited

London · New York · St Louis · San Francisco · Auckland · Bogotá
Guatemala · Hamburg · Johannesburg · Lisbon · Madrid
Mexico · Montreal · New Delhi · Panama · Paris · San Juan
São Paulo · Singapore · Sydney · Tokyo · Toronto

Published by
McGraw-HILL Book Company (UK) Limited
MAIDENHEAD · BERKSHIRE · ENGLAND

British Library Cataloging in Publication Data

Opie, Colin
    QL assembly language programming.
    1. Sinclair QL (Computer) – Programming
    2. Assembling (Electronic computers)
    I. Title
    001.64'2   QA76.8.S625

    ISBN 0-07-084777-0

Library of Congress Cataloging in Publication Data

Opie, Colin
    QL assembly language programming.

    Includes index
    1. Sinclair QL (Computer) – Programming.   2. Assembler language
    (Computer program language)
    I. Title.   II. Title: Q.L. assembly language programming.
    QA 76.8.S6216065   1984   001.64'2   84-21796
    ISBN 0-07-084777-0

12345 BBP 8654

CONTENTS

PREFACE

The microelectronic evolution recently spawned a uniquely cost
effective, yet inherently powerful, microcomputer system – the Sinclair
QL. This microcomputer is indeed unique, and certainly a 'first' in its
breed. Enclosed in the slender black light-weight case is a member of
the 68000 family of microprocessors (one of the most advanced processors
currently widely available). The QL provides true 32-bit processing, a
suite of specially designed state-of-the-art logic arrays, 128K of RAM,
a multi-tasking operating system kernel, two Microdrives for backup
storage, and a range of I/O facilities including local area networking
ports. What makes this system unique, apart from the actual electronics,
is the fact that it costs no more, and in many cases much less, than its
rival 8-bit microcomputers.

The Sinclair QL comes equipped with a powerful, and truly extensible,
'SuperBASIC'. One important feature of this extensibility is that 68000
machine code routines may be written and merged into SuperBASIC in order
to enlarge the variety of commands available. Of course, there is also
the option of writing whole application programs in 68000 code, hence
obtaining a maximum speed advantage during the running of the package.

This book is about 68000 assembly language programming on the Sinclair
QL. There are many good general texts on 68000 programming and there is
little point in reproducing such material here. The emphasis is
therefore: 'Assuming I have a detailed text on 68000 instructions and
their operation, how can I use the Sinclair QL to gain expertise and
create useful assembly language programs to run on it?' It is hoped that
such an emphasis has given rise to a vital and informative book that is
suitable for general programmers, industrial and educational training
institutions, and also for OEM design engineers, all of whom may come to
use the Sinclair QL. Even though detailed information on each of the
68000 instructions is not included, Chapters 1 and 2, and Appendix A,
will go a long way to meeting most needs in this area.

Such a text as this would not be complete unless it could provide
sound, practical experience of the theory presented. To this end a full
screen-orientated program editor and 68000 assembler/loader package has
been developed to complement this book. As will be seen from Part 4 of
this book (which describes in detail the operation of the software) the
package supports a full 68000 assembler development environment. The
actual assembler, for example, provides features normally found only in
rather more expensive minicomputer-based versions. The software is
available separately on a Microdrive cartridge. Another cartridge is
available which holds the source code for all the programs and major
subroutines listed or referred to in the text.

My sincere thanks to John Watson, Tom Blackall, Liz Nemecek, and Jenny Wright for their help in the production of this book. Special thanks go to Tony Tebby for his invaluable technical advice and support, without which this book could not have been written. As ever I remain totally grateful to my wife whose patience and support seem ever increasing.

Colin N. Opie
July 1984

ACKNOWLEDGEMENTS

The following names and trade marks are the property of SINCLAIR RESEARCH LIMITED, and are used by kind permission: QL, QDOS, Microdrive, ZX Microdrive, SuperBASIC, Microdrive cartridge, ZX, Spectrum, ZX Spectrum, ZX Net, QLUB.

The following names are registered trade marks of Psion Ltd.: Quill, QL Quill, Abacus, QL Abacus, Easel, QL Easel, Archive, QL Archive.

INTRODUCTION

'One of the pleasantest things in the
world is going a journey; ...'

William Hazlitt

In this book we are going to embark on a journey into the operating
environment of the Sinclair QL microcomputer. The excursion will hold
many new experiences for most travellers, and there is much to stretch
the imagination and inventiveness of everyone. The operating environment
of the Sinclair QL is based upon a kernel of procedures collectively
known as QDOS. In addition to QDOS there is a set of utility routines
which may be entered via well-defined vectors in ROM. These QDOS
procedures and general utilities provide the assembly language
programmer with a wealth of support ranging from simple character output
to floating point arithmetic. The main processor in the Sinclair QL is a
Motorola MC68008. This new generation 16-bit processor offers extremely
good architectural features. A direct, yet large, memory address space
is provided together with a highly consistent instruction set. This book
is about the use of this instruction set within the architecture of the
Sinclair QL.

The package tour

As this text is specifically aimed at the assembly language programmer
it makes sense to look at the general architecture of the 68000
processor, its addressing modes, and the operation of its instructions.
These topics will be covered in Part 1. A detailed discussion of each of
the 68000 instructions is not given for two reasons. First, such an
inclusion would make this text unnecessarily large and expensive.
Second, there are a number of suitable texts readily available (e.g.,
Kane,G., Hawkins,D., and Leventhal,L.: '68000 Assembly Language
Programming', Osborne/McGraw-Hill, 1981). The emphasis in the
appropriate chapters of this book is to provide a concise 68000
companion.

Part 2, comprising Chapters 3 to 8, describes in detail the QDOS and
utility procedures. These procedures are the building blocks for the
assembly language programmer's own application programs. Chapter 8
describes the options available when actually loading and running a
machine code program, as well as how machine code procedures may be
added to SuperBASIC in order to extend the language.

Part 3 contains four chapters of program examples. Chapters 9 and 10
give examples of stand-alone executable programs. Chapter 9 contains a
number of utility programs and Chapter 10 deals with graphics. Chapters
11 and 12 give examples of programs which extend the SuperBASIC
language. Chapter 11 contains some general utility procedures and

1

Chapter 12 concentrates on Microdrive file handling. The programs given are full implementations and useful, not simply as utilities, but also as examples of 'how to get the code loaded and executed'.

Part 4 describes the full screen editor and assembler/locator package used to create the assembly language programs given in Part 3. The programs within the package are easy to use and provide a professional approach to assembly language programming on the Sinclair QL. Finally, a number of appendices exist to provide quick reference guides for commonly required information.

Getting started

Exactly how you use this book will depend upon your current expertise in assembly language programming. It is assumed that you have a basic understanding of the techniques of assembly language programming, and are familiar with terms such as registers, addressing modes, stack pointers, and so on. If you already write a fair amount of assembly language code for some other processor (e.g., Z80 or 6502), you will be in a good position to start programming your Sinclair QL very soon. For those of you who already know 68000 assembly language, Part 2 of the book will probably be your starting point.

If you do know the assembly language of some other processor but are unfamiliar with the 68000, Chapters 1 and 2 and Appendix A will give you a good insight into what the 68000 is capable of. As mentioned previously, another suitable text will be required should you desire to look at detailed accounts of each of the 68000 instructions. Once you are happy with the overall design and the capabilities of the 68000, full use can be made of Part 2 in order to actually write, load, and execute an assembly language program.

Whetting the appetite

Assembly language programming on the QL is best performed using a proper assembler package. Programs developed in this way would normally be merged into SuperBASIC as an extension, or run as a separate machine code program by using the EXEC command (see Chapter 8). Very simple machine code programs can be loaded into memory and accessed through the CALL command, this being the approach adopted here simply to whet your appetite a little!

Figure 1 is a listing (output by the McGraw-Hill assembler described in Part 4) of an assembly language version of the SuperBASIC RECOL command. This command accepts a screen channel number followed by eight colour parameters:

RECOL #n, c1, c2, c3, c4, c5, c6, c7, c8

Each colour parameter defines the new pixel colour for the current respective colour: black, blue, red, magenta, green, cyan, yellow, and white. To rewrite this procedure in assembly language for use with the

CALL statement, it is necessary to know how parameters are passed across. Chapter 8 shows that up to 13 parameters may be passed, and that they will be passed over as long-words in the 68000 registers D1 to D7, and A0 to A5 (in that order). Our example requires nine parameters and they will, therefore, be passed over in registers D1 to D7, and A0 to A1. It is also necessary to know how the respective QDOS routine should be set up. The routine that we are interested in is SD.RECOL (TRAP#3, D0=$26). A full description of this QDOS procedure will be found in Chapter 6. Let us now see how the program in Fig.1 evolved.

```
                          *H Demo Program
                          ;
00030000                            org    $30000
                          ;
                          ; A short assembly language demonstration
                          ; program. Used in conjunction with SuperBASIC.
                          ; Copyright (c) 1984 McGraw-Hill(UK)
                          ;
                          ;
00030000 45FA0036         demo:   lea     data(pc),a2      ;Find buffer
00030004 15420000                 move.b  d2,0(a2)         ;Store table
00030008 15430001                 move.b  d3,1(a2)
0003000C 15440002                 move.b  d4,2(a2)
00030010 15450003                 move.b  d5,3(a2)
00030014 15460004                 move.b  d6,4(a2)
00030018 15470005                 move.b  d7,5(a2)
0003001C 3408                      move.w  a0,d2
0003001E 15420006                 move.b  d2,6(a2)
00030022 3409                      move.w  a1,d2
00030024 15420007                 move.b  d2,7(a2)
00030028 224A                      move.l  a2,a1            ;Set data ptr.
0003002A 363C0000                 move.w  #0,d3            ;Timeout=0
0003002E 2041                      move.l  d1,a0            ;Channel
00030030 103C0026                 move.b  #$26,d0          ;RECOLOUR
00030034 4E43                      trap    #3
00030036 4E75                      rts
                          ;
                          ;Workspace
                          ;
00030038 00               data:   defb    0
                                  defs    20
                          ;
                          end
Symbols:

00030038 DATA        00030000 START

0000 error(s)  detected
```

Figure 1 Assembly language version of RECOL

The QDOS procedure requires the eight colour parameters to be set up in a byte table. This means that we have to transfer the contents of the appropriate registers to a small data area. To do this we find out where the data area exists physically for this particular program, and then use byte indexed addressing to perform the transfers. But you say: 'We know where the data area is; it's at $00030038'. In a sense this is true because the program ORG statement has forced this to be the case, but most machine code programs in the QL need to be relocatable. The program shown in Fig.2 is a SuperBASIC program which uses the above machine code routine. When requesting space for the machine code (by using the RESPR command) we do not know, in advance, where SuperBASIC will allocate it. In the example shown we simply asked for 70 bytes to be reserved, and SuperBASIC returned the base address (in variable 'mc') of such an area. Our machine code must work, then, wherever it is put! The LEA instruction found at the beginning of the assembly language program is being used in its 'Program Counter Relative with Displacement' mode, and will store the true absolute position of the beginning of the data area into the designated address register. A detailed discussion of this addressing mode, together with the appropriate assembler syntax (for the McGraw-Hill assembler) will be found in Chapter 2.

Once all the colour parameters have been stored in the data table, it is a simple matter of setting up the appropriate registers for the QDOS call and then executing the TRAP#3 instruction. A final RTS instruction will effect a return to SuperBASIC.

Now let us look at the SuperBASIC program, shown in Fig.2. The program starts by drawing three circles of varying colours. Two of the circles are filled and the third circle is simply an outline. The next operation performed is the storing of the machine code routine into a reserved area of memory. The program is 56 bytes long and therefore a reserved area of 70 bytes is more than sufficient (because the data buffer need only be eight bytes long). The DATA statements hold the denary values corresponding to the hexadecimal instruction opcodes output by the assembler (shown in Fig.1, second column from left). Once this initialization has occurred a small indefinite loop is entered. The loop causes the screen display of circles to invert its colours every 10 seconds.

In SuperBASIC normal program output goes to channel #1. Our machine code subroutine requires the channel 'ID' to be passed over as the first argument in the CALL statement parameter list. You will notice that this parameter, given in lines 170 and 190, is not unity! The SuperBASIC channel numbers have no direct correspondence to the QDOS channel ID values. If no reopening of screen channels is performed the actual correspondence between SuperBASIC screen channels and QDOS channel IDs is as follows:

SuperBASIC #	QDOS ID	
	HEX.	DENARY
0	$00000	0
1	$10001	65537
2	$20002	131074

It is important to remember that the QDOS IDs will alter if you have reopened a screen channel (e.g., by performing OPEN#1,...). Standard

4

practice for assembly language programming on the QL would be for particular channel IDs to be determined by use of a suitable algorithm. Chapter 11 contains an appropriate routine.

```
100 REMark Introductory Demonstration Program
120 REMark Copyright (c) 1984 McGraw-Hill(UK)
130 REMark MAIN PROGRAM
140 display_colours
150 mc=RESPR(70): store_mcode
160 PAUSE 200
170 CALL mc,65537,7,6,5,4,3,2,1,0
180 PAUSE 200
190 CALL mc,65537,0,1,2,3,4,5,6,7
200 GO TO 160
210 :
220 REMark ROUTINES
230 DEFine PROCedure display_colours
240 INK 0: FILL 1: CIRCLE 30,60,15
250 INK 4: FILL 0: CIRCLE 60,60,15
260 INK 6: FILL 1: CIRCLE 45,30,15
270 FILL 0
280 END DEFine
290 :
300 DEFine PROCedure store_mcode
310 RESTORE 350
320 FOR c = 0 TO 55: READ n: POKE mc+c,n
330 END DEFine
340 :
350 DATA 69,250,0,54,21,66,0,0,21,67,0,1
360 DATA 21,68,0,2,21,69,0,3,21,70,0,4
370 DATA 21,71,0,5,52,8,21,66,0,6,52,9
380 DATA 21,66,0,7,34,74,54,60,0,0,32,65
390 DATA 16,60,0,38,78,67,78,117
```

Figure 2 Demonstration SuperBASIC program

It is worth stressing that assembly language programming on the QL is best performed using a proper assembler package. Programs should normally be merged into SuperBASIC as extensions to the language, or run as separate machine code programs (jobs) alongside QDOS; either by using the SuperBASIC EXEC command, or by using QDOS job creation/activation procedures. The SuperBASIC CALL command is simple, but very limited, and should only be used for small demonstration/test routines, or for performing the initial linkage of an extended set of SuperBASIC procedures.

5

PART 1 The 68000 MPU

1   THE 68000 PROCESSOR

At the heart of the Sinclair QL there is a member of the Motorola 68000 family of processors; the Motorola 68008. From a software point of view the 68008 is a full 68000 implementation. Its major difference is that the device package is smaller, and only caters for an 8-bit data bus. An effect of this is that the actual throughput of the processor is reduced, due to overheads in memory addressing. This particular detail should not deter the QL assembly language programmer, who still has at his disposal one of the most powerful state-of-the-art 16/32-bit processors currently available. Also, the 68008 only has 20 of its maximum 32 address lines brought out to its package pins. This means that the addressing range is limited to 1 Megabyte (if you can call 1 Megabyte a 'limitation'!). Before going on to see how this processor may be used within the QL, let us look first at the general features of the 68000.

1.1 Operating modes

Two distinct operating modes are available with the 68000 processor. The two modes are called 'user' mode, and 'supervisor' mode. A flag in the status register will determine which state the processor is in at any one time. Certain instructions (e.g., STOP) cannot be executed while the 68000 is in user mode, and a privilege violation exception process will be initiated by the processor if such an execution is attempted.

When the processor is in user mode, the user stack pointer (USP) will be used by stack related operations. Conversely, the supervisor stack pointer (SSP) will be used when the processor is in supervisor mode.

1.2 68000 registers

The 68000 has eighteen 32-bit registers and one 16-bit status register (see Fig.1.1). The 32-bit register set is divided up into eight data registers, seven address registers, two stack pointers, and a program counter.

DATA REGISTERS

The eight data registers are labelled D0 to D7. Data operations using these registers may be bit, BCD (nibble), byte, word (16-bit), or long-word (32-bit) orientated. Within instructions that permit a data register to be one or more of its operands, any data register may be used. In effect this means that any data register may be used as an accumulator, index register, general purpose register, or loop counter. This is an extremely flexible approach to processor register allocation, and is one of the reasons why the 68000 is so easy to program efficiently.

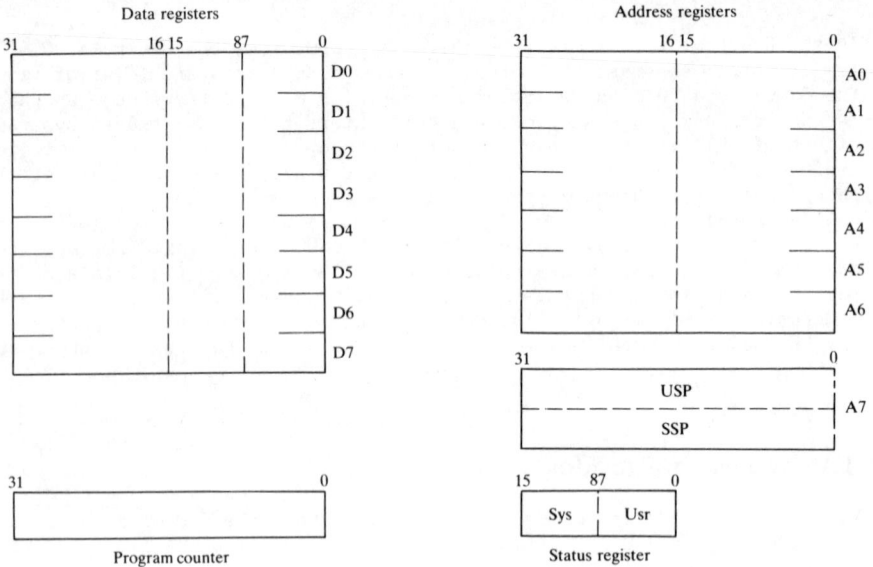

Figure 1.1 68000 internal registers

ADDRESS REGISTERS AND STACK POINTERS

The seven address registers are labelled A0 to A6. The two stack pointers are also treated as address registers and are both labelled A7. Alternative mnemonics for the two stack pointers are USP (user stack pointer) and SSP (supervisor stack pointer). A flag in the status register will determine which state the processor is in (i.e., user or supervisor) and the respective stack pointer will be used accordingly. Operations using the address registers are limited to the types word (16-bit) and long-word (32-bit). In other words, address registers cannot be the source or destination for bit, byte, or logical operations. If an address register is the destination operand, the operation will always be long-word, and the source will be sign extended, if necessary, before use. The address registers are normally used for manipulating and holding addresses rather than data. They may be used also as index registers.

Note that, because the stack pointers are in fact the address register

8

A7, any legal addressing mode for instructions using address registers will also be legal for the stack pointers. This means that stack pointer register addressing modes for the 68000 are much more versatile than for many other processors.

STATUS REGISTER

The 68000 status register is a 16-bit register split into two distinct bytes. The two bytes correspond to the system status byte (bits 8 to 15) and the user status byte (bits 0 to 7). The system status byte can only be modified when the processor is in supervisor mode. Two mnemonics are allocated to the status register. First, there is CCR, and this refers to the low order user byte of condition codes. Any instruction using this mnemonic will refer to eight bits of data only. Second, there is SR, and this refers to the whole status register. Any instruction using this mnemonic, in order to modify the contents of the status register, will only be executed if the 68000 is in supervisor mode.

Figure 1.2 shows the allocation of flags within the status word. The Carry (C), Zero (Z), Negative (N), and Overflow (V) bits are standard condition flags. There is also an Extend (X) bit flag which is always set to the same state as the Carry flag, if it is affected by any particular instruction. The Extend flag is used for multi-precision arithmetic operations. Chapter 2 describes the relevance of these flags for instructions.

The three least significant bits of the system status byte are used as the interrupt disable mask (IDM) for the 68000. Seven prioritized levels of interrupt are catered for, and each priority interrupt causes execution to be routed through an interrupt vector. The mask in the status register specifies the range of interrupts which are to be ignored. If, for example, the mask is set to binary 011 (3), interrupts 1 to 3 will be ignored by the processor.

Note that the 68008 only has three levels of interrupt (i.e., 2, 5, and 7). On the QL, a level 5 interrupt is transitory and will always generate a level 7 interrupt (non-maskable) within 20 ms.

The Supervisor flag (S) determines whether or not the 68000 is running in supervisor mode. If the bit is set (i.e., 1), the processor will be in supervisor mode. Last, but far from least, is the Trace (T) flag. This flag enables the processor to be run in single-step mode, and permits system debuggers to obtain control over instruction execution.

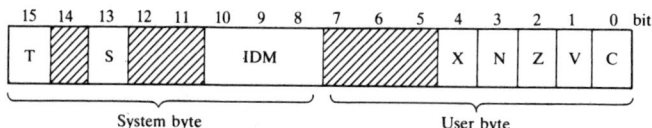

Figure 1.2 68000 status register

1.3 Use of memory

Up to 1 Megabyte of memory may be directly accessed by the 68008. A 20-bit address bus is required to address this amount of memory. Addresses can, therefore, be represented by five digit hexadecimal numbers in the range $00000 to $FFFFF. To access a byte of data in memory, any one of the possible addresses may be used. Accessing a word (i.e., 16 bits) or a long-word (i.e., 32 bits) of memory is a little more restrictive. Words or long-words can only be addressed at even addresses; that is, $00000, $00002, and so on up to $FFFFE.

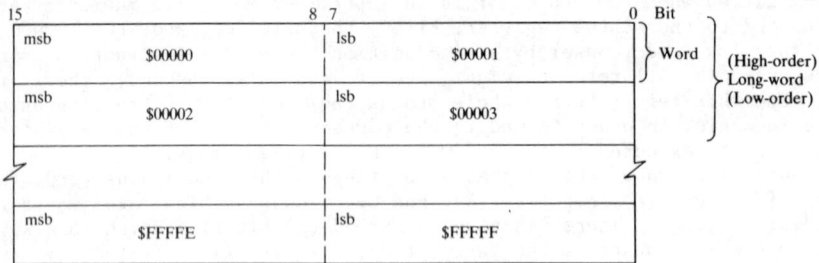

Figure 1.3 Memory usage

In the case of word addressing the most significant byte of the word will be found in the even address, and the least significant byte of the word will be found in the following odd address (see Fig.1.3). Long-word addressing is similar to word addressing in that it involves the equivalent of two word accesses. The high-order word of the long-word will be found first, followed by the low-order word of the long-word.

1.4 Moving between supervisor and user modes

To know that the 68000 has two modes of operation is not particularly useful unless you know how to swap between them. When the 68000 is reset (e.g., at power-on) the bottom eight bytes of memory are loaded into the supervisor stack pointer and the program counter, and instruction execution commences in supervisor mode.

Because we start off in supervisor mode the first thing we need to know how to do is enter user mode. The task is not onerous! Any instruction, which is capable of affecting the state of the S flag in the status register, also has the ability to transfer execution to user mode. An example is the RTE (ReTurn from Exception) instruction. This instruction will load the status register with the word on the stack, and load the program counter with the following two words on the stack. If the word loaded into the status register reset the S flag, user mode will be entered. If the S flag remains set, supervisor mode will continue.

Once you are in user mode, the method of getting back into supervisor mode is to cause some form of exception processing. Exception processing will occur under a number of conditions:

1. Addressing violation. A word or long-word was addressed on an odd byte boundary.
2. Privileged instruction violation. A privileged instruction was executed.
3. Illegal or unimplemented opcode. The instruction executed was not a legal instruction.
4. TRAP instruction execution. All TRAP instructions are treated as internal exceptions.
5. TRAPV, CHK, DIVS, DIVU exception error condition has occurred (e.g., divide by zero).
6. Trace active. If the T flag in the status register is set, exception processing will be performed after each user instruction is executed.
7. External interrupt request. One of seven (n.b., three on the QL) prioritized interrupts has been received.
8. Reset. The 68000 processor has physically been reset.
9. Bus error. An error has occurred on the physical address/data bus of the 68000 processor.

The last two of these exception processes (reset and bus error) are clearly not of much use to the applications programmer! The most common way of entering supervisor mode from a program is through the use of a TRAP instruction.

2 68000 INSTRUCTIONS AND ADDRESSING MODES

In 1971 Intel introduced the 4004, which had 46 instructions. Later on, Intel came out with the 8008. This had 48 instructions. In 1973 the Intel 8080 appeared with 78 basic instruction types, giving well over 200 instructions. The year 1974 saw the release of the Motorola 6800, and within a further couple of years the Zilog Z80 processor appeared with 158 basic instruction types and around 700 instructions. The dawn of the 1980s saw the release of the 68000. This processor has 56 basic instruction mnemonics and over a thousand instructions!

A decade of microelectronic research has clearly produced some amazing achievements. One of the most interesting points, as far as the 68000 is concerned, is that the number of instructions available has increased greatly, with only a minor increase in the number of instruction mnemonics. This has important consequences. First, the instruction set is not hard to learn. Second, the instructions must be capable of multiple addressing modes, of which the 68000 has 14. Additionally, the 68000 has the ability to deal with five basic data types. It is the merging of these basic instruction mnemonics, addressing modes, and data types that give the 68000 its large, yet simple to learn, instruction repertoire.

In this chapter we will look at the basic instructions that are available, together with the addressing modes which the instructions may variably use. Only an overview is presented, for reasons already mentioned (see Introduction). The emphasis is toward a companion to the 68000 so that anyone, with some knowledge of assembly language programming, can quickly assimilate the capabilities of the processor.

When discussing these topics it becomes important to know how the resultant instructions are actually presented to an assembler. Assembler packages vary in the form of syntax that they will allow, and therefore descriptions in this chapter will relate to the McGraw-Hill assembler documented in Chapter 14. This particular assembler was used to create all the example programs given in this book. Clearly if some other assembler package is used there will almost certainly be some syntax changes required.

In particular it will be noticed, at least by those of you who have looked also at a detailed text on the 68000 using Motorola nomenclature, that there appear to be less instruction types described (e.g., ADDI is not listed). The McGraw-Hill assembler is a full implementation and, therefore, all instructions do exist; it is simply that certain instructions, listed by Motorola as being variations, have been included here as a natural member of the parent instruction. For example, Motorola's ADDI instruction is simply an ADD instruction using immediate data as the source operand.

2.1 Addressing modes

Six basic addressing modes in the 68000 give rise to 14 actual modes. The modes of addressing are shown in Fig.2.1, together with the appropriate assembler syntax. Not every addressing mode can be used with all instructions, though the homogeneity is remarkable.

MODE	SYNTAX
Implied	
Register	SR, CCR, USP, PC
Immediate	
Immediate	#n
Quick immediate	#b
Absolute	
Short	a16
Long	a32
Register Direct	
Data register	Dn
Address register direct	An
Register Indirect	
Address register	(An)
Postincrement	(An)+
Predecrement	-(An)
Address register with offset	d16(An)
Register with index and offset	d8(An,i)
Program Counter Relative	
Address register with offset	d16(PC)
Register with index and offset	d8(PC,i)

Notes:

b = 3, 4 or 8 bits	i	= An or Dn
n = 8,16, or 32 bits	An	= address register
d8 = 8 bit offset	Dn	= data register
d16 = 16 bit offset	PC	= current location
a16 = 16 bit address	SR	= status register
a32 = 32 bit address	CCR	= condition codes
	USP	= user stack ptr

Figure 2.1 68000 addressing modes

Perhaps the major deviation is with respect to address registers as operands. When these registers are used within direct addressing modes, bit or byte data types are never permitted. There are also some instructions which are severely limited in their choice of operands. For example, the Bcc (Branch) and DBcc (Decrement and Branch) instructions may only have an absolute address as their operand. This absolute address is normally specified in terms of a label. The value entered into the instruction opcodes will be an offset, so that the instructions provide relative addressing.

Note that there is also what is termed inherent addressing. Instructions using this form of addressing mode require no operands. There are six instructions which fall into this category (viz., NOP, RESET, RTE, RTR, RTS, and TRAPV).

PROGRAM COUNTER RELATIVE ADDRESSING

A special mention must be given to the way in which the assembler will handle this form of addressing. In principle, program (counter) relative addressing modes are the same as address register indirect with offset (or offset and index), and the overall syntax is therefore the same. The difference, of course, is that the program counter (PC) is being used instead of an address register for the indirection.

However, the major purpose in using this particular form of addressing is to obtain position independent code. The offsets given to the instruction are, therefore, normally labels within the program. Clearly the assembler should not allocate the value of the label as being the offset; rather it should allocate the offset required to get from where the program counter is at the moment to where the label is. As such, the assembler will manipulate the instructions in one of two ways. First, if the offset expression starts with an integer, the absolute value of the expression will be allocated as the offset:

Opcode	Instruction
4BFA1040	lea $1040(PC),a5

Second, if the offset expression starts with a symbol, the symbol will be treated as a label (whether it was or not; the assembler has no way of knowing) and the true offset will be allocated:

Address	Opcode	Instruction
282AE	44FA0012	move lab(PC),CCR

The actual value of the symbol (label) 'lab' is $282C2, and $0012 is the offset required to reach it from the given instruction.

Note that program counter relative addressing modes can never be used as destination operands.

SOURCE AND DESTINATION OPERANDS

Instructions for the 68000 may require no operands at all, a single source or destination operand, both a source operand and a destination operand, or (in one case only - BTST) two source operands. Whenever two operands are required, the source operand is always specified first, and separated from the destination operand by a comma (,). For example:

1. **No operand:**   rts
2. **Source operand:**   clr (a0)
3. **Source and destination operand:** divs (a1)+,d1

The result of any operation involving two operands will be stored in the destination operand effective address, if this is pertinent. Source operand effective address contents will not be changed.

This declaration order for the operands is normally very helpful and readable. An exception to this is in the CMP instruction. For example, 'CMP.L D1,D2' compares D2 against D1. If D1 is less than D2, this comparison will yield the condition GT (greater than; signed) or HI (higher; unsigned).

2.2 Condition codes

In the following descriptions of the 68000 instructions there are three instructions (Bcc, DBcc, and Scc) which use a set of conditional tests. The tests are given 'one/two character' mnemonics and the full instruction mnemonic consists of the above names with 'cc' replaced by the test mnemonic (e.g., BHI, BF, DBEQ, SNE, and so on). Each test produces a true or false result depending on the state of given condition flags in the 68000 CCR register. The tests, their mnemonics, and their interpretation, are as follows:

Mnemonic	Test	Interpretation
T	1	true (always)
F	0	false (always)
HI	not(C).not(Z)	higher (unsigned)
LS	C+Z	less than or same (unsigned)
CC	not(C)	carry clear (unsigned)
CS	C	carry set (unsigned)
NE	not(Z)	not equal
EQ	Z	equal
VC	not(V)	overflow clear
VS	V	overflow set
PL	not(N)	plus
MI	N	minus
GE	not(N xor V)	greater than or equal (signed)
LT	N xor V	less than (signed)
GT	not(Z+(N xor V))	greater than
LE	Z+(N xor V)	less than or equal

Some of the above mnemonics have alternative mnemonics, in order to improve their readability under given instances (see Sec.2.4).

2.3 Condition code flag handling

The condition code flags (X, N, V, Z, and C) are manipulated, at various times and in various ways, by the instruction set of the 68000. The handling of these flags may seem a little irregular, and indeed it is, but the irregularity is not some strange quirk of the processor; rather it is a positive phenomenon. In general, the condition codes are set according to the value being sent to the destination operand. This is also true of the operand in the TST instruction and the second operand in the CMP instruction, even though these 'destination' operands are not altered. A near general exception to this rule is in the use of address registers as destination operands. In this case the condition codes are not altered. This enables the adjustment of stack pointers, and the calculation of addresses to be performed without wiping out condition flags set by a previous operation. However, note that the condition codes are set when an address register is the 'destination' register of a CMP instruction (it would be a poor state of affairs if they were not!).

The handling of the Z flag, in particular, is even more variable. The extended operations (ABCD, ADDX, NEGX, SBCD, and SUBX) cause the Z flag to be cleared if the result is non-zero, or left alone in all other cases. This means that at the end of a series of extended operations the flag will only be set if all the results were zero. For bit operations (BCHG, BCLR, BSET, BTST, and TAS) the Z flag is set according to the state of the specified bit **before** the operation.

2.4 Alternative mnemonics

A set of alternative mnemonics exists within the assembler to aid the programmer both in terms of style and readability. First is the mnemonic for 'exclusive-or' operations. There are two widely used mnemonics for this instruction and both are supported:

Standard	Alternative
EOR	XOR

Only the mnemonic EOR is listed in the following descriptions of the 68000 instructions.

Second, there is the common confusion, especially with processors which cater for signed and unsigned arithmetic, as to the true interpretation of the 'carry-clear' and 'carry-set' conditional statements. As such the assembler provides the following:

Standard	Alternative
BCC, BCS	BHS, BLO
DBCC, DBCS	DBHS, DBLO
SCC, SCS	SHS, SLO

The mnemonic part 'HS' stands for 'higher or same', and 'LO' stands for 'lower'. They differ from the 'greater or equal' (GE) and 'less than' (LT) mnemonics in that they refer to conditions set after an unsigned operation.

2.5 68000 instructions

There are 56 basic instructions for the 68000 processor. The assembler allocates a further seven variations, bringing the total to 63 instruction mnemonics. Each instruction mnemonic is discussed briefly giving, amongst other things, details of its addressing modes. The instructions are covered in alphabetical order for quick reference. Appendix A contains a summary of the instructions, showing their effect upon the CCR flags.

References will be found to items called data qualifiers. These are qualifiers that can be given to certain instructions, which specify what type of data size is to be used. For example, let us look at the MOVE instruction. We can move bytes (8 bits), words (16 bits) or long-words (32 bits). The same MOVE instruction mnemonic is used in all three cases; it is the qualifier which determines the actual instruction operation. This gives rise to the following three forms:

MOVE.B   MOVE.W   MOVE.L

The qualifier '.L', and the additional qualifier '.S', may be found also when looking at instructions that use a label as their operand (e.g., BSR - branch to subroutine). In this context, '.L' stands for long, and '.S' for short. A label addressed as being short must be within +127 bytes or -128 bytes of the current program counter position. A long label can be up to within +32767 or -32768 bytes of the current position. Short branch instructions use less bytes of opcode, and therefore it is worth specifying them as such if you know a label is in range but that it is as yet unknown to the assembler (i.e., because it is a forward reference during pass 1). There is no need to specify a qualifier for backward references because the assembler will always use a short addressing mode wherever possible.

ABCD ADD DECIMAL WITH EXTEND

Addressing modes: -(An),-(An)
                                Dn,Dn

Flags affected: X N Z V C

Privileged instruction: no

Byte data size only. Adds two BCD digits in source byte, with extend, to two BCD digits in destination byte.

ADD ADD

Addressing modes:

#n	
a16	
a32	
Dn	
(An)	
(An)+	,Dn
-(An)	,An
d16(An)	
d8(An,i)	
d16(PC)	
d8(PC,i)	

	a16
	a32
#n,	(An)
Dn,	(An)+
	-(An)
	d16(An)
	d8(An,i)

An,An
An,Dn

Flags affected: X N Z V C

Privileged instruction: no

Register An may not be used as destination for byte operations. Adds source to destination.

ADDQ ADD QUICK

Addressing modes:

#b,
$\left\{\begin{array}{l} \text{Dn} \\ \text{An} \\ \text{a16} \\ \text{a32} \\ \text{(An)} \\ \text{(An)+} \\ \text{-(An)} \\ \text{d16(An)} \\ \text{d8(An,i)} \end{array}\right.$

Flags affected: X N Z V C

Privileged instruction: no

Register An may not be used as destination for byte operations. Word and long-word operations are identical. Adds data (1 to 8) to destination.

ADDX ADD WITH EXTEND

Addressing modes: -(An),-(An)
                             Dn,Dn

Flags affected: X N Z V C

Privileged instruction: no

Adds source, with extend, to destination.

AND LOGICAL AND

Addressing modes:
$\left.\begin{array}{l} \text{\#n} \\ \text{a16} \\ \text{a32} \\ \text{Dn} \\ \text{(An)} \\ \text{(An)+} \\ \text{-(An)} \\ \text{d16(An)} \\ \text{d8(An,i)} \\ \text{d16(PC)} \\ \text{d8(PC,i)} \end{array}\right\}$,Dn

$$\left.\begin{array}{c}\text{\#n,}\\\text{Dn,}\end{array}\right\}\begin{array}{l}\text{a16}\\\text{a32}\\\text{(An)}\\\text{(An)+}\\\text{-(An)}\\\text{d16(An)}\\\text{d8(An,i)}\end{array}$$

#n,SR

Flags affected: N Z V C

Privileged instruction: no, except for AND.W #n,SR

Register SR may not be used with long-word operations. CCR is least
significant byte of SR, and accessed by 'AND.B #n,SR'. Logically ANDs
all bits of source with corresponding bits of destination.

ASL   ARITHMETIC SHIFT LEFT

Addressing modes: a16   (no data qualifier)
                          a32
                          (An)
                          (An)+
                          -(An)
                          d16(An)
                          d8(An,i)

                          #b,Dn   (data qualifier used)
                          Dn,Dn

Flags affected: X N Z V C

Privileged instruction: no

Data size is always word. Destination shift is always by one bit when no
qualifier is present, or by a count of up to 63. An immediate shift
count can be given of 0 to 7 only. Zero signifies a shift of eight
places. Sets V flag if sign bit changes at any time during shift.

ASR   ARITHMETIC SHIFT RIGHT

Addressing modes: a16   (no data qualifier)
                          a32
                          (An)
                          (An)+
                          -(An)
                          d16(An)
                          d8(An,i)

```
                    #b,Dn              (data qualifier used)
                    Dn,Dn
```

Flags affected: X N Z V C

Privileged instruction: no

Data size is always word. Destination shift is always by one bit when no
qualifier is present, or by a count of up to 63. An immediate shift
count can be given of 0 to 7 only. Zero signifies a shift of eight
places. Sign bit is replicated.

Bcc   BRANCH CONDITIONALLY

Addressing modes: label

Flags affected: none

Privileged instruction: no

Label may be declared short (.S) or long (.L). Byte or word offsets are
used.

BCHG   BIT TEST AND CHANGE

Addressing modes:
```
                                    a16
                                    a32
                                    Dn
                    #n,             (An)
                    Dn,             (An)+
                                    -(An)
                                    d16(An)
                                    d8(An,i)
```

Flags affected: Z

Privileged instruction: no

Byte operations only, except when data register is destination. If Dn is
destination then data size is long—word. Tests (setting Z flag) and then
inverts the specified bit of destination.

BCLR BIT TEST AND CLEAR

Addressing modes:

$$\left.\begin{matrix} \\ \\ \\ \#n, \\ Dn, \\ \\ \\ \\ \end{matrix}\right\{ \quad \begin{matrix} a16 \\ a32 \\ Dn \\ (An) \\ (An)+ \\ -(An) \\ d16(An) \\ d8(An,i) \end{matrix}$$

Flags affected: Z

Privileged instruction: no

Byte operations only, except when data register is destination. If Dn is destination then data size is long-word. Tests (setting Z flag) and then clears the specified bit of destination to zero.

BRA BRANCH ALWAYS

Addressing modes: label

Flags affected: none

Privileged instruction: no

Label may be declared short (.S) or long (.L). Byte or word offsets are used.

BSET BIT TEST AND SET

Addressing modes:

$$\left.\begin{matrix} \\ \\ \\ \#n, \\ Dn, \\ \\ \\ \\ \end{matrix}\right\{ \quad \begin{matrix} a16 \\ a32 \\ Dn \\ (An) \\ (An)+ \\ -(An) \\ d16(An) \\ d8(An,i) \end{matrix}$$

Flags affected: Z

Privileged instruction: no

Byte operations only, except when data register is destination. If Dn is destination then data size is long-word. Tests (setting Z flag) and then sets the specified bit of destination to one.

BSR BRANCH TO SUBROUTINE

Addressing modes: label

Flags affected: none

Privileged instruction: no

Label may be declared short (.S) or long (.L). Pushes address of next instruction and then branches by a byte or word offset.

BTST BIT TEST

Addressing modes:

$$
\text{\#n,} \quad \text{Dn,} \quad \left\{ \begin{array}{l} \text{a16} \\ \text{a32} \\ \text{Dn} \\ \text{(An)} \\ \text{(An)+} \\ \text{-(An)} \\ \text{d16(An)} \\ \text{d8(An,i)} \\ \text{d16(PC)} \\ \text{d8(PC,i)} \end{array} \right.
$$

Flags affected: Z

Privileged instruction: no

Byte operations only, except when data register is destination. If Dn is destination then data size is long-word. Tests (setting Z flag) the specified bit.

CHK CHECK REGISTER AGAINST BOUNDS

Addressing modes:

$$
\left. \begin{array}{l} \text{\#n} \\ \text{a16} \\ \text{a32} \\ \text{Dn} \\ \text{(An)} \\ \text{(An)+} \\ \text{-(An)} \\ \text{d16(An)} \\ \text{d8(An,i)} \\ \text{d16(PC)} \\ \text{d8(PC,i)} \end{array} \right\} \quad \text{,Dn}
$$

Flags affected: N Z V C

Privileged instruction: no

Data size is word only. Will generate an exception if Dn is less than zero or greater than operand contents.

CLR CLEAR OPERAND

Addressing modes: a16
                              a32
                              Dn
                              (An)
                              (An)+
                              -(An)
                              d16(An)
                              d8(An,i)

Flags affected: N Z V C

Privileged instruction: no

Operand data size is cleared to zero.

CMP COMPARE

Addressing modes: #n
                              a16
                              a32
                              Dn
                              (An)
                              (An)+   ⎫ ,Dn
                              -(An)   ⎬ ,An
                              d16(An)
                              d8(An,i)
                              d16(PC)
                              d8(PC,i)

                                            a16
                                            a32
                                            (An)
                              #n,   (An)+
                                            -(An)
                                            d16(An)
                                            d8(An,i)

                              An,An
                              An,Dn

Flags affected: N Z V C

Privileged instruction: no

Register An may not be used as destination for byte operations. Subtracts source from destination but does not store the result.

CMPM COMPARE MEMORY

Addressing modes: (An)+,(An)+

Flags affected: N Z V C

Privileged instruction: no

Subtracts source from destination but does not store the result. Not an extended operation.

DBcc DECREMENT AND BRANCH CONDITIONALLY

Addressing modes: Dn,label

Flags affected: none

Privileged instruction: no

If condition is not met, data register word is decremented, then if result is not -1, branches by word offset. (DBT is a 4-byte no-op).

DBRA DECREMENT AND BRANCH ALWAYS

Addressing modes: Dn,label

Flags affected: none

Privileged instruction: no

Decrements data register word and then branches by word offset.

DIVS   SIGNED DIVIDE

Addressing modes:

```
                #n
                a16
                a32
                Dn
                (An)
                (An)+         ,Dn
                -(An)
                d16(An)
                d8(An,i)
                d16(PC)
                d8(PC,i)
```

Flags affected: N Z V C

Privileged instruction: no

Divides destination long—word by source word. Quotient is put in low
order word, remainder (same sign as dividend!) is put in high order
word.

DIVU   UNSIGNED DIVIDE

Addressing modes:

```
                #n
                a16
                a32
                Dn
                (An)
                (An)+         ,Dn
                -(An)
                d16(An)
                d8(An,i)
                d16(PC)
                d8(PC,i)
```

Flags affected: N Z V C

Privileged instruction: no

Divides destination long—word by source word. Quotient is put in low
order word, remainder in high order word.

26

EOR EXCLUSIVE OR

Addressing modes:

#n, Dn,	Dn a16 a32 (An) (An)+ -(An) d16(An) d8(An,i)

#n,SR

Flags affected:　　　N Z V C

Privileged instruction:　　　no, except for EOR.W #n,SR

Register SR may not be used with long-word operations. CCR is least significant byte of SR, and accessed by 'AND.B #n,SR'. Exclusive ORs all bits of source with corresponding bits of destination.

EXG EXCHANGE REGISTERS

Addressing modes:　　An,Dn
　　　　　　　　　　　　Dn,Dn
　　　　　　　　　　　　An,An
　　　　　　　　　　　　Dn,An

Flags affected:　　　none

Privileged instruction:　　　no

Long-word operations only. Exchanges complete contents of two registers.

EXT SIGN EXTEND

Addressing modes:　　Dn

Flags affected:　　　N Z V C

Privileged instruction:　　　no

Byte operations not allowed. Extends sign bit of low order half of destination, through the entire high order half of destination.

JMP JUMP

Addressing modes: a16
a32
(An)
d16(An)
d8(An,i)
d16(PC)
d8(PC,i)

Flags affected: none

Privileged instruction: no

Sets program counter to destination address.

JSR JUMP TO SUBROUTINE

Addressing modes: a16
a32
(An)
d16(An)
d8(An,i)
d16(PC)
d8(PC,i)

Flags affected: none

Privileged instruction: no

Pushes address of next instruction, and sets program counter to destination address.

LEA LOAD EFFECTIVE ADDRESS

Addressing modes: a16
a32
(An)
d16(An)   ,An
d8(An,i)
d16(PC)
d8(PC,i)

Flags affected: none

Privileged instruction: no

Puts the effective address of the source into the destination register.

28

LINK LINK STACK

Addressing modes: An,#n

Flags affected: none

Privileged instruction: no

The contents of An are pushed onto the stack. Register An is then loaded from the updated stack pointer. Finally, the sign-extended dispacement is added to the stack pointer.

LSL LOGICAL SHIFT LEFT

Addressing modes:
```
a16            (no data qualifier)
a32
(An)
(An)+
-(An)
d16(An)
d8(An,i)

#b,Dn          (data qualifier used)
Dn,Dn
```

Flags affected: X N Z V C

Privileged instruction: no

Data size is always word. Shift is always by one bit when no qualifier is present, or by a count of up to 63. An immediate shift count can be given of 0 to 7 only. Zero signifies a shift of eight places.

LSR LOGICAL SHIFT RIGHT

Addressing modes:
```
a16            (no data qualifier)
a32
(An)
(An)+
-(An)
d16(An)
d8(An,i)

#b,Dn          (data qualifier used)
Dn,Dn
```

Flags affected: X N Z V C

Privileged instruction: no

Data size is always word. Shift is always by one bit when no qualifier is present, or by a count of up to 63. An immediate shift count can be given of 0 to 7 only. Zero signifies a shift of eight places.

MOVE MOVE

Two categories of MOVE instruction exist; those that use a data qualifier and those that do not.

1. MOVE instructions that require a data qualifier

Addressing modes:	#n		a16
	a16		a32
	a32		Dn
	Dn		An **
** An			(An)
	(An)	,	(An)+
	(An)+		-(An)
	-(An)		d16(An)
	d16(An)		d8(An,i)
	d8(An,i)		
	d16(PC)		
	d8(PC,i)		

(** An address register may not be used as a source
    or destination operand if the data type is byte)

Flags affected: N Z V C
                         (No flags are affected if
                           the destination is An)

Privileged instruction: no

2. MOVE instructions that do not use a data qualifier

Addressing modes:	#n	
	a16	
	a32	
	Dn	
	(An)	,CCR
	(An)+	,SR
	-(An)	
	d16(An)	
	d8(An,i)	
	d16(PC)	
	d8(PC,i)	

```
                    An,USP
                    USP,An

                              ⎧   a16
                              ⎪   a32
                              ⎪   Dn
              SR,             ⎨   (An)
                              ⎪   (An)+
                              ⎪   -(An)
                              ⎪   d16(An)
                              ⎩   d8(An,i)
```

Flags affected: X N Z V C
                          (No flags are affected if
                          the source is SR or USP)

Privileged instruction: yes, unless moving
                                   from SR or
                                   to CCR

Moving to CCR or SR is always word. When moving to CCR only least
significant byte is used to update condition codes. Moving from SR is
always word. USP operations are always long-word.

MOVEM   MOVE MULTIPLE REGISTERS

```
**Addressing modes:**     a16        ⎫
                          a32        ⎪
                          (An)       ⎪
                          (An)+      ⎬   ,<reg-list>
                          d16(An)    ⎪
                          d8(An,i)   ⎪
                          d16(PC)    ⎪
                          d8(PC,i)   ⎭

                                        ⎧   a16
                                        ⎪   a32
                                        ⎪   (An)
                          <reg-list>,   ⎨   -(An)
                                        ⎪   d16(An)
                                        ⎩   d8(An,i)
```

Flags affected: none

Privileged instruction: no

Data size is word or long-word. Register list can be any list of data or
address registers separated by a comma (no ranges allowed by assembler).
         For example: MOVEM.L locstore, A1,A2,A3,D4,D6
Organization in memory is D0 at lowest address, A7 at highest.

MOVEP MOVE PERIPHERAL DATA

Addressing modes: Dn,d16(An)
                                d16(An),Dn

Flags affected: none

Privileged instruction: no

Data size is word or long-word only. Bytes are transferred to/from alternate memory locations. If address is even, transfer is on high order half of data bus (68000 only; 68008 has 8-bit data bus).

MOVEQ MOVEQ

Addressing modes: #b,Dn

Flags affected: N Z V C

Privileged instruction: no

Moves data (-128 to +127) to complete data register.

MULS SIGNED MULTIPLY

Addressing modes: #n
                            a16
                            a32
                            Dn
                            (An)
                            (An)+   ,Dn
                            -(An)
                            d16(An)
                            d8(An,i)
                            d16(PC)
                            d8(PC,i)

Flags affected: N Z V C

Privileged instruction: no

The low order half of destination long-word is multiplied by source word.

MULU   UNSIGNED MULTIPLY

Addressing modes: #n
                             a16
                             a32
                             Dn
                             (An)
                             (An)+   ,Dn
                             -(An)
                             d16(An)
                             d8(An,i)
                             d16(PC)
                             d8(PC,i)

Flags affected: N Z V C

Privileged instruction: no

The low order half of destination long-word is multiplied by source word.

NBCD   NEGATE DECIMAL WITH EXTEND

Addressing modes: a16
                             a32
                             Dn
                             (An)
                             (An)+
                             -(An)
                             d16(An)
                             d8(An,i)

Flags affected: X N Z V C

Privileged instruction: no

Byte data size only. Subtracts the two BCD digits of destination, with extend, from zero.

NEG   NEGATE

Addressing modes: a16
                             a32
                             Dn
                             (An)
                             (An)+
                             -(An)
                             d16(An)
                             d8(An,i)

Flags affected: X N Z V C

Privileged instruction: no

Subtracts the destination from zero.

NEGX   NEGATE WITH EXTEND

Addressing modes: a16
a32
Dn
(An)
(An)+
-(An)
d16(An)
d8(An,i)

Flags affected: X N Z V C

Privileged instruction: no

Subtracts the destination, with extend, from zero.

NOP   NO OPERATION

Addressing modes: inherent

Flags affected: none

Privileged instruction: no

NOT   ONE'S COMPLEMENT

Addressing modes: a16
a32
Dn
(An)
(An)+
-(An)
d16(An)
d8(An,i)

Flags affected: N Z V C

Privileged instruction: no

34

Inverts all bits of the destination.

OR LOGICAL OR

Addressing modes:

```
#n          ⎫
a16         ⎪
a32         ⎪
Dn          ⎪
(An)        ⎪
(An)+       ⎬    ,Dn
-(An)       ⎪
d16(An)     ⎪
d8(An,i)    ⎪
d16(PC)     ⎪
d8(PC,i)    ⎭
```

```
              ⎧   a16
              ⎪   a32
    #n,       ⎪   (An)
    Dn,       ⎨   (An)+
              ⎪   -(An)
              ⎪   d16(An)
              ⎩   d8(An,i)
```

```
    #n,SR
```

Flags affected: N Z V C

Privileged instruction: no, except for OR.W #n,SR

Register SR may not be used with long-word operations. CCR is least significant byte of SR, and accessed by 'AND.B #n,SR'. Logically ORs all bits of the source with corresponding bits of destination.

PEA PUSH EFFECTIVE ADDRESS

Addressing modes:
```
a16
a32
(An)
d16(An)
d8(An,i)
d16(PC)
d8(PC,i)
```

Flags affected: none

Privileged instruction: no

Pushes the effective address of the source.

RESET   RESET EXTERNAL DEVICES

Addressing modes: inherent

Flags affected: none

Privileged instruction: yes

Asserts the reset pin.

ROL   ROTATE LEFT

Addressing modes: a16   (no data qualifier)
                          a32
                          (An)
                          (An)+
                          -(An)
                          d16(An)
                          d8(An,i)

                          #b,Dn   (data qualifier used)
                          Dn,Dn

Flags affected: N Z V C

Privileged instruction: no

Data size is always word. Rotate is always by one bit when no qualifier
is present, or by a count of up to 63. An immediate rotate count can be
given of 0 to 7 only. Zero signifies a rotate of eight places. Does not
set extend flag.

ROR   ROTATE RIGHT

Addressing modes: a16   (no data qualifier)
                          a32
                          (An)
                          (An)+
                          -(An)
                          d16(An)
                          d8(An,i)

                          #b,Dn   (data qualifier used)
                          Dn,Dn

Flags affected: N Z V C

Privileged instruction: no

Data size is always word. Rotate is always by one bit when no qualifier is present, or by a count of up to 63. An immediate rotate count can be given of 0 to 7 only. Zero signifies a rotate of eight places. Does not set extend flag.

ROXL ROTATE LEFT THROUGH EXTEND

Addressing modes:

a16   (no data qualifier)
a32
(An)
(An)+
-(An)
d16(An)
d8(An,i)

#b,Dn   (data qualifier used)
Dn,Dn

Flags affected: X N Z V C

Privileged instruction: no

Data size is always word. Rotate is always by one bit when no qualifier is present, or by a count of up to 63. An immediate rotate count can be given of 0 to 7 only. Zero signifies a rotate of eight places. Rotates through extend flag.

ROXR ROTATE RIGHT THROUGH EXTEND

Addressing modes:

a16   (no data qualifier)
a32
(An)
(An)+
-(An)
d16(An)
d8(An,i)

#b,Dn   (data qualifier used)
Dn,Dn

Flags affected: X N Z V C

Privileged instruction: no

Data size is always word. Rotate is always by one bit when no qualifier is present, or by a count of up to 63. An immediate rotate count can be given of 0 to 7 only. Zero signifies a rotate of eight places. Rotates through extend flag.

RTE RETURN FROM EXCEPTION

Addressing modes: inherent

Flags affected: X N Z V C

Privileged instruction: yes

Pops status register and program counter.

RTR RETURN AND RESTORE CCR

Addressing modes: inherent

Flags affected: X N Z V C

Privileged instruction: no

Pops condition code register and program counter.

RTS RETURN FROM SUBROUTINE

Addressing modes: inherent

Flags affected: none

Privileged instruction: no

Pops program counter.

SBCD SUBTRACT DECIMAL WITH EXTEND

Addressing modes: -(An),-(An)
Dn,Dn

Flags affected: X N Z V C

Privileged instruction: no

Byte data size only. Subtracts two BCD digits in source, with extend, from two BCD digits in destination.

Scc SET CONDITIONAL

Addressing modes: a16
        a32
        Dn
        (An)
        (An)+
        -(An)
        d16(An)
        d8(An,i)

Flags affected: none

Privileged instruction: no

Byte operations only. If condition is true, sets destination byte to $FF, else clears destination byte to zero.

STOP STOP

Addressing modes: #n

Flags affected: X N Z V C

Privileged instruction: yes

Loads status register and stops until interrupt or reset.

SUB SUBTRACT

Addressing modes: #n
        a16
        a32
        Dn
        (An)
        (An)+ ,Dn
        -(An)   ,An
        d16(An)
        d8(An,i)
        d16(PC)
        d8(PC,i)

              a16
              a32
       #n,   (An)
       Dn,   (An)+
             -(An)
             d16(An)
             d8(An,i)

```
                              An,An
                              An,Dn

Flags affected:               X N Z V C

Privileged instruction:   /      no
```

Register An may not be used as destination for byte operations.
Subtracts source from destination.

SUBQ   SUBTRACT QUICK

```
Addressing modes:                      ⎫   Dn
                                       ⎪   An
                                       ⎪   a16
                                       ⎪   a32
                              #b,   ⎬   (An)
                                       ⎪   (An)+
                                       ⎪   -(An)
                                       ⎪   d16(An)
                                       ⎭   d8(An,i)

Flags affected:               X N Z V C

Privileged instruction:          no
```

Register An may not be used as destination for byte operations. Word and
long-word operations are identical. Subtracts data (1 to 8) from
destination.

SUBX   SUBTRACT WITH EXTEND

```
Addressing modes:            -(An),-(An)
                             Dn,Dn

Flags affected:              X N Z V C

Privileged instruction:          no
```

Subtracts source, with extend, from destination.

SWAP   SWAP DATA REGISTER HALVES

```
Addressing modes:            Dn

Flags affected:              N Z V C
```

Privileged instruction: no

Swaps low order word with high order word.

TAS   TEST AND SET BIT 7

Addressing modes: a16
a32
Dn
(An)
(An)+
-(An)
d16(An)
d8(An,i)

Flags affected: N Z V C

Privileged instruction: no

Byte operations only. Tests bit 7 of byte (setting N and Z flags) and then sets bit 7 to one.

TRAP   TRAP

Addressing modes: #b

Flags affected: none

Privileged instruction: no

Immediate value is vector between 0 and 15. Generates the specified TRAP exception.

TRAPV   TRAP ON OVERFLOW

Addressing modes: inherent

Flags affected: none

Privileged instruction: no

If overflow flag (V) is set, generates a TRAPV exception.

TST TEST

Addressing modes:
a16
a32
Dn
(An)
(An)+
-(An)
d16(An)
d8(An,i)

Flags affected: N Z V C

Privileged instruction: no

Tests the destination. Destination is not altered.

UNLK UNLINK

Addressing modes: An

Flags affected: none

Privileged instruction: no

Stack pointer is loaded from register An. Register An is then loaded from long-word pulled off stack.

PART 2 QL System Procedures

3 THE QDOS PACKAGE

'The whole world is in
a state of chassis.'

Sean O'Casey

Conceptually, QDOS is the chassis, and you are the coach-builder. It is important to view the QDOS system in this way. There are perhaps many programmers who are accustomed to thinking of operating systems as resource allocation programs, under which their own application programs run. Strictly speaking this is not true of QDOS.

QDOS is a chassis of procedures. Application programs which you may write are at liberty to use any of these procedures. Furthermore QDOS has the appropriate hooks to enable its collection of procedures to be expanded or modified as required. It is this structure which provides the assembly language programmer with so much flexibility.

3.1 System memory map

The physical memory map of the Sinclair QL, and the RAM map imposed by QDOS, are so important to the assembly language programmer that we will look at these first. Figure 3.1 shows the layout of the two maps. Map 1 is the physical memory map of the microcomputer, and map 2 is the map of the RAM.

PHYSICAL MEMORY MAP

The total amount of memory that can be accessed is 1 Megabyte. The system ROM, together with the address space for the plug-in ROM, occupy the bottom 64 Kilobytes ($00000 to $0FFFF). The next 64 Kilobytes ($10000 to $1FFFF) are dedicated to I/O devices. Only 16 Kilobytes of this area are currently allocated. Above the first I/O block lies the RAM. The RAM always has a base address of $20000. The top of the RAM area will, on a standard 128K machine, be $3FFFF. With the 0.5 Megabyte expansion RAM module plugged in, the top of RAM becomes $BFFFF. The final 256 Kilobytes of memory address space is reserved for additional I/O. This final area, together with the I/O area that exists further down the map, supplies the user with a total of 304 Kilobytes of expansion I/O. This may seem rather large but it serves to act not simply as device address space, but also as device driver program space. An advantage is clearly evident here because it means that no RAM space needs to be taken up in the process of adding additional I/O facilities.

QDOS RAM MEMORY MAP

Now that we know how the memory space is divided up physically, let us look at how the RAM space is allocated. The bottom 32 Kilobytes ($20000 to $27FFF) are dedicated to the screen display. The remaining 96 Kilobytes ($28000 to $3FFFF), or 608 Kilobytes ($28000 to $BFFFF), are managed by QDOS in the form of five major areas. There are a number of system variables that are used to determine, at any one point in time, the sizes and free RAM pointer values of these QDOS areas. The variables, their use, and their absolute position in the memory map are shown in Fig.3.2. Each variable is stored as a long–word, i.e., is 32 bits in length. The mnemonics given to the variables (e.g., SV_BASIC) are for reference only – they will not be recognized either by SuperBASIC or QDOS.

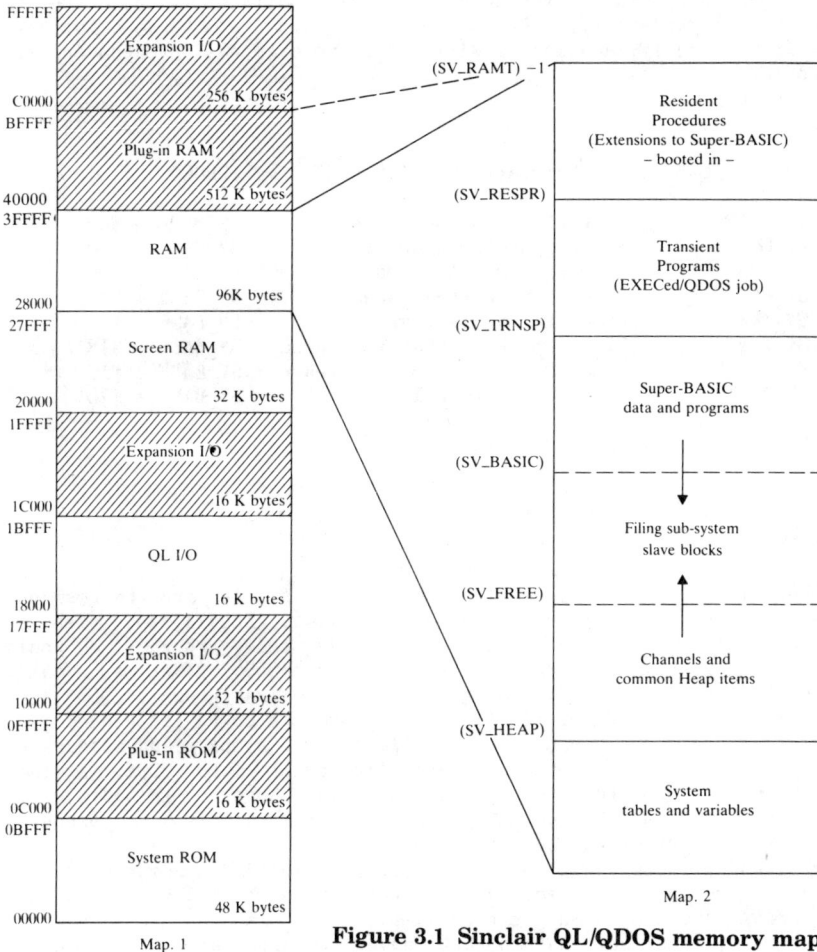

Figure 3.1 Sinclair QL/QDOS memory map

RESIDENT PROCEDURE AREA

At the very top of the available RAM are the Resident Procedures. These procedures, and any tables that may accompany them, are loaded into memory when the system is booted (i.e., reset). The only way to change the area allocation after it has been set up is to re-boot the system. More will be said of this in Chapter 8. The term resident procedure area is used because this is an area that, once booted in, will be permanently resident. Also the most common use of this area is the storage of user-defined SuperBASIC procedures. By adding the entry point names of the procedures into the procedure name list of the SuperBASIC interpreter utility, the procedures themselves will become extensions to the SuperBASIC language.

Any procedure added to the system in this way must be re-entrant (i.e., contain no local variables or self-modifying code), and be position independent. Clearly the resident procedure area does not have to exist physically, and indeed will not if no external procedures are booted in.

Base of system variables (SV_BASE)   = $28000

SV_HEAP	Base of common heap area	SV_BASE + $04
SV_CHPFR	First space in heap area	SV_BASE + $08
SV_FREE	Base of free RAM area	SV_BASE + $0C
SV_BASIC	Base of SuperBASIC area	SV_BASE + $10
SV_TRNSP	Base of transient area	SV_BASE + $14
SV_TRNFR	First space in transient area	SV_BASE + $18
SV_RESPR	Base of resident proc. area	SV_BASE + $1C
SV_RAMT	Top of RAM (plus 1)	SV_BASE + $20

Figure 3.2   RAM system variables

TRANSIENT PROGRAM AREA

The next area is the transient program area (TPA). As with the resident procedure area, the TPA does not have to exist. Should you wish to implement and execute a transient machine code program, you would allocate an appropriate amount of memory using a QDOS 'TRAP #1' call. Once a TPA had been set up, a program within the TPA (known to QDOS as a job) can be made active or inactive. The job can also be suspended, or the TPA discarded. This process of allocating TPA space and scheduling jobs is part of the multi-tasking capability built into QDOS. A full discussion of such processes will be found in Chapter 4. In addition to being executed as a QDOS job, a transient program can also be executed from SuperBASIC by using the EXEC command.

Each TPA program must be written in position independent code, but need not be re-entrant. Also, each program must have its own data and stack areas. A TPA area may be used simply as a data area. In such cases it is clearly important that the job never becomes active and hence executed! Owing to the fact that jobs can be created and discarded almost at will, the total TPA area will grow and shrink dynamically. Note, however, that any one TPA program will always take up a pre-declared amount of space.

SUPERBASIC AREA

This area contains all currently loaded SuperBASIC programs and all related data (i.e., both program data and SuperBASIC interpreter utility data). Clearly there is no way of telling, a priori, how much space is going to be required by a SuperBASIC program. In view of this, QDOS makes a special allowance for the SuperBASIC area and permits it to grow and shrink dynamically. The total transient program area, immediately above the SuperBASIC area, can grow and shrink dynamically also, and therefore the entire SuperBASIC area can shift dynamically.

SYSTEM TABLES AND VARIABLES

All general purpose computer systems require a minimal amount of RAM in which to store important variables, pointers, and so on. QDOS also requires tables to be set up in RAM for operations such as job and channel management. In the Sinclair QL this small amount of memory is located at the base of the RAM map.

The 68000 processor is capable of running in either a user mode or a supervisor mode. The two modes use different stack pointers and stack areas. The supervisor stack lies between the system variables and the tables.

CHANNELS AND HEAP AREA

This is an area of RAM, directly above the system variables and tables area, used both for the setting up and permitting of I/O through specified channels, and also for common heap items. Working storage for I/O drivers (e.g., the keyboard routine) would be one use for this area. In cases such as this it is the device drivers themselves that allocate space within the area. QDOS jobs may also request space from this region. When a particular job is removed any heap allocations owned by it will be removed also.

This area of RAM is conceptually the same as the transient program area (in that they are both heaps) and, like the SuperBASIC area, it is not possible, a priori, to know the actual size of it. As such it too grows and shrinks dynamically. So, there are now two areas which vary in size dynamically; the TPA+SuperBASIC area, and this area. This is exactly the situation that is present in simple single user systems utilizing a single stack. The easiest way of implementing such a system is to have one region grow from one end of the memory toward the middle, and the second region growing from the other end of the memory toward the middle. When the two regions meet you have run out of memory! Figure 3.1 shows that the same form of implementation is used in QDOS. The TPA+SuperBASIC area grows downwards and the channel and heap area grows upwards. Any memory left in the middle of these two areas is given over to filing sub-system slave blocks.

FILING SUB-SYSTEM SLAVE BLOCK AREA

This area exists between the dynamically variable SuperBASIC and channel and heap areas. All the remaining RAM, at any one point in time, is given over to filing sub-system slave blocks. These slave blocks are invisible to the user and merely duplicate data held on the Microdrives. Their use enables QDOS I/O to make Microdrive accesses as efficient as possible. The bigger the amount of free RAM, the greater will be the efficiency of Microdrive accesses. This mechanism means that QDOS is constantly using all available memory to its greatest advantage.

3.2 Bootstrapping

When the system is first turned on, or a reset is performed, execution will start at the base of the system ROM. Once the system variables have been determined, and a RAM test carried out, a system scan will be performed to find out the true configuration of the machine.

First the plug-in ROM address map will be checked (at $0C000) for the characteristic long-word '$4AFB0001'. If this word is found it is assumed that a ROM exists and that it contains appropriate code. Next the expansion areas are checked for device drivers. Assuming control is returned to the bootstrap routine, an attempt will finally be made to open either a device called 'BOOT', or the file 'MDV1_BOOT'. If this attempt is successful then the respective file will be loaded into memory (as a SuperBASIC program) and executed.

3.3 System calls and utilities

There are two major types of routine that assembly language programmers can access from within their own application programs and subroutines. The first type is that of 'TRAP #n' calls made to QDOS procedures; the second are those general utilities that are accessed through vectors.

QDOS ROUTINES

System calls to QDOS may either be treated as atomic or partially atomic. Most QDOS routines are atomic in nature. Atomic routines are executed with the 68000 processor in supervisor mode. In this mode no other job can take priority over use of the processor and, therefore, the routine will be executed from start to finish before being 'swapped-out'. Note that this is the general case only; the routine could be interrupted by an interrupt service procedure. Routines which are partially atomic will complete some sort of primary operation, but will then allow another job to swap-out the original calling process until a later moment in time. All the I/O calls are partially atomic unless specifically accessed as being fully atomic. Scheduler calls are partially atomic.

Note that executing a TRAP #0 instruction, on the QL, will force a switch to supervisor mode. No registers will be altered (except, of course, the stack pointer, which will become the SSP). User mode can be re-entered simply by altering the status register.

QDOS procedures are accessed via 'TRAP #n' calls with register D0 indicating which particular call is required. Chapters 4 to 6 describe these trap calls in detail, but some generalities are worth mentioning at this point. Register D0, as well as containing the procedure index on entry (as a byte), is used also to return an error status (as a long-word) to the calling process. If the error code returned is not zero then an error has occurred. Small negative error codes are used to indicate standard errors. These error codes are listed in Appendix C. If the trap call invoked some form of additional device driver, the error code returned can be a pointer to a specific error message. In order that the two types of error return code might never be confused, the pointer type error code is in fact a pointer to an address $8000 below that of the true error message. Potentially, all QDOS routines can return the error 'ERR.BP' (-15), signifying 'bad parameter'.

In addition to the use of register D0, data registers D1 to D3 and address registers A0 to A3 are variably used to pass values to and from the QDOS procedures. When the appropriate registers have been set for any one call the appropriate routine is accessed by simply executing the appropriate 68000 trap instruction. For example, to suppress the cursor in the window belonging to channel ID $10001, the following may be used:

```
        :
        :
move.b  #15,d0          ;Suppress cursor routine
move.w  #0,d3           ;Return immediately
move.l  #$10001,a0      ;Channel ID
trap    #3
        :
        :
```

The full description of this QDOS routine, given in Chapter 6, shows that it is capable of returning three errors (the two listed and the more general 'bad parameter' error). It would of course be wise to check for these errors after the trap call has been made.

UTILITY ROUTINES

These routines are, as far as this text is concerned, a mixture of simplified trap routines and SuperBASIC utility routines. Each routine is discussed in detail in Chapter 7. By using these routines the assembly language programmer can greatly simplify basic I/O code and can even incorporate floating point calculations into application programs!

The method of accessing either type of utility is the same, and simply involves setting up the appropriate call parameters and then performing a subroutine call to the required vector. For example, to send out the ASCII representation of an integer word in the memory location labelled 'RESULT' to the command channel (#0), the following could be used:

```
        :
        :
move.w    result(PC),d1      ;Get result
sub.1     a0,a0              ;Select channel zero
move.w    #$CE,a4            ;Convert and print routine
jsr       (a4)
        :
        :
result:   defs 2             ;Integer result register
        :
        :
```

Once again it would be normal to check for all possible error return conditions.

There are four Microdrive support routines available that have to be handled in a slightly different way. First, their access vectors actually point to an address $4000 bytes before the true entry points. It is important therefore to add on this offset when making the vectored calls:

```
e.g.    move.w    md.verin,a4
        jsr       $4000(a4)
```

Second, they do not return an error code. Instead, they have multiple return points.

50

4 MACHINE RESOURCE MANAGEMENT (TRAP #1)

The QDOS procedures, within this classification, control the allocation of machine resources. QDOS supports multi-tasking (i.e., the pseudo-concurrent execution of multiple jobs) and the appropriate allocation of both CPU and RAM resources is, therefore, of prime importance.

4.1   QDOS multi-tasking

System calls to QDOS may either be treated as atomic or partially atomic. Most QDOS routines are atomic in nature. Atomic routines are executed with the 68000 processor in supervisor mode. In this mode no other job can take priority over use of the processor and, therefore, the routine will be executed from start to finish before being 'swapped-out'. Note that this is the general case only; the routine could be interrupted by an interrupt service procedure. Routines which are partially atomic will complete some sort of primary operation, but will then allow another job to swap-out the original calling process until a later moment in time. All the I/O calls are partially atomic unless specifically accessed as being fully atomic. Scheduler calls are partially atomic.

JOB STATUS

When a job is set up by QDOS procedures it can exist in a number of states. First, the job can be active. This means that the job has a priority, within the multi-tasking environment, and will obtain a share of the 68000 CPU resources in line with that priority. If the job has a low priority then it will be allocated a relatively small percentage of CPU resources.

Second, the job may be suspended, either for a limited time or for an indefinite period. Jobs are normally suspended to force them to wait for some I/O or another job.

Third, the job may be inactive. The job will still use up space within the memory, but it will never be allocated any CPU resources. A job at priority level 0 is identical to an inactive job. A major difference between an inactive job and a job that has been suspended indefinitely is that the latter cannot be removed by the simple version of the 'remove job' call (i.e., MT.RJOB (TRAP #1, D0=4)). The reason for the difference between suspended/released jobs and inactive/active jobs is as follows. Suspending and releasing a job does not alter the flow of execution of code; it merely interrupts it. On the other hand, an inactivated job has completed its execution. When re-activated, the job will start again at the beginning.

SCHEDULING

The allocation of CPU resources to jobs, in line with job priorities, is known as scheduling. QDOS re-scheduling is related to the frame rate of the monitor (i.e., 50/60 Hz). Certain QDOS routines will cause re-scheduling to take place (e.g., MT.SUSJB (TRAP #1, D0=8)).

TIMEOUTS

A number of QDOS calls permit a timeout to be specified. The procedure to suspend a job (i.e., MT.SUSJB) is one example. The timeout period is a multiple of the monitor frame rate (i.e., 50/60 Hz). A timeout period of unity is therefore equivalent to 20 ms for a 50 Hz timebase, and 16.666 ms for a 60 Hz timebase.

With respect to QDOS procedures, a timeout value of -1 signifies that an indefinite period is required. No other negative value should be used. A maximum timeout period of 32767 times the unit timebase period is permitted. This gives a maximum period of 10 minutes, 55.3 seconds for a 50 Hz timebase, and 9 minutes, 6.1 seconds for a 60Hz timebase.

4.2 Use of 68000 registers

The TRAP #1 procedures are accessed with register D0 (byte) indicating which particular call is required. This register is also used to return an error status (long-word) to the calling process. If the error code returned is not zero then an error has occurred. Small negative error codes are used to indicate standard errors. These error codes are listed in Appendix C. If the trap call invoked some form of additional device driver, the error code returned can be a pointer to a specific error message. In order that the two types of error return code might never be confused, the pointer type error code is in fact a pointer to an address $8000 below that of the true error message. Potentially, all QDOS routines can return the error 'ERR.BP' (-15), signifying 'bad parameter'. The full descriptions of the TRAP #1 procedures state which additional errors can be returned. It would of course be wise to check for any errors after the trap call has been made.

In addition to the use of register D0, data registers D1 to D3 and address registers A0 to A3 are variably used to pass values to and from the QDOS procedures. When the appropriate registers have been set for any one call the appropriate routine is accessed by simply executing the TRAP #1 instruction. In cases where the data size qualifier (i.e., '.B',

'.W', or '.L') is not specified within the description, the default is long-word (i.e., '.L').

.

MT.INF $00 (0)

Get system information

Entry parameters: none

Return parameters: D1.L   Current job ID
                       D2.L   QDOS version (in ASCII)
                       AO   Pointer to system variables

Affected registers: D1, D2, AO

Additional errors: none

Description

MT.INF returns the specified system information. The version number of
QDOS is returned as a 4-byte ASCII string in the form:

          v.xx

where 'v' is the major revision, and 'xx' is the update code. The most
significant word of D2 will contain the major revision code and the full
stop. The update code will be in the least significant word of D2.
   The system variable pointer returned in AO is the value of the base
pointer SV.BASE (normally $28000).

MT.CJOB $01 (1)

Create a job in transient program area

Entry parameters:	D1.L	Owner job ID
	D2.L	Code length (bytes)
	D3.L	Data length (bytes)
	A1	Start address
Return parameters:	D1.L	Job ID
	A0	Base of area allocated
Affected registers:	D1, A0	
Additional errors:	OM (-3) out of memory	
	NJ (-2) not a valid job	

Description

QDOS jobs are created in the transient program area. Each job has a fixed allocation of memory, which must allow for all data and working areas (including stack space). It is advisable to use at least an extra 64 bytes on top of any calculated stack space, to allow for QDOS utility stack requirements. On entry to MT.CJOB, registers D2 and D3 will specify the total memory requirement for the job. Stack space is included in the data length specification.

The specified start address will be zero if the start address is at the base of the job. Any other address specified must be absolute. The owner job ID will be zero if the job is to be independent. If the current job is to be this new job's owner then the owner job ID may be passed as -1 (i.e., a negative value).

(A6,A5)

Memory

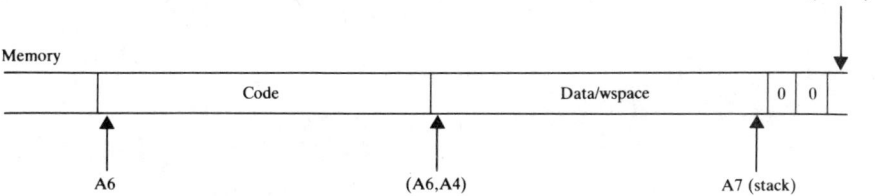

| A6 | (A6,A4) | A7 (stack) |

Figure 4.1 Job area pointers

Note that this procedure does not load or execute the actual job; it simply attempts to allocate space in the TPA and set up a job entry in the scheduler tables. The job program would normally be loaded by another job after this call had been successfully completed. Job programs must be written in position independent code. When a job is made active, register A6 will be pointing to the base of the job area, A6 indexed by A4 will be pointing to the base of the data area, and A6 indexed by A5 will be pointing to the top of the area. The stack pointer register A7 will, in the simple case, be pointing to two words of zero placed on the stack by the MT.CJOB procedure (see Fig.4.1).

The two words of zero placed on the stack are a standard format information packet. In non-simple cases these zeros would be replaced by more detailed information packets consisting of, for example, a word of data representing the number of channels opened for the job, long-word channel IDs, and a job command string. The command string would also be in standard format, i.e., a word of data representing the length of the command string followed by the string itself.

Note that the SuperBASIC command EXEC performs the setting up of a TPA, and the loading and activation of a job program, all in one go! Unless there is the requirement for one job to set up and control its own sub-job, the use of EXEC would be the normal way to invoke a transient program (see Chapter 8).

MT.JINF $02 (2)

Get job information

Entry parameters:	D1.L	Job ID
	D2.L	Job ID at top of tree
Return parameters:	D1.L	Next job ID in tree
	D2.L	Owner job ID
	D3.L	Status/priority
	A0	Base address of job
Affected registers:	D1 – D3, A0, A1	
Additional errors:	NJ (-2) not a valid job	

Description

This procedure returns the status of a specified job. Jobs may be independent or they may be owned by other jobs (except for job zero which cannot be owned by any other job). The structure of job ownership can be viewed as a tree (see Fig.4.2). It is possible, using this procedure, to scan the status of an entire tree of jobs. To do so is a simple matter of setting D1 and D2 to the top of the tree, and then continuously calling MT.JINF until D1 is returned as zero (which signifies that there is no next job).

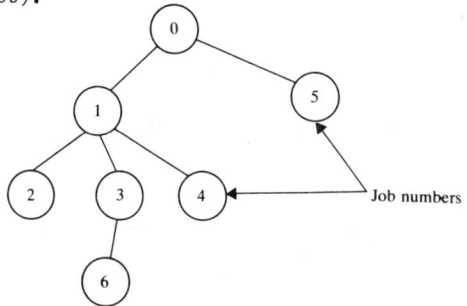

Figure 4.2 Job ownership tree

On exit, D2 will contain zero if the scanned job is independent. The most significant byte of D3 will be negative if the job is suspended, and the least significant byte of D3 will contain the priority of the job.

MT.RJOB $04 (4)

Remove inactive job from TPA

Entry parameters:	D1.L	Job ID
	D3.L	Error code
Return parameters:	none	
Affected registers:	D1 - D3, A0 - A3	
Additional errors:	NJ (-2) not a valid job	
	NC (-1) job is not inactive	

Description

This procedure removes a specified job from the transient program area.
Any sub-jobs owned by the job will also be removed. For the procedure to
work, the job(s) must be inactive. On entry, D3 should contain the error
code that is to be returned from the activation call which created the
job (see MT.ACTIV; D0=$0A). If no such error exists then D3 will contain
zero.

Note that job zero cannot be removed. The procedure is not guaranteed to
be atomic.

MT.FRJOB $05 (5)

Force remove job(s) from TPA

Entry parameters: D1.L   Job ID
                      D3.L   Error code

Return parameters: none

Affected registers: D1 – D3, A0 – A3

Additional errors: NJ (-2) not a valid job

Description

This procedure will inactivate and remove a complete job tree. On entry, D1 may be negative if the job to remove is the current job. Also, D3 should contain the error code that is to be returned from the activation call which created the job (see MT.ACTIV; D0=$0A). If no such error exists then D3 will contain zero.

If there is another job waiting for the completion of the job being removed, it will be released with D0 set to the error code that was initially returned from the activation call which created the job.

Note that job zero cannot be removed. The procedure is not guaranteed to be atomic.

MT.FREE $06 (6)

Length of largest space in TPA

Entry parameters: none

Return parameters: D1.L   Length of space found

Affected registers: D1 – D3, A0 – A3

Additional errors: none

Description

This will return the length of the largest contiguous area of memory
that could be subsequently allocated to a transient program area. Note
that the value returned can only be used as a guide if there are
numerous active jobs. The scheduling system may have allowed another job
to grab some (or all) of the free memory in between the time this call
was made and the time the current job attempts to use it.

MT.TRAPV $07 (7)

Set job trap vector pointer

Entry parameters:	D1.L	Job ID
	A1	Pointer to vector table
Return parameters:	D1.L	Job ID
	A0	Base address of job
Affected registers:	D1, A0, A1	
Additional errors:	none	

Description

The traps and exception vectors of the 68000 CPU that are not used by
QDOS may be redirected through a table set up by a particular job. If a
job does set up such a table, the table vectors will be used while the
job is being executed. Additionally, any job set up by a job with its
own vector table will automatically adopt the same table until it is
redefined locally.

Vector tables set up by jobs (with the exception of adoption as
mentioned above) are entirely local and do not affect tables within
other jobs. If on entry, D1 is negative, the table will be set up for
the job that called the procedure. The vector table pointed to by A1 on
entry must contain long-word addresses for each trap and exception. The
table order, together with the offset address for each vector (with
respect to the base of the table), is as follows:

Offset	Vector/exception	Offset	Vector/exception
00	address error	28	TRAP #7
04	illegal instruction	2C	TRAP #8
08	zero divide	30	TRAP #9
0C	CHK	34	TRAP #10
10	TRAPV	38	TRAP #11
14	privilege violation	3C	TRAP #12
18	trace	40	TRAP #13
1C	interrupt level 7	44	TRAP #14
20	TRAP #5	48	TRAP #15
24	TRAP #6		< end of table >

MT.SUSJB $08 (8)

Suspend a job

Entry parameters:	D1.L	Job ID
	D3.W	Timeout period
	A1	Flag byte address
Return parameters:	D1.L	Job ID
	AO	Base of job control area
Affected registers:	D1, AO	
Additional errors:	NJ (-2) not a valid job	

Description

This procedure will suspend a job, either indefinitely or for a given time. If on entry, D1 is negative, the current job will be suspended. Suspension for an indefinite time will occur if the word value of D3 is passed as -1. No other negative value should be used. Suspending an already suspended job will have the effect of resetting the suspension period.

The flag byte, which exists in the job control area, will be cleared when the job is later released. The flag is used to indicate to a job, which is suspending another job, that either the suspension has timed-out, or yet another job has released the suspended job. Use of the job control area is rather specialised and it is, therefore, not normally accessed by the applications programmer. As such register A1, on entry to the procedure, should be set to zero.

All jobs will be re-sheduled and therefore (as a result of accessing the scheduler) MT.SUSJB cannot be fully atomic.

MT.RELJB $09 (9)

Release a job and re-schedule

Entry parameters: D1.L   Job ID

Return parameters: D1.L   Job ID
                       A0   Base of job control area

Affected registers: D1, A0

Additional errors: NJ (-2) not a valid job

Description

This call will release (i.e., un-suspend) a specified job and cause all
jobs to be re-scheduled. The act of releasing a job does not imply that
the job will become active. Job activity is also related to job
priority, and a job that has a priority of zero will be inactive.

Because all jobs are re-sheduled MT.RELJB cannot be fully atomic.

MT.ACTIV $0A (10)

Activate a job

Entry parameters:	D1.L	Job ID
	D2.B	Job priority (0 to 127)
	D3.W	Timeout (0 or -1)
Return parameters:	D1.L	Job ID
	AO	Base of job control area
Affected registers:	D1, AO, A3	
Additional errors:	NJ (-2) not a valid job	
	NC (-1) job already active	
	<any job run-time error>	

Description

The specified job, in the transient program area, will be made active. Execution, on obtaining CPU resources, will begin at the address specified when the job was created (see MT.CJOB (TRAP #1, DO=1)). A priority of 127 is the highest priority possible.

Two timeout options are available. First, if a timeout of zero is given, execution of the current (calling) job will continue. The newly activated job will begin execution at some later moment in time, as and when the scheduler invokes it. In this case the two errors, ERR.NJ (-2) and ERR.NC (-1), are the only additional errors that will be returned.

Second, if a timeout of -1 is given, the current job will be suspended until the newly activated job has finished execution. In this case any error could be returned when the job completes (i.e., when the job removes itself, or is removed by some other job. See MT.RJOB; DO=4, and MT.FRJOB; DO=5).

MT.PRIOR $0B (11)

Change job priority

Entry parameters: D1.L   Job ID
                       D2.B   Job priority (0 to 127)

Return parameters: D1.L   Job ID
                       A0   Base of job control area

Affected registers: D1, A0

Additional errors: NJ (-2) not a valid job

Description

This call can be used to change the priority of a job. If, on entry, D1
is negative, the priority of the current job will be changed. A priority
of zero will effect inactivation. This procedure invokes the scheduler
and therefore a job will immediately inactivate itself if it sets its
own priority to zero.

MT.ALRES $0E (14)

Allocate resident procedure area

Entry parameters:	D1.L	Number of bytes required
Return parameters:	A0	Base address of area
Affected registers:	D1 - D3, A0 - A3	
Additional errors:	OM (-3) out of memory	
	NC (-1) TPA not empty	

Description

This procedure is used to allocate memory to the resident procedure area. It should only be used when the TPA is completely empty (i.e., when no transient programs exist).
  Note that the SuperBASIC function RESPR is normally used to perform this task from a 'BOOT' device or file (see Chapter 8).

MT.RERES $0F (15)

Release resident procedure area

Entry parameters:	none
Return parameters:	none
Affected registers:	D1 – D3, A0 – A3
Additional errors:	NC (–1) TPA not empty

Description

This procedure will release the resident procedure area. A paradox is
evident here. The call cannot be made if the TPA is not empty, but a
program must exist to make the call. It is no good having the call as
part of a program in the resident procedure area because it will
annihilate itself in the process!

There is a way of circumventing this apparent paradox but it is not to
be encouraged. In practice, therefore, this call will never be used and
the resident procedure area will only be released or reset by re-booting
the entire system.

MT.DMODE $10 (16)

Set/read display mode

Entry parameters:	D1.B	Set/read display mode flag
	D2.B	Set/read display type flag
Return parameters:	D1.B	Display mode
	D2.B	Display type
Affected registers:	D1, D2, A4	
Additional errors:	none	

Description

This procedure is used for one of two purposes. First, if D1 and D2 are set to −1 on entry, the display mode (i.e., four or eight colour) and display type (i.e., TV or monitor) will be returned in the respective registers. The return values are as follows:

Display mode:	0	−	4 colour
	8	−	8 colour

Display type:	0	−	monitor
	1	−	TV (625 line)

Second, if one each of the above display mode and display type codes are placed into the respective registers on entry to the call, the display will be set accordingly. This form of the procedure should only be invoked when there are no other jobs attempting to access the display. All windows are cleared and the character sizes may change. In some cases (e.g., as shown in the example 'clock' program in Chapter 9) programs may be written such that the display mode may be changed by a job, without serious side-effects.

MT.IPCOM $11 (17)

Intelligent peripheral controller (IPC) command
(keyboard row scan, sound)

Entry parameters:	A3	Pointer to command
Return parameters:	D1.B	Return parameter
Affected registers:	D1, D5, D7	
Additional errors:	none	

Description

Extreme care must be taken when using this procedure. IPC communication
is entirely unprotected and a total loss of machine operations may occur
if an error exists in the call. Additionally, most of the IPC commands
are for sole use by QDOS, and any attempt to use such commands is likely
to effect a loss of data or something equally belligerent.

  Three commands to the IPC are usable. Each command is a string of
bytes consisting of a command byte, a parameter block, and a
reply-length byte. The parameter block consists of a parameter byte
count (in one byte), a long-word holding up to 16 2-bit codes, and the
actual parameter bytes. The 2-bit codes are used to determine how many
bits of each parameter byte should be sent to the IPC, as follows:

00	-	send least significant four bits
01	-	send nothing
10	-	send all eight bits

Bits 1,0 of the long-word refer to parameter byte 0. Bits 3,2 refer to
parameter byte 1, and so on. The final reply-length byte of the command
is encoded in a similar fashion using bits 1,0 (i.e., a byte value of
$02 will signify that the return value in register D1 should be eight
bits long).

The three commands available are:

1. Keyboard row scan
   The command byte is $09. There is one parameter of four bits
   specifying the row to scan. The reply is eight bits long and it has
   one bit set for each column position that has a key pressed. The
   relationship between rows, columns, and actual keys can be found in
   the QL User Manual in the section on the SuperBASIC command KEYROW.

2. Create sound
   The command byte is $0A. There are eight parameters:

pitch-1	8 bits
pitch-2	8 bits
step interval	16 bits
duration	16 bits
pitch step	4 bits
wrap	4 bits
randomness	4 bits
fuzz	4 bits

There is no reply.

3. Kill sound
   The command byte is $0B. There are no parameters and no reply is given.

MT.BAUD $12 (18)

Set baud rate

Entry parameters:	D1.W	Baud rate
Return parameters:	none	
Affected registers:	D1	
Additional errors:	none	

Description

This procedure is used to set the baud rate for the two serial
interfaces, SER1 and SER2. The same baud rate must be applied to both
interfaces. The rate is passed to the procedure as a pure binary value.
For example, to set a rate of 9600 baud the following could be used:

```
        :
move.w    #9600,d1      ;9600 baud
move.b    #$12,d0       ;Set baud rate proc.
trap      #1
        :
```

MT.RCLCK $13 (19)

Read real-time clock

Entry parameters:	none
Return parameters:	D1.L Time in seconds
Affected registers:	D1, D2, A0
Additional errors:	none

Description

This procedure will return the time in seconds and may be used in one of two ways. First, it can be used in conjunction with the clock set and adjust traps, and date, day, and time utilities to obtain a true calendar clock for as long as the machine is turned on. In this case, time is assumed to have started at 00.00 hours on 1 January 1961.

   Second, the value returned can be used simply to measure elapsed time between two successive calls.

MT.SCLCK $14 (20)

Set real-time clock

Entry parameters:	D1.L	Time in seconds
Return parameters:	D1.L	Time in seconds
Affected registers:	D1 – D3, A0	
Additional errors:	none	

Description

This procedure is used to set the real-time clock so that utilities can be used to display a true calendar clock. Time is assumed to have started at 00.00 hours on 1 January 1961.

MT.ACLCK $15 (21)

Adjust real-time clock

Entry parameters:	D1.L	Adjustment in seconds
Return parameters:	D1.L	Time in seconds
Affected registers:	D1 - D3, AO	
Additional errors:	none	

Description

This call can be used to adjust the real-time clock. A negative adjustment can be made. Because it takes a significant time to set the clock, no adjustment will be made if D1 is zero on entry to the call.

MT.ALCHP $18 (24)

Allocate common heap area

Entry parameters:	D1.L	Number of bytes required
	D2.L	Owner job ID
Return parameters:	D1.L	Number of bytes allocated
	A0	Base address of area
Affected registers:	D1 – D3, A0 – A3	
Additional errors:	OM (-3) out of memory	
	NJ (-2) not a valid job	

Description

Space may be grabbed from the common heap area by jobs. The space may be allocated by one job on behalf of another job, and all heap space allocated using this procedure will be released when the owner job (rather than the 'allocater' job) is removed. The allocated space is cleared and all of it is available to the job.

MT.RECHP $19 (25)

Release common heap area

Entry parameters: A0   Base of area to be freed

Return parameters: none

Affected registers: D1 - D3, A0 - A3

Additional errors: none

Description

This procedure will release the specified space from the common heap
area. It is the programmer's responsibility to ensure that the area is
completely finished with before this procedure is called.

5 INPUT/OUTPUT ALLOCATION (TRAP #2)

Input and output QDOS procedures fall into two major categories. First, there are those that are concerned with the actual allocation of channels for devices and files. Second, there are those that actually perform input and output operations on the allocated channels. The first category comprises the TRAP #2 calls discussed in this chapter. The second category comprises the TRAP #3 calls discussed in Chapter 6.

5.1 Redirectable input and output

An important concept within QDOS is that of redirectable I/O. It is not necessary for an applications programmer to know what physical device is actually attached to an I/O channel. Opening a channel for use with a Microdrive involves accessing exactly the same routine as when opening an extra screen window channel. The real task of getting information in and out of channels is the job of the device driver.

Sometimes it is necessary for certain aspects of physical devices to be specified alongside the actual device name. This additional information is used by the appropriate device driver to configure the channel as necessary.

5.2 Standard device names

QDOS supports a range of standard device drivers. Each driver can accept a pre-defined name followed by any appropriate configuration parameters. Known devices, and their parameters, are as follows:

CON_wXhAxXy_k   Console I/O. A window is defined as width 'w' by height 'h', at location 'x', 'y'. The keyboard type-ahead buffer is set to length 'k'. Note that the size and position of the window is defined in terms of pixels on a 512 by 256 pixel grid. The width 'w' and the 'x' coordinate should both be specified in multiples of two pixels.
The default definition is: CON_448x180a32x16_128

SCR_wXhAxXy	Screen output. This has the same window definition as for the I/O device 'CON_'. The default definition is: SCR_448x180a32x16
SERnpz	Serial I/O. The port number is specified by 'n'. Parity (Even, Odd, Mark, or Space) is defined by 'p' being one of E, O, M, or S. Parameter 'z' specifies protocol by taking on one of the values R (raw data), Z (CTRL Z is eof), or C (<CR> is changed to <LF> on input, <LF> is changed to <CR> on output, and CTRL Z is eof). The default definition is: SER1R
NETI_nn	Serial network link from node 'nn'.
NETO_nn	Serial network link to node 'nn'.
MDVn_name	Microdrive. Microdrive number 'n' and file name given by 'name'. There is no default.

5.3 Use of 68000 registers

The TRAP #2 procedures are accessed with register D0 (byte) indicating which particular call is required. This register is used also to return an error status (long-word) to the calling process. If the error code returned is not zero then an error has occurred. Small negative error codes are used to indicate standard errors. These error codes are listed in Appendix C. If the trap call invoked some form of additional device driver, the error code returned can be a pointer to a specific error message. In order that the two types of error return code might never be confused, the pointer type error code is in fact a pointer to an address $8000 below that of the true error message. Potentially, all QDOS routines can return the error 'ERR.BP' (-15), signifying 'bad parameter'. The full descriptions of the TRAP #2 procedures state which additional errors can be returned. It would of course be wise to check for any errors after the trap call has been made.

In addition to the use of register D0, data registers D1 to D3 and address registers A0 to A3 are variably used to pass values to and from the QDOS procedures. When the appropriate registers have been set for any one call the appropriate routine is accessed by simply executing the TRAP #2 instruction. In cases where the data size qualifier (i.e., '.B', '.W', or '.L') is not specified within the description, the default is long-word (i.e., '.L').

IO.OPEN $01 (1)

Open a channel

Entry parameters:	D1.L	Job ID
	D3.L	Access code
	A0	Address of channel name
Return parameters:	D1	Job ID
	A0	Channel ID
Affected registers:	D1, A0	
Additional errors:	NJ (-2)	not a valid job
	OM (-3)	out of memory
	NO (-6)	too many channels open
	NF (-7)	file or device not found
	EX (-8)	file already exists
	IU (-9)	file or device in use
	BN (-12)	bad device or file name

Description

A channel is opened by specifying the appropriate device and/or file
name. On entry, A0 is a pointer to the name, which is a string of ASCII
characters preceded by a character count (data length .W), this being
the standard format for a string parameter. Register A0 points to the
word of data representing the character count.

Each job requires its own list of I/O channels and therefore the job
ID must be supplied on entry to the procedure. If the job ID is passed
as a negative integer (e.g., -1), the channel will be associated with
the current job.

More than one type of open is available, and on entry D3 may hold a
code specifying which open option is required. The options available,
together with their access codes, are as follows:

Access code	Type
0	Opens existing file/device. Exclusive use. R/W.
1	Opens existing file/device. Shared use. R/O.
2	Opens new file. Exclusive use. R/W.
3	Opens new file (overwrite).
4	Opens directory file. R/O.

Most device drivers ignore the access code. QDOS does support the
'overwrite' type of access, but the Microdrive device driver does not.

The error ERR.BN (-12) is usually given when the name of the device
has been recognized, but the parameter information is in an incorrect
form. A channel will not be opened if any error occurs.

IO.CLOSE $02 (2)

Close a channel

Entry parameters:	AO	Channel ID
Return parameters:	none	
Affected registers:	AO	
Additional errors:	NO (-6) channel not open	

Description

This procedure simply closes the specified channel.

IO.FORMT $03 (3)

Format a sectored medium

Entry parameters:	AO	Pointer to medium name
Return parameters:	D1.W	Number of good sectors
	D2.W	Total number of sectors
Affected registers:	D1, D2, AO	
Additional errors:	OM (-3)	out of memory
	NF (-7)	drive not found
	IU (-9)	drive in use
	FF (-14)	format failed

Description

The medium name pointed to by AO on entry to the procedure must be in the standard string parameter form. This means that AO will be pointing to a word of data (specifying the length of the string) followed by the ASCII string itself.
   The string should consist of the drive name, followed by the drive number, then an underscore, and finally the medium name (up to 10 characters). The medium name is that name which will be supplied when a directory is performed on the medium. For example, the command string:

MDV1_MYPROGS

will format the medium in Microdrive-1, and label the medium 'MYPROGS'.

IO.DELET $04 (4)

Delete a file

Entry parameters:	D1.L	Job ID
	AO	Address of device/file name

Return parameters: none

Affected registers: D1, D3, AO - A2

Additional errors:
- OM (-3) out of memory
- NO (-6) too many channels open
- NF (-7) file or device not found
- BN (-12) bad device or file name

Description

Deleting a file is a form of 'open' operation and therefore a job ID must be supplied. Any job ID may be used; -1 being the most convenient (i.e., the current job). On entry, AO is a pointer to the name, which is a string of ASCII characters preceded by a character count (data length .W), this being the standard format for a string parameter. Register AO points to the word of data representing the character count.

No delete operation will have been performed if any error has occurred.

6 INPUT/OUTPUT OPERATIONS (TRAP #3)

Input and output QDOS procedures fall into two major categories. First, there are those that are concerned with the actual allocation of channels for devices and files. Second, there are those that actually perform input and output operations on the allocated channels. The first category comprises the TRAP #2 calls, as discussed in Chapter 5. The second category comprises the TRAP #3 calls which we will discuss now.

6.1 Timeouts

All TRAP #3 procedures require a timeout to be specified. The timeout period is a multiple of the monitor frame rate (i.e., 50/60 Hz). A timeout period of unity is therefore equivalent to 20 ms for a 50 Hz timebase, and 16.666 ms for a 60 Hz timebase.

If a routine is called with the timeout set to zero, the call will return immediately after attempting its task, regardless of whether or not it succeeded. A positive timeout will make the call return immediately on completion, or at the end of the timeout, whichever occurs first. A maximum timeout period of 32767 times the unit timebase period is permitted. This gives a maximum period of 10 minutes, 55.3 seconds for a 50 Hz timebase, and 9 minutes, 6.1 seconds for a 60Hz timebase. A timeout value of -1 signifies that an indefinite period is required. No other negative value should be used.

The IO.FBYTE procedure is a worthy example. Suppose the procedure was being used to input a byte (character) from the keyboard. If a timeout of zero is used, the procedure will return a character if one is waiting, or return the error ERR.NC (not complete) if no character exists. Either way, an immediate return is made. A positive timeout will force the routine to look for a character for the specified length of time. If a character is entered within the time, an immediate return is made with the character. If no character arrives within the time specified, the routine will return at the end of the timeout with the ERR.NC error. A timeout of -1 will force the procedure to wait until complete, that is, wait until a character is entered.

6.2 Important principles

It must be remembered that QDOS supports multi-tasking and, therefore, there may be more than one job trying to get access to a particular channel. If your job call requests access to a channel that is already being waited on, one of two things will happen. If your timeout was given as zero, your call will return immediately as incomplete. If your timeout was not zero, your job will get re-scheduled until such time as the I/O channel request can be serviced. Note particularly that your specified timeout period commences from the moment your job obtains access to the channel, and not from the moment the original request was made. This means, of course, that the actual timeout period may be longer than the programmed timeout.

Incompletion of a job has important side-effects when dealing with output. In such cases, incompletion means that the QDOS procedure could not finish outputting its data. Any data not sent, because of an incomplete return from a procedure, must be re-sent at some later stage. The case of single character (byte) output is trivial; you would simply re-send the byte. When a string of characters is being sent, the QDOS procedure will return a count of the number of characters actually sent.

The input and output of large amounts of data should be handled carefully. It is inefficient to perform such I/O a byte at a time. The QL comes with a large amount of RAM and reasonable decisions over the use of memory buffers should be made. Characters would then be imported and exported in as large a block as possible at any one time.

6.3   Screen channel definition blocks

Approximately 70% of QDOS TRAP #3 procedures are related to screen operations. The procedure to redefine a window (SD.WDEF) is one example. All of the procedures require a channel ID to be specified. The topic of channel IDs and screen channels is, therefore, so important that we will look at these in some detail.

THE CHANNEL ID

A channel ID is a long-word holding two bits of information (no pun intended!). First, in the high order word of the ID, there is a tag value. This value will get incremented each time a channel is opened. Second, in the low order word of the ID, there is a channel index code. This code is used internally by QDOS. For information only (you would never normally use the fact), the channel value, stored in the ID, multiplied by four will supply an appropriate index into a channel table (see Fig.6.1).

When the machine is first switched on, there are three screen channels open. In SuperBASIC the channels are designated #0, #1, and #2. The actual correspondence between these SuperBASIC screen channels and the QDOS channel IDs will be as follows:

SuperBASIC #	QDOS ID		
	HEX.		DENARY
	TAG	CHAN.	
0	0000	0000	0
1	0001	0001	65537
2	0002	0002	131074

If, for example, SuperBASIC channel #2 is re-opened, it will still be channel #2 as far as SuperBASIC is concerned, but its internal QDOS ID will be $00030002 (denary 196610).

It is important to realise that, in practice, you should never need to know this correspondence. When writing pure assembly language application programs you will always have a copy of the QDOS channel ID, and that is all you need. If you are passing a SuperBASIC channel number over to an assembly language utility, the utility will collect the standard channel integer (i.e., #0, #1, etc.) and use it to calculate the internal QDOS channel ID (see Chapters 8 and 11).

SCREEN CHANNELS

QDOS maintains a channel resource management table, which holds such information as the highest known channel number, and so on (see Fig.6.1). Two pointers within this table, SV_CHBAS and SV_CHTOP, point to the base and top of the channel table respectively. The pointers within the channel table (long-words) point, in turn, to the corresponding channel definition blocks. Figure 6.1 shows the layout of screen channel definition blocks.

If it is a requirement of an applications program to obtain information about a particular screen channel, it should be obtained by calling your 'get the information' subroutine via the TRAP #3 extended operation procedure (SD.EXTOP; D0=9). The SD.EXTOP call will assume that your subroutine is a standard device driver and perform a couple of important operations. First, it will pass the base of the system variables (SV_BASE) to the subroutine in register A6. Second, register A7 will be set to the supervisor stack in such a way that you may use up to 64 bytes of stack space within your subroutine. Note that your subroutine actually will be running in supervisor mode. Third, the channel ID passed over to SD.EXTOP in register A0 will be converted to a pointer (in A0) to the base of the corresponding channel definition block. These operations provide your subroutine with vital pointer information in a very neat and convenient manner. When the return from subroutine (RTS) instruction is executed at the end of your subroutine (note: RTS not RTE), register A0 will be reset to the channel ID specified on entry to SD.EXTOP.

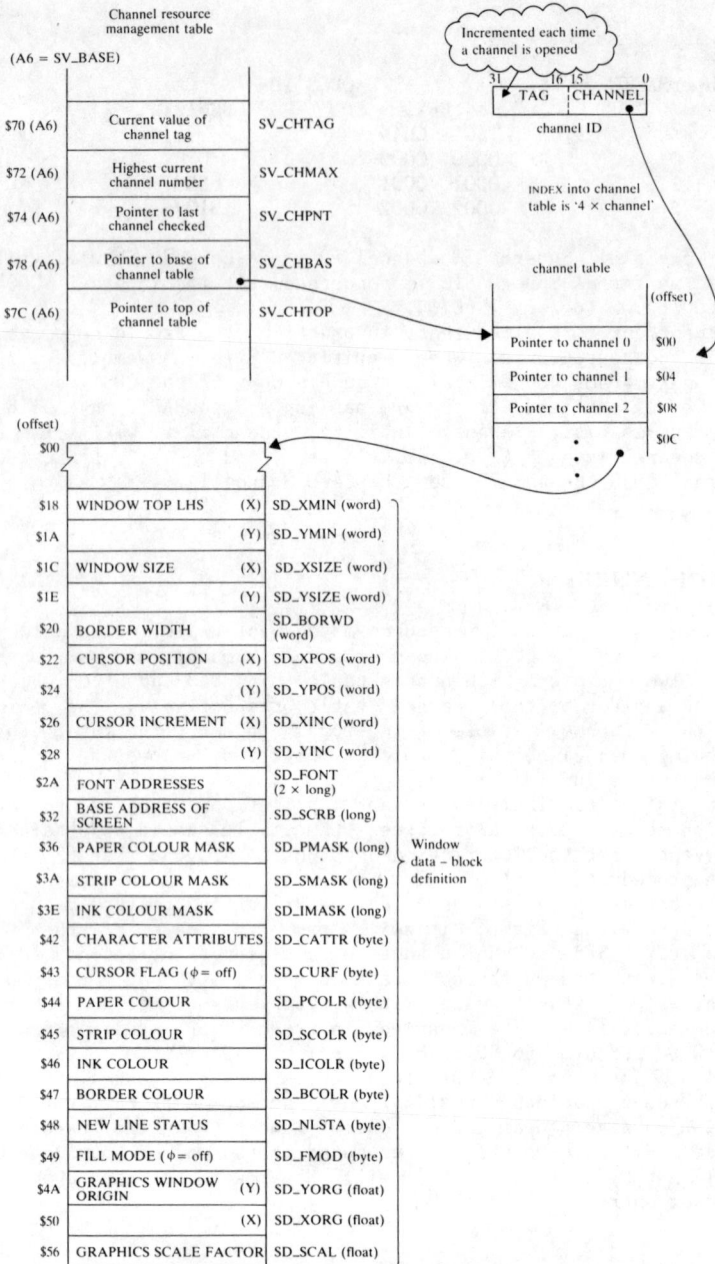

Channel resource management table

(A6 = SV_BASE)

Offset	Description	Name
$70 (A6)	Current value of channel tag	SV_CHTAG
$72 (A6)	Highest current channel number	SV_CHMAX
$74 (A6)	Pointer to last channel checked	SV_CHPNT
$78 (A6)	Pointer to base of channel table	SV_CHBAS
$7C (A6)	Pointer to top of channel table	SV_CHTOP

Incremented each time a channel is opened

31	16	15		0
	TAG		CHANNEL	

channel ID

INDEX into channel table is '4 × channel'

channel table

	(offset)
Pointer to channel 0	$00
Pointer to channel 1	$04
Pointer to channel 2	$08
⋮	$0C

(offset)

Offset	Description	Name
$00		
$18	WINDOW TOP LHS (X)	SD_XMIN (word)
$1A	(Y)	SD_YMIN (word)
$1C	WINDOW SIZE (X)	SD_XSIZE (word)
$1E	(Y)	SD_YSIZE (word)
$20	BORDER WIDTH	SD_BORWD (word)
$22	CURSOR POSITION (X)	SD_XPOS (word)
$24	(Y)	SD_YPOS (word)
$26	CURSOR INCREMENT (X)	SD_XINC (word)
$28	(Y)	SD_YINC (word)
$2A	FONT ADDRESSES	SD_FONT (2 × long)
$32	BASE ADDRESS OF SCREEN	SD_SCRB (long)
$36	PAPER COLOUR MASK	SD_PMASK (long)
$3A	STRIP COLOUR MASK	SD_SMASK (long)
$3E	INK COLOUR MASK	SD_IMASK (long)
$42	CHARACTER ATTRIBUTES	SD_CATTR (byte)
$43	CURSOR FLAG (ϕ = off)	SD_CURF (byte)
$44	PAPER COLOUR	SD_PCOLR (byte)
$45	STRIP COLOUR	SD_SCOLR (byte)
$46	INK COLOUR	SD_ICOLR (byte)
$47	BORDER COLOUR	SD_BCOLR (byte)
$48	NEW LINE STATUS	SD_NLSTA (byte)
$49	FILL MODE (ϕ = off)	SD_FMOD (byte)
$4A	GRAPHICS WINDOW ORIGIN (Y)	SD_YORG (float)
$50	(X)	SD_XORG (float)
$56	GRAPHICS SCALE FACTOR	SD_SCAL (float)

Window data – block definition

Figure 6.1 Screen channels and definition block

6.4 Colour

A number of the TRAP #3 procedures allow a colour to be specified as one of their parameters. Setting the ink colour (SD.SETIN) is one example of this. Three colours are used by the screen drivers. There is the 'paper' colour which is the background colour; the 'ink' colour which is the main printing and graphical plotting colour; and the 'strip' colour used for highlighting.

The solid colours which may be specified for the two screen modes are as follows:

Mode 8 (256)			Mode 4 (512)		
0	–	black	0	–	black
1	–	blue	1	–	black
2	–	red	2	–	red
3	–	magenta	3	–	red
4	–	green	4	–	green
5	–	cyan	5	–	green
6	–	yellow	6	–	white
7	–	white	7	–	white

In addition to the solid colours there are four stipple patterns that can be specified. Stipple patterns exist within a 2x2 pixel matrix, and can be selected by setting appropriate bits in the colour byte (see Fig.6.2).

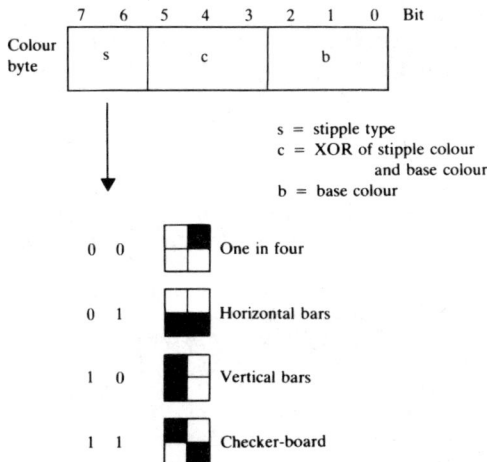

Figure showing the colour byte bit layout:

```
        7   6   5   4   3   2   1   0   Bit
Colour
byte      s       c           b

s = stipple type
c = XOR of stipple colour
        and base colour
b = base colour

0  0    One in four
0  1    Horizontal bars
1  0    Vertical bars
1  1    Checker-board
```

Figure 6.2 Exploded view of colour byte

Bits 7 and 6 will specify the stipple pattern as shown. Bits 0 to 2 specify the base colour (0..7), and bits 3 to 5 hold a value corresponding to the XOR (exclusive_OR) of the base colour and the stipple pattern colour. Suppose we want a base colour of blue and a stipple colour of yellow. The base colour has the binary value '001', and the stipple colour the binary value '110'. The XOR of these two values is the binary value '111', and it is this value that must be put into bits 3 to 5 of the colour byte. If we also wanted a checker-board type of stipple, the whole colour byte would be binary encoded as '11 111 001', which is the denary colour 249.

This method of encoding the pattern colours enables the standard solid colours to be obtained quite naturally. For example, take the solid colour green (value 4). This has a colour byte binary pattern of '00 000 100'. The stipple pattern is type 0 (one dot in four). The XOR value is zero and, therefore, the stipple colour must be 4 (binary 100), which is green! This gives us a base colour and a stipple colour that are the same, and hence we get our solid colour.

6.5 Use of 68000 registers

The TRAP #3 procedures are accessed with register D0 (byte) indicating which particular call is required. This register is used also to return an error status (long-word) to the calling process. If the error code returned is not zero then an error has occurred. Small negative error codes are used to indicate standard errors. These error codes are listed in Appendix C. If the trap call invoked some form of additional device driver, the error code returned can be a pointer to a specific error message. In order that the two types of error return code might never be confused, the pointer type error code is in fact a pointer to an address $8000 below that of the true error message. Potentially, all QDOS routines can return the error 'ERR.BP' (-15), signifying 'bad parameter'. The full descriptions of the TRAP #3 procedures state which additional errors can be returned. It would of course be wise to check for any errors after the trap call has been made.

In addition to the use of register D0, data registers D1 to D3 and address registers A0 to A3 are variably used to pass values to and from the QDOS procedures. When the appropriate registers have been set for any one call the appropriate routine is accessed by simply executing the TRAP #3 instruction. In cases where the data size qualifier (i.e., '.B', '.W', or '.L') is not specified within the description, the default is long-word (i.e., '.L').

The channel ID, which specifies the channel to be used for the I/O transfer, is always passed as a long-word in A0, and is never modified by the TRAP #3 procedure. The timeout is always passed as a word in D3, and it also is never modified by the call. If register A1 points to an array of bytes on entry to the TRAP #3 procedure, on exit from the procedure A1 will be pointing to the next byte in the array. Registers D2 to D7, A0, and A2 to A7 are always preserved by the I/O procedures.

IO.PEND $00 (0)

Check for pending input

Entry parameters:	D3.W	Timeout
	A0	Channel ID
Return parameters:	none	
Affected registers:	D1, A1	
Additional errors:	NC (-1)	not complete (no pending input)
	NO (-6)	channel not open
	EF (-10)	end of file

Description

This trap call can be used to check for pending input on a channel. Note that only a check for input is performed; the input channel is not modified in any way, and no input of data is performed.

IO.FBYTE $01 (1)

Fetch a byte

Entry parameters: D3.W   Timeout
                         AO   Channel ID

Return parameters: D1.B   Byte fetched

Affected registers: D1, A1

Additional errors: NC (-1) not complete
                         NO (-6) channel not open
                         EF (-10) end of file

Description

This procedure will fetch a byte from the specified input channel.

IO.FLINE $02 (2)

Fetch a line (terminated by ASCII <LF>)

Entry parameters:	D2.W	Length of buffer
	D3.W	Timeout
	A0	Channel ID
	A1	Base of buffer

Return parameters:	D1.W	Number of bytes fetched
	A1	Updated buffer pointer

Affected registers: D1, A1

Additional errors:	NC (-1)	not complete
	BO (-5)	buffer overflow
	NO (-6)	channel not open
	EF (-10)	end of file

Description

When dealing with console input, this procedure has special properties. First, the characters read from the keyboard will be echoed in the appropriate window. Second, the standard cursor keys (LEFT and RIGHT) can be used for simple editing as follows:

LEFT	–	move cursor left
RIGHT	–	move cursor right
CTRL-LEFT	–	delete character left
CTRL-RIGHT	–	delete character under cursor

Note that the cursor, within the specified window, will only be enabled for the duration of the procedure call. The count of the number of bytes fetched, as returned in D1, will include the line terminator (ASCII <LF>) if it was found.

The line-feed terminator may not be found if the timeout is exhausted, and will never be found if the buffer overflows. In such cases the cursor will be left enabled.

On exit, the pointer in register A1 will point to the byte following the last character entered.

IO.FSTRG $03 (3)

Fetch a string of bytes

Entry parameters:

D2.W	Length of buffer	
D3.W	Timeout	
A0	Channel ID	
A1	Base of buffer	

Return parameters:

D1.W	Number of bytes fetched	
A1	Updated buffer pointer	

Affected registers: D1, A1

Additional errors:

NC	(-1)	not complete
NO	(-6)	channel not open
EF	(-10)	end of file

Description

This procedure will fetch a string or block of bytes from the specified input channel. The bytes fetched will not be echoed on the screen, even if the channel device is a window. A return will be effected either when the timeout is exhausted or when the buffer becomes full.

IO.EDLIN $04 (4)

Edit a line (console only)

Entry parameters:	D1.L	Line/cursor parameters
	D2.W	Length of buffer
	D3.W	Timeout
	A0	Channel ID
	A1	Pointer to end of line
Return parameters:	D1	Line/cursor parameters
	A1	Pointer to end of line
Affected registers:	D1, A1	
Additional errors:	NC (-1)	not complete
	BO (-5)	buffer overflow
	NO (-6)	channel not open

Description

This is similar to the procedure IO.FLINE ($02) except that an initial
line, on which to start the editing, is supplied to the user. On entry,
register D1 must hold two words of information about the line. The high
order word must contain the current cursor position (0..n), and the low
order word must specify the total line length. The line specified should
not contain the terminating character (ASCII <LF>). Only the part of the
line starting from the current cursor position up to the end of the line
will be given to the user.

  On exit, the procedure will have updated the parameters in registers
D1 and A1 to correspond to the edited line. Valid terminating characters
are <LF>, <CURSOR-UP>, and <CURSOR-DOWN>. The terminating character will
be included in the line (and hence the line length) when the procedure
returns. Note that the pointer in register A1 always points to the
character byte following the last character entered.

IO.SBYTE $05 (5)

Send a byte

Entry parameters:	D1.B	Byte to be sent
	D3.W	Timeout
	A0	Channel ID
Return parameters:	none	
Affected registers:	D1, A1	
Additional errors:	NC (-1)	not complete
	OR (-4)	out of range
	NO (-6)	channel not open
	DF (-11)	drive full

Description

This procedure will send a byte out to the specified output channel.
   Special provisions exist for the output of a line-feed (<LF>) to a screen or console device. First, a newline is inserted on receipt of the line-feed terminator, or when the cursor reaches the right-hand side of the window. If the cursor is suppressed, the newline will be held pending. To release it one of the following may be performed:

   1. another byte may be sent
   2. the character size may be changed
   3. the cursor may be enabled
   4. the cursor position may be requested

If the cursor is explicitly positioned, the pending newline will be cancelled. Note especially that an explicit newline will replace an implicit one, thus providing sensible output with no unwanted blank lines.

The error code ERR.OR (-4) will be returned if any newline operation has taken place.

IO.SSTRG $07 (7)

Send a string of bytes

Entry parameters:	D2.W	Number of bytes to send
	D3.W	Timeout
	A0	Channel ID
	A1	Base of buffer
Return parameters:	D1.W	Number of bytes sent
	A1	Updated pointer to buffer
Affected registers:	D1, A1	
Additional errors:	NC (-1)	not complete
	NO (-6)	channel not open
	DF (-11)	drive full

Description

This procedure will send a string of bytes out to the specified channel.
Special provisions exist for the output of a line-feed (<LF>) to a
screen or console device. First, a newline is inserted on receipt of the
line-feed terminator, or when the cursor reaches the right-hand side of
the window. If the cursor is suppressed, the newline will be held
pending. To release it one of the following may be performed:

1. another string may be sent
2. the character size may be changed
3. the cursor may be enabled
4. the cursor position may be requested

If the cursor is explicitly positioned, the pending newline will be
cancelled. Note especially that an explicit newline will replace an
implicit one, thus providing sensible output with no unwanted blank
lines.

SD.EXTOP $09 (9)

Call an extended operation

Entry parameters:	D1	Parameter (if required)
	D2	Parameter (if required)
	D3.W	Timeout
	A0	Channel ID
	A1	Parameter (if required)
	A2	Address of routine
Return parameters:	D1	Parameter (if used)
	A1	Parameter (if used)
Affected registers:	D1, A1	
Additional errors:	NC (-1)	not complete
	NO (-6)	channel not open

Description

This trap call provides a mechanism for accessing a user supplied routine in supervisor mode. The routine specified on entry must conform to device driver rules. A detailed description of device driver routines is outside the scope of this book, but Sec.6.3 discusses the pertinent points.

The registers available for parameter passing (i.e., the three for importing, and the two for exporting) do not have to be used. It is simply the case that the values in these registers will not become corrupted in the 'interface' between the TRAP routine and the user-supplied device driver.

SD.PXENQ $0A (10)

Return window size & cursor position in pixel coords.

Entry parameters:	D3.W	Timeout
	AO	Channel ID
	A1	Base of enquiry block
Return parameters:	(Updated enquiry block)	
Affected registers:	A1	
Additional errors:	NC (-1)	not complete
	NO (-6)	channel not open

Description

An enquiry block is required for this procedure call, consisting of four
words:

Block offset	Use
$00	Window size (X)
$02	Window size (Y)
$04	Cursor position (X)
$06	Cursor position (Y)

The top left-hand corner of the window will have the coordinates [0,0].
If a newline is pending on the specified window channel, it will be
activated (i.e., released).

SD.CHENQ $0B (11)

Return window size & cursor position in character coords.

Entry parameters:	D3.W	Timeout
	AO	Channel ID
	A1	Base of enquiry block

Return parameters: (Updated enquiry block)

Affected registers: A1

Additional errors: NC (-1) not complete
                        NO (-6) channel not open

Description

An enquiry block is required for this procedure call, consisting of four
words:

Block offset	Use
$00	Window size (X)
$02	Window size (Y)
$04	Cursor position (X)
$06	Cursor position (Y)

The top left-hand corner of the window will have the coordinates [0,0].
If a newline is pending on the specified window channel, it will be
activated (i.e., released).

98

SD.BORDR $0C (12)

Set border width & colour

Entry parameters:
	D1.B	Colour
	D2.W	Width
	D3.W	Timeout
	A0	Channel ID

Return parameters: none

Affected registers: D1

Additional errors: NC (-1)   not complete
                       NO (-6)   channel not open

Description

This procedure will redefine the border of the specified window. A border is, by default, of zero width. When the border is set up it will lie inside the window limits, and the vertical edges will be of double width. All subsequent screen calls will use the reduced window size (except a subsequent call to SD.BORDR). The cursor will be homed if the border width is changed.

The standard colour codes are as described in Sec.6.4. There is also the colour $80 (128) which is treated as a special case, and will create a transparent border, leaving the original border contents intact.

SD.WDEF $0D (13)

Define a window and its border

Entry parameters:	D1.B	Border colour
	D2.W	Border width
	D3.W	Timeout
	A0	Channel ID
	A1	Base of window block

| Return parameters: | none |

| Affected registers: | D1, A1 |

Additional errors:	NC (-1)	not complete
	OR (-4)	range error - window too big
	NO (-6)	channel not open

Description

This call is used to redefine the shape and position of a window. The
original contents of the screen will not be changed or moved, but the
cursor will be set to the top left-hand corner of the new window.
   A window definition block consisting of four words must be set up
before the TRAP call is made, and should contain:

Block offset	Use
$00	Window size (X)
$02	Window size (Y)
$04	Window origin (X)
$06	Window origin (Y)

The window origin corresponds to the top left-hand corner of the defined
window.

SD.CURE $0E (14)

Enable the cursor

Entry parameters:	D3.W	Timeout
	AO	Channel ID
Return parameters:	none	
Affected registers:	D1, A1	
Additional errors:	NC (-1)	not complete
	NO (-6)	channel not open

Description

This procedure will enable the cursor in the specified window channel.
Note that the cursor will automatically be enabled when a 'read line'
(IO.FLINE) or 'edit line' (IO.EDLIN) procedure is invoked.

SD.CURS $0F (15)

Suppress the cursor

Entry parameters: D3.W   Timeout
                         AO   Channel ID

Return parameters: none

Affected registers: D1, A1

Additional errors: NC (-1) not complete
                         NO (-6) channel not open

Description

This procedure will disable the cursor in the specified window channel.
Note that the cursor will automatically be disabled when a 'read line'
(IO.FLINE) or 'edit line' (IO.EDLIN) procedure terminates normally.

SD.POS $10 (16)

Move cursor absolute using character coordinates

Entry parameters: D1.W   Column position
                       D2.W   Row position
                       D3.W   Timeout
                       A0   Channel ID

Return parameters: none

Affected registers: D1, A1

Additional errors: NC (-1)   not complete
                       OR (-4)   range error - not in window
                       NO (-6)   channel not open

Description

This procedure will position the cursor at a specified absolute position. The top left-hand corner of the window is position [0,0].

If a newline is pending, it will be cleared by this call. The original cursor position will not be altered if an error occurs.

SD.TAB $11 (17)

Tabulate

Entry parameters:	D1.W	Column position
	D3.W	Timeout
	A0	Channel ID
Return parameters:	none	
Affected registers:	D1, A1	
Additional errors:	NC (-1)	not complete
	OR (-4)	range error - not in window
	NO (-6)	channel not open

Description

This procedure will position the cursor at the specified tab-stop position. The specified position may be anywhere on the current cursor line.

   If a newline is pending, it will be cleared by this call. The original cursor position will not be altered if an error occurs.

SD.NL $12 (18)

Newline

Entry parameters: D3.W   Timeout
                         A0   Channel ID

Return parameters: none

Affected registers: D1, A1

Additional errors: NC (-1)   not complete
                          OR (-4)   range error - not in window
                          NO (-6)   channel not open

Description

This procedure will force a newline to be given in the specified window
channel.
   If a newline is pending, it will be cleared by this call. The original
cursor position will not be altered if an error occurs.

SD.PCOL $13 (19)

Cursor back

Entry parameters:	D3.W	Timeout
	A0	Channel ID
Return parameters:	none	
Affected registers:	D1, A1	
Additional errors:	NC (-1)	not complete
	OR (-4)	range error - not in window
	NO (-6)	channel not open

Description

This procedure will backspace the cursor non-destructively (i.e., the
cursor will not rub out the previous character).
   If a newline is pending, it will be cleared by this call. The original
cursor position will not be altered if an error occurs.

SD.NCOL $14 (20)

Cursor forward

Entry parameters:	D3.W	Timeout
	A0	Channel ID
Return parameters:	none	
Affected registers:	D1, A1	
Additional errors:	NC (-1)	not complete
	OR (-4)	range error - not in window
	NO (-6)	channel not open

Description

This procedure will move the cursor forward one character position, non-destructively.

If a newline is pending, it will be cleared by this call. The original cursor position will not be altered if an error occurs.

SD.PROW $15 (21)

Cursor up

Entry parameters:	D3.W	Timeout
	AO	Channel ID
Return parameters:	none	
Affected registers:	D1, A1	
Additional errors:	NC (-1)	not complete
	OR (-4)	range error - not in window
	NO (-6)	channel not open

Description

This procedure will move the cursor up one line non-destructively. The
column position of the cursor will be unchanged.
   If a newline is pending, it will be cleared by this call. The original
cursor position will not be altered if an error occurs.

SD.NROW $16 (22)

Cursor down

Entry parameters:	D3.W	Timeout
	A0	Channel ID
Return parameters:	none	
Affected registers:	D1, A1	
Additional errors:	NC (-1)	not complete
	OR (-4)	range error - not in window
	NO (-6)	channel not open

Description

This procedure will move the cursor down one line non-destructively. The
column position of the cursor will be unchanged.

   If a newline is pending, it will be cleared by this call. The original
cursor position will not be altered if an error occurs.

SD.PIXP $17 (23)

Move cursor absolute pixel using pixel coordinates

Entry parameters: D1.W   X coordinate
                         D2.W   Y coordinate
                         D3.W   Timeout
                         AO   Channel ID

Return parameters: none

Affected registers: D1, A1

Additional errors: NC (-1)   not complete
                         OR (-4)   range error - not in window
                         NO (-6)   channel not open

Description

This procedure will position the cursor at a specified absolute
position. The top left-hand corner of the window is position [0,0].
Pixel coordinates should correspond to the top left-hand corner of the
required character rectangle.
   If a newline is pending, it will be cleared by this call. The original
cursor position will not be altered if an error occurs.

SD.SCROL $18 (24)

Scroll entire window

Entry parameters: D1.W   Distance to scroll
                         D3.W   Timeout
                         A0   Channel ID

Return parameters: none

Affected registers: D1, A1

Additional errors: NC (-1) not complete
                         NO (-6) channel not open

Description

This procedure will scroll the whole of the specified channel window. An upward scroll can be obtained by specifying a negative distance. The distance to scroll is always specified in terms of pixels. Vacated pixel rows will be filled with the 'paper' colour.

The cursor position will not be altered.

SD.SCRTP $19 (25)

Scroll top of window

Entry parameters: D1.W   Distance to scroll
D3.W   Timeout
AO   Channel ID

Return parameters: none

Affected registers: D1, A1

Additional errors: NC (-1) not complete
NO (-6) channel not open

Description

This procedure will scroll the top part of the specified channel window.
An upward scroll can be obtained by specifying a negative distance. The
distance to scroll is always specified in terms of pixels. Vacated pixel
rows will be filled with the 'paper' colour.
  The top part of the window is defined as the area of the window above
(and not including) the cursor line. The cursor position will not be
altered.

SD.SCRBT $1A (26)

Scroll bottom of window

Entry parameters:	D1.W	Distance to scroll
	D3.W	Timeout
	A0	Channel ID

Return parameters:	none

Affected registers:	D1, A1

Additional errors:	NC (-1) not complete
	NO (-6) channel not open

Description

This procedure will scroll the bottom part of the specified channel
window. An upward scroll can be obtained by specifying a negative
distance. The distance to scroll is always specified in terms of pixels.
Vacated pixel rows will be filled with the 'paper' colour.
   The bottom part of the window is defined as the area of the window
below (and not including) the cursor line. The cursor position will not
be altered.

SD.PAN $1B (27)

Pan entire window

Entry parameters: D1.W   Distance to pan
                       D3.W   Timeout
                       A0   Channel ID

Return parameters: none

Affected registers: D1, A1

Additional errors: NC (-1) not complete
                       NO (-6) channel not open

Description

This procedure will pan the whole of the specified channel window. A pan
to the left can be obtained by specifying a negative distance. The
distance to pan is always specified in terms of pixels. Vacated pixel
positions will be filled with the 'paper' colour.

The cursor position will not be altered.

SD.PANLN $1E (30)

Pan cursor line

Entry parameters: D1.W   Distance to pan
                       D3.W   Timeout
                       A0   Channel ID

Return parameters: none

Affected registers: D1, A1

Additional errors: NC (-1) not complete
                       NO (-6) channel not open

Description

This procedure will pan the whole of the current cursor line in the
specified channel window. A pan to the left can be obtained by
specifying a negative distance. The distance to pan is always specified
in terms of pixels. Vacated pixel positions will be filled with the
'paper' colour.
   The height of the cursor line will depend upon the character font size
(i.e., either 10 or 20 pixel rows). The cursor position will not be
altered.

SD.PANRT $1F (31)

Pan RHS of cursor line

Entry parameters:	D1.W	Distance to pan
	D3.W	Timeout
	A0	Channel ID
Return parameters:	none	
Affected registers:	D1, A1	
Additional errors:	NC (-1) not complete	
	NO (-6) channel not open	

Description

This procedure will pan the whole of the right-hand side of the current cursor line in the specified channel window. A pan to the left can be obtained by specifying a negative distance. The distance to pan is always specified in terms of pixels. Vacated pixel positions will be filled with the 'paper' colour.

The height of the cursor line will depend upon the character font size (i.e., either 10 or 20 pixel rows). The right-hand end includes the character at the current cursor position. The cursor position will not be altered.

SD.CLEAR $20 (32)

Clear entire window

Entry parameters:	D3.W	Timeout
	A0	Channel ID
Return parameters:	none	
Affected registers:	D1, A1	
Additional errors:	NC (-1) not complete	
	NO (-6) channel not open	

Description

This procedure will clear the whole of the specified channel window.
Cleared pixel positions will be filled with the 'paper' colour.

SD.CLRTP $21 (33)

Clear top of window

Entry parameters: D3.W   Timeout
                       A0   Channel ID

Return parameters: none

Affected registers: D1, A1

Additional errors: NC (-1) not complete
                       NO (-6) channel not open

Description

This procedure will clear the top part of the specified channel window.
Cleared pixel positions will be filled with the 'paper' colour.
   The top part of the window is defined as the area of the window above
(and not including) the cursor line. The cursor position will not be
altered.

118

SD.CLRBT $22 (34)

Clear bottom of window

Entry parameters:	D3.W	Timeout
	A0	Channel ID
Return parameters:	none	
Affected registers:	D1, A1	
Additional errors:	NC (-1) not complete	
	NO (-6) channel not open	

Description

This procedure will clear the bottom part of the specified channel
window. Cleared pixel positions will be filled with the 'paper' colour.
   The bottom part of the window is defined as the area of the window
below (and not including) the cursor line. The cursor position will not
be altered.

SD.CLRLN $23 (35)

Clear cursor line

Entry parameters:	D3.W	Timeout
	AO	Channel ID
Return parameters:	none	
Affected registers:	D1, A1	
Additional errors:	NC (-1) not complete	
	NO (-6) channel not open	

Description

This procedure will clear the whole of the current cursor line in the specified channel window. Cleared pixel positions will be filled with the 'paper' colour.

The height of the cursor line will depend upon the character font size (i.e., either 10 or 20 pixel rows). The cursor position will not be altered.

SD.CLRRT $24 (36)

Clear RHS of cursor line

Entry parameters:	D3.W	Timeout
	A0	Channel ID
Return parameters:	none	
Affected registers:	D1, A1	
Additional errors:	NC (-1) not complete	
	NO (-6) channel not open	

Description

This procedure will clear the whole of the right-hand end of the current cursor line in the specified channel window. Cleared pixel positions will be filled with the 'paper' colour.

The height of the cursor line will depend upon the character font size (i.e., either 10 or 20 pixel rows). The right-hand end includes the character at the current cursor position. The cursor position will not be altered.

SD.FONT $25 (37)

Set/reset character font

Entry parameters:	D3.W	Timeout
	A0	Channel ID
	A1	Base of first font
	A2	Base of second font

Return parameters: none

Affected registers: D1, A1

Additional errors: NC (-1) not complete
                       NO (-6) channel not open

Description

A character font consists of a 5x9 array of pixels within a 6x10 character rectangle. The top row of any character is implicitly blank, as is the right-hand column of the character. Two character fonts already exist within the QL, but other fonts may be selected if desired. The normal font caters for characters in the range $20 to $7F.

  If, on entry, the base addresses of the fonts are zero, the default fonts will be used. Switching fonts will not alter the current contents of the screen.

The specified font tables must have the following structure:

Offset	Use
00	lowest valid character in the set (e.g., $20 <space>)
01	number of valid characters - 1
02 - 0A	nine bytes specifying first valid character
0B - 13	nine bytes specifying next valid character
14 - 1C	etc.

Figure 6.3 illustrates how the nine definition bytes are used to define any one character. Bits 7, 1, and 0 should always be set to zero. Byte 0 should be first in the font definition table.

  If a character to be written is found to be illegal (i.e., it is outside the specified range) for the first font, it will be written from the second font. If it is found to be illegal for the second font, the lowest valid character of the second font will be used.

122

EXAMPLE

If the character shown in Fig.6.3 was the second valid character in the font, the byte definition would be as follows:

Offset	Byte
$0B	$40
$0C	$20
$0D	$10
$0E	$08
$0F	$04
$10	$08
$11	$10
$12	$20
$13	$40

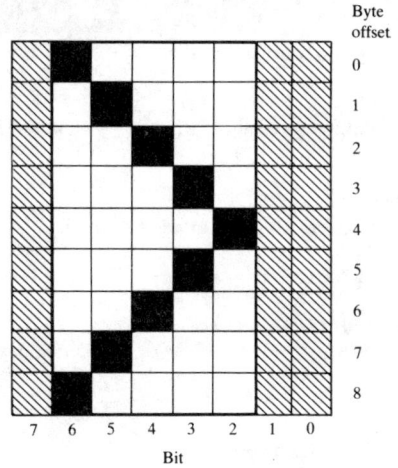

Figure 6.3

Note that you are not redefining a default character set, you are simply setting up an entirely new one. There is no limit, apart from physical memory constraints, to the number of character set fonts that can be defined.

SD.RECOL $26 (38)

Re-colour a window

Entry parameters:	D3.W	Timeout
	A0	Channel ID
	A1	Pointer to colour list

Return parameters: none

Affected registers: D1, A1

Additional errors: NC (-1) not complete
                      NO (-6) channel not open

Description

A window may be re-coloured via this procedure. The display information in the window will not be altered. A maximum of eight colours are permitted for each pixel on any one screen, and on entry to the procedure, register A1 must be pointing to a colour list of eight bytes which defines the new colour (in the range 0..7) for each possible original colour:

Byte offset	Use
0	new colour for black pixel
1	new colour for blue pixel
2	new colour for red pixel
3	new colour for magenta pixel
4	new colour for green pixel
5	new colour for cyan pixel
6	new colour for yellow pixel
7	new colour for white pixel

Two points are worth noting here. First, the above table will only refer to the eight colour mode of screen. The four colour mode screen only requires bytes 0, 2, 4, and 6 to be specified in order to re-colour black, red, green, and white. Second, we are only concerned with re-colouring each individual pixel on the screen. Clearly a pixel cannot have a stipple pattern and, therefore, the range of colours specified must be between 0 and 7. Any stipple patterns on the screen will get re-coloured according to the alteration of pixel colour.

SD.SETPA $27 (39)

Set paper colour

Entry parameters: D1.B   Colour
                       D3.W   Timeout
                       A0   Channel ID

Return parameters: none

Affected registers: A1

Additional errors: NC (-1) not complete
                       NO (-6) channel not open

Description

This procedure will set the colour of the paper (i.e., the background
colour) for the specified channel window. Any colour may be specified,
including stipple colours (see Sec.6.4).

SD.SETST $28 (40)

Entry parameters:	D1.B	Colour
	D3.W	Timeout
	A0	Channel ID

Return parameters:	none

Affected registers:	A1

Additional errors:	NC (-1) not complete
	NO (-6) channel not open

Description

This procedure will set the colour of the highlight strip (i.e., the
local background when printing characters) for the specified channel
window. Any colour may be specified, including stipple colours (see
Sec.6.4).

SD.SETIN $29 (41)

Set ink colour

Entry parameters:	D1.B	Colour
	D3.W	Timeout
	A0	Channel ID

Return parameters:	none
Affected registers:	A1
Additional errors:	NC (-1) not complete
	NO (-6) channel not open

Description

This procedure will set the colour of the ink (i.e., the foreground colour used when printing or plotting) for the specified channel window. Any colour may be specified, including stipple colours (see Sec.6.4).

SD.SETFL $2A (42)

Set/reset flash

Entry parameters:	D1.B	Attribute flag
	D3.W	Timeout
	A0	Channel ID

Return parameters: none

Affected registers: D1, A1

Additional errors: NC (-1) not complete
NO (-6) channel not open

Description

This procedure can be used to set (i.e., turn on) or reset (i.e., turn off) the flash mode for the specified window. If the attribute flag on entry is set to zero, flash mode will be suppressed. If the attribute flag is any other value, flash mode will be enabled.

Note that switching flash mode on will only affect subsequent printing (not plotting). Current window contents will not be affected. Likewise when flash mode is switched off, any current flashing items will continue to flash.

SD.SETUL $2B (43)

Set/reset underscore

Entry parameters:	D1.B	Attribute flag
	D3.W	Timeout
	A0	Channel ID

Return parameters: none

Affected registers: D1, A1

Additional errors: NC (-1) not complete
NO (-6) channel not open

Description

This procedure can be used to set (i.e., turn on) or reset (i.e., turn off) the underline mode for the specified window. If the attribute flag on entry is set to zero, underline mode will be suppressed. If the attribute flag is any other value, underline mode will be enabled.

Note that switching underline mode on will only affect subsequent printing (not plotting). Current window contents will not be affected. Likewise when underline mode is switched off, any current items underlined will remain as such.

SD.SETMD $2C (44)

Set writing/plotting mode

Entry parameters: D1.W   Mode byte
                       D3.W   Timeout
                       A0   Channel ID

Return parameters: none

Affected registers: D1, A1

Additional errors: NC (-1) not complete
                       NO (-6) channel not open

Description

This procedure will affect both subsequent printing and plotting. The
mode byte may take one of three values:

Mode	Effect
-1	ink colour is XORed (exclusive-ORed) with the background colour
0	character background becomes strip colour, and plotting is in ink colour
1	character background is transparent (i.e., only the character foreground replaces original screen contents), and plotting is in ink colour.

SD.SETSZ $2D (45)

Set character size

Entry parameters:	D1.W	Character width/space
	D2.W	Character height/space
	D3.W	Timeout
	A0	Channel ID
Return parameters:	none	
Affected registers:	D1, A1	
Additional errors:	NC (-1) not complete	
	NO (-6) channel not open	

Description

The character generator in the QL supports two widths and two heights of
character. In eight colour mode only double width, single/double height
characters may be used. Additionally, two alternative width spacings are
supported directly. In theory the spacing of characters is entirely
flexible, but access must be made to the variables SD.XINC and SD.YINC
in the window definition block for this flexibility to be fully
realized.

The entry parameters for specifying the character width, height, and
spacing may be set to any of the following:

D1.W	Character	
	Width /	Spacing
0	single	6 pixel
1	single	8 pixel
2	double	12 pixel
3	double	16 pixel

D2.W	Character	
	Height /	Spacing
0	single	10 pixel
1	double	20 pixel

Because of the limitation of only having double width type characters in
the eight colour mode, a call to this procedure (while in eight colour
mode) with D1 set to 0 or 1 will produce the same effect as if the call
had been made with D1 set to 2 or 3 respectively.

Note that if you change the screen mode from four colour to eight
colour, or vice versa, the width will automatically switch between
double and single as appropriate. Character height will remain
unchanged.

SD.FILL $2E (46)

Fill rectangle

Entry parameters:	D1.B	Colour
	D3.W	Timeout
	A0	Channel ID
	A1	Base of definition block

Return parameters:	none

Affected registers:	D1, A1

Additional errors:	NC (-1) not complete
	OR (-4) range error - block outside window
	NO (-6) channel not open

Description

This procedure will fill a rectangular block, in the specified channel window, with the specified colour. Any colour may be chosen, including stipple colours (see Sec.6.4).

On entry to the procedure, register A1 must hold a pointer to a four word definition block that defines the size and position of the rectangle:

Offset	Use
0	width of rectangle
2	height of rectangle
4	X position of top left-hand corner
6	Y position of top left-hand corner

The X and Y coordinates are specified relative to the origin of the window.

This procedure can be used to provide a fast horizontal or vertical line drawing operation. Additionally, it may be used as a fast 're-colour block within window' procedure, by setting the character/plotting mode to -1 (XOR mode) before calling it (see SD.SETMD; D0=$2C).

SD.POINT $30 (48)

Plot a point

Entry parameters: D3.W   Timeout
                           A0   Channel ID
                           A1   Arithmetic stack pointer

Return parameters: none

Affected registers: D1, A1

Additional errors: NC (−1) not complete
                           NO (−6) channel not open

Description

On entry to this procedure, register A1 must point to a local arithmetic
parameter stack of at least 240 bytes. At the top of the stack there
should be two floating point parameters (each of six bytes) as follows:

Stack position	Use
0(A1)	Y coordinate of point
6(A1)	X coordinate of point

Remember that stacks grow downwards and therefore the top of the stack
is at a physically lower address than the bottom of the stack.

The coordinates referred to are relative to an arbitrary origin (default
[0,0]) and an arbitrary scale (default 0..100). Any point which lies
outside the specified channel window will not be plotted. No error is
returned in such cases.

SD.LINE $31 (49)

Plot a line

Entry parameters: D3.W   Timeout
                           A0   Channel ID
                           A1   Arithmetic stack pointer

Return parameters: none

Affected registers: D1, A1

Additional errors: NC (−1) not complete
                           NO (−6) channel not open

Description

On entry to this procedure, register A1 must point to a local arithmetic parameter stack of at least 240 bytes. At the top of the stack there should be four floating point parameters (each of six bytes) as follows:

Stack position	Use
00(A1)	Y coordinate of end of line
06(A1)	X coordinate of end of line
0C(A1)	Y coordinate of start of line
12(A1)	X coordinate of start of line

Remember that stacks grow downwards and therefore the top of the stack is at a physically lower address than the bottom of the stack.

The coordinates referred to are relative to an arbitrary origin (default [0,0]) and an arbitrary scale (default 0..100). Any part of a line which lies outside the specified channel window will not be plotted. No error is returned in such cases.

SD.ARC $32 (50)

Plot an arc

Entry parameters: D3.W   Timeout
                          AO   Channel ID
                          A1   Arithmetic stack pointer

Return parameters: none

Affected registers: D1, A1

Additional errors: NC (-1) not complete
                          NO (-6) channel not open

Description

On entry to this procedure, register A1 must point to a local arithmetic
parameter stack of at least 240 bytes. At the top of the stack there
should be five floating point parameters (each of six bytes) as follows:

Stack position	Use
00(A1)	angle subtended by the arc
06(A1)	Y coordinate of end of arc
0C(A1)	X coordinate of end of arc
12(A1)	Y coordinate of start of arc
18(A1)	X coordinate of start of arc

Remember that stacks grow downwards and therefore the top of the stack
is at a physically lower address than the bottom of the stack.

The coordinates referred to are relative to an arbitrary origin (default
[0,0]) and an arbitrary scale (default 0..100). Any part of the arc
which lies outside the specified channel window will not be plotted. No
error is returned in such cases.

SD.ELIPS $33 (51)

Plot an ellipse

Entry parameters: D3.W   Timeout
                         AO   Channel ID
                         A1   Arithmetic stack pointer

Return parameters: none

Affected registers: D1, A1

Additional errors: NC (-1) not complete
                         NO (-6) channel not open

Description

On entry to this procedure, register A1 must point to a local arithmetic
parameter stack of at least 240 bytes. At the top of the stack there
should be five floating point parameters (each of six bytes) as follows:

Stack position	Use
00(A1)	rotation angle
06(A1)	radius of ellipse
OC(A1)	eccentricity of ellipse
12(A1)	Y coordinate of centre
18(A1)	X coordinate of centre

Remember that stacks grow downwards and therefore the top of the stack
is at a physically lower address than the bottom of the stack.

The coordinates referred to are relative to an arbitrary origin (default
[0,0]) and an arbitrary scale (default 0..100). Any point on the ellipse
which lies outside the specified channel window will not be plotted. No
error is returned in such cases.

SD.SCALE $34 (52)

Set scale

Entry parameters: D3.W   Timeout
                               A0   Channel ID
                               A1   Arithmetic stack pointer

Return parameters: none

Affected registers: D1, A1

Additional errors: NC (-1) not complete
                               NO (-6) channel not open

Description

On entry to this procedure, register A1 must point to a local arithmetic
parameter stack of at least 240 bytes. At the top of the stack there
should be three floating point parameters (each of six bytes) as
follows:

Stack position	Use
00(A1)	Y position of bottom line of window
06(A1)	X position of left-hand pixel of window
0C(A1)	length of Y axis (height of window)

Remember that stacks grow downwards and therefore the top of the stack
is at a physically lower address than the bottom of the stack.

This procedure sets the arbitrary scale for use for all subsequent
graphic plotting calls.

SD.FLOOD $35 (53)

Set/reset area flood

Entry parameters: D1.L   Flood flag
                       D3.W   Timeout
                       A0   Channel ID

Return parameters: none

Affected registers: D1, A1

Additional errors: NC (-1) not complete
                       NO (-6) channel not open

Description

This procedure can be used to set (i.e., turn on), or reset (i.e., turn off) the area flood mode for the specified window. If the attribute flag on entry is set to zero, area flood will be suppressed. If the attribute flag is set to 1, area flood will be enabled.

Note that switching flood mode on will only affect subsequent plotting. Current window contents will not be affected. Likewise when flood mode is switched off, any currently filled areas will remain as such.

SD.GCUR $36 (54)

Set graphic cursor position

Entry parameters: D3.W   Timeout
                           AO   Channel ID
                           A1   Arithmetic stack pointer

Return parameters: none

Affected registers: D1, A1

Additional errors: NC (-1) not complete
                           NO (-6) channel not open

Description

On entry to this procedure, register A1 must point to a local arithmetic parameter stack of at least 240 bytes. At the top of the stack there should be four floating point parameters (each of six bytes) as follows:

Stack position	Use
00(A1)	graphics X coordinate
06(A1)	graphics Y coordinate
0C(A1)	pixel offset to right
12(A1)	pixel offset downwards

Remember that stacks grow downwards and therefore the top of the stack is at a physically lower address than the bottom of the stack.

The coordinates referred to are relative to an arbitrary origin (default [0,0]) and an arbitrary scale (default 0..100).

FS.CHECK $40 (64)

Check pending file operations

Entry parameters:	D3.W	Timeout
	AO	Channel ID
Return parameters:	none	
Affected registers:	D1, A1	
Additional errors:	NC (-1) not complete	
	NO (-6) channel not open	

Description

Implicit buffering operations will be carried out by the standard device drivers whenever a file is read from, written to, or had its file pointer adjusted. These buffering operations, which are carried out in the background and which continue even if the calls which invoked them return 'not complete', will cause physical blocks of a file to be loaded into the slave block area (see Chapter 3).

This TRAP procedure can be used to check whether all of the pending operations have been completed.

FS.FLUSH $41 (65)

Flush file buffers

Entry parameters:	D3.W	Timeout
	A0	Channel ID
Return parameters:	none	
Affected registers:	D1, A1	
Additional errors:	NC (-1) not complete	
	NO (-6) channel not open	

Description

This procedure does not flush the specified file buffer in the sense of throwing the contents of the buffer away. When write operations to a file are complete, as far as an applications program is concerned, the data written may still be in the internal slave blocks rather than physically in the backing store file.

This procedure can, therefore, be used to ensure that all data are written out to the physical device file. It could be called during file operations for the purposes of security, but closing a channel will flush the buffers anyway.

FS.POSAB $42 (66)

Set file pointer absolute

Entry parameters:	D1.L	File pointer position
	D3.W	Timeout
	A0	Channel ID

Return parameters:	D1.L	New file pointer position

Affected registers:	D1, A1

Additional errors:	NC (-1)	not complete
	NO (-6)	channel not open
	EF (-10)	end of file

Description

This procedure enables byte positioning of a file pointer. The specified position is absolute.

The error ERR.EF (-10) will be returned if the pointer is set either to a position before the start, or to a position after the end. In both cases the pointer will be set to the respective extreme limit (i.e., 0 or end of file).

FS.POSRE $43 (67)

Set file pointer relative

Entry parameters: D1.L   Relative file pointer position
                       D3.W   Timeout
                       A0   Channel ID

Return parameters: D1.L   New file pointer position

Affected registers: D1, A1

Additional errors: NC (-1) not complete
                       NO (-6) channel not open
                       EF (-10) end of file

Description

This procedure enables byte positioning of a file pointer. The specified position is relative to the current position. Note that the procedure could be used to obtain the current absolute position of the file pointer, simply by calling it with D1 set to zero.

The error ERR.EF (-10) will be returned if the pointer is set either to a position before the start, or to a position after the end. In both cases the pointer will be set to the respective extreme limit (i.e., 0 or end of file).

FS.MDINF $45 (69)

Get medium information

Entry parameters: D3.W   Timeout
                       AO   Channel ID
                       A1   Pointer to buffer

Return parameters: D1.L   Sector count
                       A1   Pointer to end of buffer

Affected registers: D1, A1 - A3

Additional errors: NC (-1)   not complete
                       NO (-6)   channel not open

Description

Provided a file or device is open, information about the medium may be obtained using this procedure.

On entry, register A1 should point to the beginning of a 10-byte buffer that will be used to store the medium name.
  On return, register A1 will point to the byte following the end of the specified buffer. Also, the most significant word of D1 will hold a count of the number of empty sectors, and the least significant word of D1 will hold a count of the total number of good sectors.

A sector holds 512 bytes.

FS.HEADS $46 (70)

Set file header

Entry parameters:	D3.W	Timeout
	A0	Channel ID
	A1	Base of header table
Return parameters:	D1.W	Length of header set
	A1	Pointer to end of header table
Affected registers:	D1, A1	
Additional errors:	NC (-1)	not complete
	NO (-6)	channel not open

Description

Each file has a header containing information about the file. For standard files that can be listed by a directory command this header is 64 bytes long, as follows:

Offset	Use
00	file length (long-word)
04	file access byte
05	file type byte
06	eight bytes of type information
0E	length of file name (word)
10	file name (maximum 36 bytes)
34	reserved

The access byte is normally set to zero. For data files and SuperBASIC programs the file type is also zero. Executable programs have a file type of 1, and the first four bytes of the type information field will contain the default size of the data space for the program.

This procedure enables the first 14 ($0E) bytes of the header to be set. The filing system will normally, however, overwrite the file length parameter. The procedure cannot be used to rename the file.
    The length of the header set, as returned by the procedure, will be spurious if the channel ID refers to a pure serial device. Also, when the header is sent over such a device, the 14 bytes will be preceded by the byte $FF (255).

FS.HEADR $47 (71)

Read file header

Entry parameters:

	D2.W	Buffer length
	D3.W	Timeout
	A0	Channel ID
	A1	Base of buffer

Return parameters:

	D1.W	Length of header read
	A1	Top of read buffer

Affected registers: D1, A1

Additional errors:

	NC (-1)	not complete
	BO (-5)	buffer overflow
	NO (-6)	channel not open

Description

Each file has a header containing information about the file. For standard files that can be listed by a directory command this header is 64 bytes long, as follows:

Offset	Use
00	file length (long-word)
04	file access byte
05	file type byte
06	eight bytes of type information
0E	length of file name (word)
10	file name (maximum 36 bytes)
34	reserved

The access byte is normally set to zero. For data files and SuperBASIC programs the file type is also zero. Executable programs have a file type of 1, and the first four bytes of the type information field will contain the default size of the data space for the program.

This procedure enables a specified buffer length of bytes (or the first 14 ($0E) bytes in the case of a serial device) of the header to be read. The information provided is useful for allocating space for a file load operation, and also for determining certain characteristics of files. The buffer length must be at least 14 bytes.

Position zero for a file pointer is at the first byte following the header block. The header block is part of a normal sector block and therefore sector block boundaries will be found at file positions 512*n-64.

The length of the header set, as returned by the procedure, will be spurious if the channel ID refers to a pure serial device.

146

FS.LOAD $48 (72)

Load a file

Entry parameters:	D2.L	Length of file
	D3.W	Timeout
	A0	Channel ID
	A1	Base address for load
Return parameters:	A1	Top address after load
Affected registers:	D1, A1	
Additional errors:	NO (-6)	channel not open

Description

This procedure will transfer a file into memory in its entirety. If the transient program area is being used for the load, enough space must have been allocated (via TRAP #1, MT.CJOB; D0=1) prior to the call.

On entry, register D3 should be set to -1 (indefinite timeout), and the base address specified by A1 must be even.

When the procedure returns, register A1 will point to the byte following the last byte loaded.

FS.SAVE $49 (73)

Save a file

Entry parameters:

D2.L	Length of file
D3.W	Timeout
A0	Channel ID
A1	Base address of file

Return parameters: A1   Top address of file

Affected registers: D1, A1

Additional errors: NO (-6)   channel not open

Description

This procedure will transfer a file from memory to backing store in its
entirety. On entry, register D3 should be set to -1 (indefinite
timeout), and the base address specified by A1 must be even.

When the procedure returns, register A1 will point to the byte
following the last byte saved.

7 UTILITY ROUTINES

There are a number of useful routines within the QL ROM that would be of great benefit to application programmers. For example, how about a routine to compare two strings, or even better, a complete floating point arithmetic package? All such routines are available to you!

SIMPLIFIED TRAP ROUTINES

It is possible to class a number of the utility routines (seven to be precise) as being simplified TRAP routines. They offer a reduced overhead in accessing common I/O procedures, but they must be called in user mode.

SUPERBASIC UTILITY ROUTINES

The second group of utility routines described in this chapter are the SuperBASIC utility routines. They may be called from any code (i.e., code running in user or supervisor mode). An enforcement on routine accesses is that all addresses passed to a routine must be relative to register A6. If this rule is not obeyed, for every address passed over, there is no telling what the routine may actually do!

As a general rule, to make life easy for yourself, you may set register A6 to zero at the start of your program (e.g., by using SUB.L A6,A6), if your program resides in the transient program area. In this way you can forget about A6 and just concentrate on making the code program counter relative (i.e., position independent). Alternatively you can assemble your code starting at address zero. In this way your position independent code will always end up with addresses relative to a zero base address. TPA jobs are executed with A6 pointing to the base of the code and, therefore, the addresses in your code will automatically be relative to A6.

It is advisable to allocate at least 64 bytes of stack space before using any of these utilities. In the case of the arithmetic package, 96 bytes would be more appropriate. Note that these are minimal requirements.

7.1 Use of 68000 registers

Each utility routine is accessed through its own vector (see Chapter 3) and therefore there is no need to pass over a code indicating which operation is to be performed.

If an error status is returned by a routine it will be as a long-word in register D0. In such cases, if the code returned is not zero then an error has occurred. Small negative error codes are used to indicate standard errors. These error codes are listed in Appendix C. If the trap call invoked some form of additional device driver, the error code returned can be a pointer to a specific error message. In order that the two types of error return code might never be confused, the pointer type error code is in fact a pointer to an address $8000 below that of the true error message. The full descriptions of the routines which return this kind of error status list which additional errors can be returned. It would of course be wise to check for any errors after a routine has been called.

It is important to realize that not all the routines return an error status. Also, some routines will use register D0 to return a result to the calling program (not an error!). It is the programmers responsibility to know whether or not an error status will be returned, and, if not, whether register D0 will be used for some other purpose.

In addition to the use of registers D0 and A6, data registers D1 to D3 and address registers A0 to A3 are variably used to pass values to and from the routines. A few routines will also use D7 or A4. When the appropriate registers have been set for any one call the appropriate routine is accessed via its well-defined vector (see Chapter 3). In cases where the data size qualifier (i.e., '.B', '.W', or '.L') is not specified within the description, the default is long-word (i.e., '.L').

UT.WINDW   Vector $C4 (196)

Set window using name

Entry parameters: A0   Pointer to name
                            A1   Pointer to parameter block

Return parameters: A0   Channel ID

Affected registers: D1 – D3, A0 – A3

Additional errors: OM (–3) out of memory
                            OR (–4) range error
                            NO (–6) channel not available
                            BN (–12) bad device name

Description

This routine will set up a window defined by the specified name, and with the attributes given in the parameter block. The name should conform to the standard format for a screen device name (see Sec.5.2). The parameter block consists of four bytes as follows:

Byte	Use
0	Border colour
1	Border width
2	Paper colour
3	Ink colour

The strip colour for the window will be set to the same colour as the paper.

Note that the supplied name should be in the form of a standard string. The string definition will consist of a data word, defining the length of the string, followed by the string itself.

UT.CON   Vector $C6 (198)

Set up console window

Entry parameters: A1   Pointer to parameter block

Return parameters: AO   Channel ID

Affected registers: D1 – D3, AO – A3

Additional errors: OM (–3)   out of memory
                       OR (–4)   range error
                       NO (–6)   channel not available

Description

This routine will set up a console window defined by the attributes
given in the parameter block. The block consists of four bytes, and four
words, as follows:

Offset	Use	
00	Border colour	(byte)
01	Border width	
02	Paper colour	
03	Ink colour	
04	Width of window	(word)
06	Height of window	
08	X origin	
OA	Y origin	

The strip colour for the window will be set to the same colour as the
paper. The default keyboard buffer length of 128 bytes will be used.

UT.SCR   Vector $C8 (200)

Set up screen window

Entry parameters:	A1	Pointer to parameter block
Return parameters:	A0	Channel ID
Affected registers:	D1 - D3, A0 - A3	
Additional errors:	OM (-3)	out of memory
	OR (-4)	range error
	NO (-6)	channel not available

Description

This routine will set up a screen window defined by the attributes given in the parameter block. The block consists of four bytes, and four words, as follows:

Offset	Use	
00	Border colour	(byte)
01	Border width	
02	Paper colour	
03	Ink colour	
04	Width of window	(word)
06	Height of window	
08	X origin	
0A	Y origin	

The strip colour for the window will be set to the same colour as the paper.

UT.ERRO   Vector $CA (202)

Write error message to channel 0

Entry parameters: DO.L   Error code

Return parameters: none ·

Affected registers: none

Additional errors: none

Description

This routine will write the error message, defined by DO on entry, to
channel zero. If the error code is in fact an address to a specific
error message (see Sec.7.1), the message must be in the form of a
standard string and it must be terminated by an ASCII <LF> ($0A). The
string definition will consist of a data word, defining the length of
the string, followed by the string itself. The defined length of the
string will include the <LF>.

UT.ERR   Vector $CC (204)

Write error message to channel n

Entry parameters:	DO.L	Error code
	AO	Channel ID
Return parameters:	none	
Affected registers:	none	
Additional errors:	NC (-1) not complete	
	NO (-6) channel not open	

Description

This routine will write the error message, defined by DO on entry, to
the specified channel. If the error code is in fact an address to a
specific error message (see Sec.7.1), the message must be in the form of
a standard string and it must be terminated by an ASCII <LF> ($0A). The
string definition will consist of a data word, defining the length of
the string, followed by the string itself. The defined length of the
string will include the <LF>.

UT.MINT   Vector $CE (206)

Convert integer to ASCII and write it to channel n.

Entry parameters:	D1.W	Integer value
	A0	Channel ID
Return parameters:	none	
Affected registers:	D1 - D3, A1 - A3	
Additional errors:	NC (-1) not complete	
	NO (-6) channel not open	

Description

This routine will convert the integer, specified by register D1, into an
ASCII string. It will then add an ASCII space to the end of the string
and send the whole string to the specified channel.

UT.MTEXT   Vector $D0 (208)

Send message to channel n

Entry parameters:	A0	Channel ID
	A1	Base of message

Return parameters: none

Affected registers: D1 – D3, A1 – A3

Additional errors: NC (–1) not complete
                          NO (–6) channel not open

Description

This routine will send the specified message to the specified channel.
The message must be in the standard format for a string. The string
definition will consist of a data word, defining the length of the
string, followed by the string itself. The defined length of the string
will include any ASCII <LF> terminator, which may be present if desired.

UT.CSTR   Vector $E6 (230)

Compare two strings

Entry parameters:	DO.B	Comparison type
	AO	Base of string 0
	Al	Base of string 1
Return parameters:	DO.L	Result
Affected registers:	none	
Additional errors:	none	

Description

This is a SuperBASIC utility. All addresses must be relative to A6.

The comparison type, specified by register DO on entry, defines the mode of operation of the comparison operation. Valid types are:

Type	Comparison
0	Simple, character by character
1	As type 0, case of characters ignored
2	As type 0, value of embedded numbers is significant
3	As type 1, value of embedded numbers is significant

The result returned in register DO will be one of three values:

Result	Reason
-1	String 0 is less than string 1
0	String 0 and string 1 are the same
+1	String 1 is less than string 0

The string definitions will consist of a data word, defining the length of the string, followed by the string itself.

CN.DATE   Vector $EC (236)

Get date and time

Entry parameters:	D1.L	Date (internal value)
	A1	Pointer to stack area
Return parameters:	A1	Updated stack pointer
Affected registers:	A1	
Additional errors:	none	

Description

This is a SuperBASIC utility. All addresses must be relative to A6.

This routine will return the data and time as a 20-byte string in standard string format. The date string will have the form:

yyyy mmm dd hh:mm:ss

On entry to the routine, register A1 must point to the top of a stack area. At least 22 bytes must be available at the top of this stack for the routine to store the string, and its length. On returning to the calling program, the pointer will be pointing to the new top of the stack area (which will be holding the length of the string).

CN.DAY   Vector $EE (238)

Get day of week

Entry parameters:	D1.L	Date (internal value)
	A1	Pointer to stack area
Return parameters:	A1	Updated stack pointer
Affected registers:	A1	
Additional errors:	none	

Description

This is a SuperBASIC utility. All addresses must be relative to A6.

This routine will return the day of the week as a 3-byte string in standard string format. On entry to the routine, register A1 must point to the top of a stack area. At least six bytes must be available at the top of this stack for the routine to store the string, and its length. On returning to the calling program, the pointer will be pointing to the new top of the stack area (which will be holding the length of the string).

CN.FTOD   Vector $F0 (240)

Convert floating point to ASCII

Entry parameters:	A0	Pointer to buffer
	A1	Pointer to stack
Return parameters:	A0	Updated buffer pointer
	A1	Updated stack pointer
Affected registers:	D1 – D3, A0 – A3	
Additional errors:	none	

Description

This is a SuperBASIC utility. All addresses must be relative to A6.

This routine will convert a floating point number into a string of ASCII characters. The string will not be in standard format and, therefore, will not be preceded by a word of data giving the byte count.
  On entry, the floating point number must be on the top of a stack area pointed to by A1, and register A0 must point to a buffer area. On return, the string will be stored in the buffer. The buffer must be at least 14 bytes long. Both the stack pointer and the buffer pointer will be updated. The stack pointer will be incremented by 6, and the buffer pointer will point to the byte following the last character stored.

CN.ITOD   Vector $F2 (242)

Convert integer to ASCII

Entry parameters:	A0	Pointer to buffer
	A1	Pointer to stack

Return parameters:	A0	Updated buffer pointer
	A1	Updated stack pointer

Affected registers: D1 – D3, A0 – A3

Additional errors: none

Description

This is a SuperBASIC utility. All addresses must be relative to A6.

This routine will convert an integer number into a string of ASCII characters. The string will not be in standard format and, therefore, will not be preceded by a word of data giving the byte count.

On entry, the integer must be on the top of a stack area pointed to by A1, and register A0 must point to a buffer area. On return, the string will be stored in the buffer. The buffer must be at least six bytes long. Both the stack pointer and the buffer pointer will be updated. The stack pointer will be incremented by 2, and the buffer pointer will point to the byte following the last character stored.

CN.ITOBB   Vector $F4 (244)

Convert byte (binary) to ASCII

Entry parameters:	A0	Pointer to buffer
	A1	Pointer to stack
Return parameters:	A0	Updated buffer pointer
	A1	Updated stack pointer
Affected registers:	D1 – D3, A0 – A3	
Additional errors:	none	

Description

This is a SuperBASIC utility. All addresses must be relative to A6.

This routine will convert a binary number, of size byte, into a string of ASCII characters. The string will not be in standard format and, therefore, will not be preceded by a word of data giving the byte count. On entry, the byte must be on the top of a stack area pointed to by A1, and register A0 must point to a buffer area. On return, the string will be stored in the buffer. The buffer must be at least eight bytes long. Both the stack pointer and the buffer pointer will be updated. The stack pointer will be incremented by 1, and the buffer pointer will point to the byte following the last character stored.

CN.ITOBW   Vector $F6 (246)

Convert word (binary) to ASCII

Entry parameters: A0   Pointer to buffer
                      A1   Pointer to stack

Return parameters: A0   Updated buffer pointer
                      A1   Updated stack pointer

Affected registers: D1 – D3, A0 – A3

Additional errors: none

Description

This is a SuperBASIC utility. All addresses must be relative to A6.

This routine will convert a binary number, of size word, into a string of ASCII characters. The string will not be in standard format and, therefore, will not be preceded by a word of data giving the byte count.
  On entry, the word of data must be on the top of a stack area pointed to by A1, and register A0 must point to a buffer area. On return, the string will be stored in the buffer. The buffer must be at least 16 bytes long. Both the stack pointer and the buffer pointer will be updated. The stack pointer will be incremented by 2, and the buffer pointer will point to the byte following the last character stored.

CN.ITOBL   Vector $F8 (248)

Convert long—word (binary) to ASCII

Entry parameters:	A0	Pointer to buffer
	A1	Pointer to stack
Return parameters:	A0	Updated buffer pointer
	A1	Updated stack pointer
Affected registers:	D1 – D3, A0 – A3	
Additional errors:	none	

Description

This is a SuperBASIC utility. All addresses must be relative to A6.

This routine will convert a binary number, of size long—word, into a string of ASCII characters. The string will not be in standard format and, therefore, will not be preceded by a word of data giving the byte count.
  On entry, the long—word must be on the top of a stack area pointed to by A1, and register A0 must point to a buffer area. On return, the string will be stored in the buffer. The buffer must be at least 32 bytes long. Both the stack pointer and the buffer pointer will be updated. The stack pointer will be incremented by 4, and the buffer pointer will point to the byte following the last character stored.

CN.ITOHB   Vector $FA (250)

Convert byte to hexadecimal ASCII

Entry parameters:	A0	Pointer to buffer
	A1	Pointer to stack
Return parameters:	A0	Updated buffer pointer
	A1	Updated stack pointer
Affected registers:	D1 - D3, A0 - A3	
Additional errors:	none	

Description

This is a SuperBASIC utility. All addresses must be relative to A6.

This routine will convert a single byte into a string of ASCII characters. The string will not be in standard format and, therefore, will not be preceded by a word of data giving the byte count.
  On entry, the byte must be on the top of a stack area pointed to by A1, and register A0 must point to a buffer area. On return, the string will be stored in the buffer. The buffer must be at least two bytes long. Both the stack pointer and the buffer pointer will be updated. The stack .pointer will be incremented by 1, and the buffer pointer will point to the byte following the last character stored.

CN.ITOHW   Vector $FC (252)

Convert word to hexadecimal ASCII

Entry parameters:	A0	Pointer to buffer
	A1	Pointer to stack
Return parameters:	A0	Updated buffer pointer
	A1	Updated stack pointer
Affected registers:	D1 – D3, A0 – A3	
Additional errors:	none	

Description

This is a SuperBASIC utility. All addresses must be relative to A6.

This routine will convert a word of data into a string of ASCII characters. The string will not be in standard format and, therefore, will not be preceded by a word of data giving the byte count.
  On entry, the data word must be on the top of a stack area pointed to by A1, and register A0 must point to a buffer area. On return, the string will be stored in the buffer. The buffer must be at least four bytes long. Both the stack pointer and the buffer pointer will be updated. The stack pointer will be incremented by 2, and the buffer pointer will point to the byte following the last character stored.

CN.ITOHL   Vector $FE (254)

Convert long-word to hexadecimal ASCII

Entry parameters:	A0	Pointer to buffer
	A1	Pointer to stack
Return parameters:	A0	Updated buffer pointer
	A1	Updated stack pointer
Affected registers:	D1 – D3, A0 – A3	
Additional errors:	none	

Description

This is a SuperBASIC utility. All addresses must be relative to A6.

This routine will convert a long-word of data into a string of ASCII characters. The string will not be in standard format and, therefore, will not be preceded by a word of data giving the byte count.
   On entry, the long-word must be on the top of a stack area pointed to by A1, and register A0 must point to a buffer area. On return, the string will be stored in the buffer. The buffer must be at least eight bytes long. Both the stack pointer and the buffer pointer will be updated. The stack pointer will be incremented by 4, and the buffer pointer will point to the byte following the last character stored.

CN.DTOF   Vector $100 (256)

Convert ASCII to floating point

Entry parameters:	D7	Pointer to end of buffer
	AO	Pointer to buffer
	A1	Pointer to stack

Return parameters:	AO	Updated buffer pointer
	A1	Updated stack pointer

Affected registers: D1 - D3, AO - A3

Additional errors: XP (-17) expression error

Description

This is a SuperBASIC utility. All addresses must be relative to A6.

This routine will convert a string of ASCII characters into a floating point number. The string should not be in standard format and, therefore, will not be preceded by a word of data giving the byte count. Conversion will stop either when AO equals D7, or when a non-permissible character is found in the ASCII string.
   On entry, register A1 must point to the top of a stack area, and register AO must point to the buffer area containing the string. The stack must have at least six bytes free. Register D7 may either point to the end of the buffer, or be zero. On return, the floating point number will be loaded onto the top of the stack. Both the stack pointer and the buffer pointer will be updated if no error occurs. The stack pointer will be decremented by 6, and the buffer pointer will point to the byte following the last valid character scanned.

CN.DTOI   Vector $102 (258)

Convert ASCII to integer

Entry parameters: D7   Pointer to end of buffer
                        AO   Pointer to buffer
                        A1   Pointer to stack

Return parameters: AO   Updated buffer pointer
                        A1   Updated stack pointer

Affected registers: D1 - D3, AO - A3

Additional errors: XP (-17) expression error

Description

This is a SuperBASIC utility. All addresses must be relative to A6.

This routine will convert a string of ASCII characters into an integer.
The string should not be in standard format and, therefore, will not be
preceded by a word of data giving the byte count. Conversion will stop
either when AO equals D7, or when a non-permissible character is found
in the ASCII string.
  On entry, register A1 must point to the top of a stack area, and
register AO must point to the buffer area containing the string. The
stack must have at least four bytes free. Register D7 may either point
to the end of the buffer, or be zero. On return, the integer will be
loaded onto the top of the stack. Both the stack pointer and the buffer
pointer will be updated if no error occurs. The stack pointer will be
decremented by 2, and the buffer pointer will point to the byte
following the last valid character scanned.

CN.BTOIB   Vector $104 (260)

Convert ASCII to byte

Entry parameters:	D7	Pointer to end of buffer
	A0	Pointer to buffer
	A1	Pointer to stack
Return parameters:	A0	Updated buffer pointer
	A1	Updated stack pointer
Affected registers:	D1 – D3, A0 – A3	
Additional errors:	XP (–17) expression error	

Description

This is a SuperBASIC utility. All addresses must be relative to A6.

This routine will convert a string of ASCII ones and zeros into a byte
of data. The string should not be in standard format and, therefore,
will not be preceded by a word of data giving the byte count. Conversion
will stop either when A0 equals D7, or when a non-permissible character
is found in the ASCII string.
   On entry, register A1 must point to the top of a stack area (at an
even address boundary), and register A0 must point to the buffer area
containing the string. The stack must have at least four bytes free.
Register D7 may either point to the end of the buffer, or be zero. On
return, the byte (as the least significant byte of a word) will be
loaded onto the top of the stack. Both the stack pointer and the buffer
pointer will be updated if no error occurs. The stack pointer will be
decremented by 1, and the buffer pointer will point to the byte
following the last valid character scanned.
   This routine will not work on QDOS versions 1.03 and earlier.

CN.BTOIW   Vector $106 (262)

Convert ASCII to word

Entry parameters:	D7	Pointer to end of buffer
	A0	Pointer to buffer
	A1	Pointer to stack
Return parameters:	A0	Updated buffer pointer
	A1	Updated stack pointer
Affected registers:	D1 - D3, A0 - A3	
Additional errors:	XP (-17) expression error	

Description

This is a SuperBASIC utility. All addresses must be relative to A6.

This routine will convert a string of ASCII ones and zeros into a word of data. The string should not be in standard format and, therefore, will not be preceded by a word of data giving the byte count. Conversion will stop either when A0 equals D7, or when a non-permissible character is found in the ASCII string.

  On entry, register A1 must point to the top of a stack area, and register A0 must point to the buffer area containing the string. The stack must have at least four bytes free. Register D7 may either point to the end of the buffer, or be zero. On return, the word of data will be loaded onto the top of the stack. Both the stack pointer and the buffer pointer will be updated if no error occurs. The stack pointer will be decremented by 2, and the buffer pointer will point to the byte following the last valid character scanned.

  This routine will not work on QDOS versions 1.03 and earlier.

CN.BTOIL   Vector $108 (264)

Convert ASCII to long-word

Entry parameters: D7   Pointer to end of buffer
                         AO   Pointer to buffer
                         A1   Pointer to stack

Return parameters: AO   Updated buffer pointer
                         A1   Updated stack pointer

Affected registers: D1 - D3, AO - A3

Additional errors: XP (-17) expression error

Description

This is a SuperBASIC utility. All addresses must be relative to A6.

This routine will convert a string of ASCII ones and zeros into a long-word of data. The string should not be in standard format and, therefore, will not be preceded by a word of data giving the byte count. Conversion will stop either when AO equals D7, or when a non-permissible character is found in the ASCII string.

On entry, register A1 must point to the top of a stack area, and register AO must point to the buffer area containing the string. The stack must have at least four bytes free. Register D7 may either point to the end of the buffer, or be zero. On return, the long-word will be loaded onto the top of the stack. Both the stack pointer and the buffer pointer will be updated if no error occurs. The stack pointer will be decremented by 4, and the buffer pointer will point to the byte following the last valid character scanned.

This routine will not work on QDOS versions 1.03 and earlier.

CN.HTOIB   Vector $10A (266)

Convert hexadecimal ASCII to byte

Entry parameters:	D7	Pointer to end of buffer
	AO	Pointer to buffer
	A1	Pointer to stack

Return parameters:	AO	Updated buffer pointer
	A1	Updated stack pointer

Affected registers: D1 - D3, AO - A3

Additional errors: XP (-17) expression error

Description

This is a SuperBASIC utility. All addresses must be relative to A6.

This routine will convert a string of ASCII characters into a byte of data. The string should not be in standard format and, therefore, will not be preceded by a word of data giving the byte count. Conversion will stop either when AO equals D7, or when a non-permissible character is found in the hexadecimal ASCII string.

On entry, register A1 must point to the top of a stack area (at an even address boundary), and register AO must point to the buffer area containing the string. The stack must have at least four bytes free. Register D7 may either point to the end of the buffer, or be zero. On return, the byte (as the least significant byte of a word) will be loaded onto the top of the stack. Both the stack pointer and the buffer pointer will be updated if no error occurs. The stack pointer will be decremented by 1, and the buffer pointer will point to the byte following the last valid character scanned.

This routine will not work on QDOS versions 1.03 and earlier.

CN.HTOIW   Vector $10C (268)

Convert hexadecimal ASCII to word

Entry parameters:	D7	Pointer to end of buffer
	A0	Pointer to buffer
	A1	Pointer to stack
Return parameters:	A0	Updated buffer pointer
	A1	Updated stack pointer
Affected registers:	D1 – D3, A0 – A3	
Additional errors:	XP (–17) expression error	

Description

This is a SuperBASIC utility. All addresses must be relative to A6.

This routine will convert a string of ASCII characters into a word of data. The string should not be in standard format and, therefore, will not be preceded by a word of data giving the byte count. Conversion will stop either when A0 equals D7, or when a non-permissible character is found in the hexadecimal ASCII string.
   On entry, register A1 must point to the top of a stack area, and register A0 must point to the buffer area containing the string. The stack must have at least four bytes free. Register D7 may either point to the end of the buffer, or be zero. On return, the word of data will be loaded onto the top of the stack. Both the stack pointer and the buffer pointer will be updated if no error occurs. The stack pointer will be decremented by 2, and the buffer pointer will point to the byte following the last valid character scanned.
   This routine will not work on QDOS versions 1.03 and earlier.

CN.HTOIL   Vector $10E (270)

Convert hexadecimal ASCII to long—word

Entry parameters:	D7	Pointer to end of buffer
	A0	Pointer to buffer
	A1	Pointer to stack
Return parameters:	A0	Updated buffer pointer
	A1	Updated stack pointer
Affected registers:	D1 - D3, A0 - A3	
Additional errors:	XP (-17) expression error	

Description

This is a SuperBASIC utility. All addresses must be relative to A6.

This routine will convert a string of ASCII characters into a long—word of data. The string should not be in standard format and, therefore, will not be preceded by a word of data giving the byte count. Conversion will stop either when A0 equals D7, or when a non—permissible character is found in the hexadecimal ASCII string.
   On entry, register A1 must point to the top of a stack area, and register A0 must point to the buffer area containing the string. The stack must have at least four bytes free. Register D7 may either point to the end of the buffer, or be zero. On return, the long—word of data will be loaded onto the top of the stack. Both the stack pointer and the buffer pointer will be updated if no error occurs. The stack pointer will be decremented by 4, and the buffer pointer will point to the byte following the last valid character scanned.
   This routine will not work on QDOS versions 1.03 and earlier.

RI.EXEC   Vector $11C (284)

Execute single arithmetic operation

Entry parameters:	DO.B	Operation code
	D7	0
	A1	Pointer to arithmetic stack
	A4	Pointer to base of load/store area

Return parameters:	A1	Updated stack pointer

Affected registers: A1

Additional errors: OV (-18) arithmetic overflow

Description

This is a SuperBASIC utility. All addresses must be relative to A6. Also, it is advised that data register D7 be set to zero.

The arithmetic package operates on floating point numbers that exist on a specified arithmetic stack. The package will operate on the floating point number at the top of the stack (TOS), which is pointed to by '0(A6,A1.L)', and if required for any one operation the package will also operate on the next floating point number on the stack (NOS), which is pointed to by '6(A6,A1.L)'. The format of floating point numbers is discussed in Chapter 8.

  The package will accept one of two types of operation code. First, there are the true arithmetic operations. These have codes in the range $02 to $30 inclusive:

Code	Name	Operation
02	RI.NINT	TOS to nearest integer, A1=A1+4
04	RI.INT	TOS to truncated integer, A1=A1+4
06	RI.NLINT	TOS to nearest long integer, A1=A1+2
08	RI.FLOAT	Integer TOS to floating point, A1=A1-4
0A	RI.ADD	Add TOS to NOS, A1=A1+6
0C	RI.SUB	Subtract TOS from NOS, A1=A1+6
0E	RI.MULT	Multiply TOS by NOS, A1=A1+6
10	RI.DIV	Divide TOS into NOS, A1=A1+6
12	RI.ABS	Positive value of TOS
14	RI.NEG	Negate TOS
16	RI.DUP	Duplicate TOS, A1=A1-6
18	RI.COS	Cosine of TOS
1A	RI.SIN	Sine of TOS
1C	RI.TAN	Tangent of TOS
1E	RI.COT	Cotangent of TOS
20	RI.ASIN	Arcsine of TOS

22	RI.ACOS	Arccosine of TOS
24	RI.ATAN	Arctangent of TOS
26	RI.ACOT	Arccotangent of TOS
28	RI.SQRT	Square root of TOS
2A	RI.LN	Natural logarithm of TOS
2C	RI.LOG	LOG10 of TOS
2E	RI.EXP	Exponential of TOS
30	RI.POWFP	NOS to power of TOS, A1=A1+6

Some of these operations are seen to affect the stack. Remember that stacks grow downwards. A few examples will clarify the situation. First, let us look at RI.COS (code $18). This does not affect the stack pointer (A1). The floating point number on the top of the stack is taken as the argument for the cosine operation, and the resultant cosine is placed on the top of the stack. A floating point number is removed, and a floating point number is put back, so the stack pointer remains unmoved. Second, let us look at RI.NINT (code $02). This will take the floating point number from the top of the stack and convert it to the nearest integer. This integer result is then placed on the stack. Floating point numbers are six bytes long, but integers are only two bytes long, therefore the stack pointer is incremented by 4 (i.e., four less bytes will now be required on the stack). By looking at the effect on the stack pointer (A1), you should now be able to deduce what is happening to the stack for each of the operations listed.

The second type of operation code is a negative code in the range $FF to $31 (interpreted as the range $FFFF to $FF31 inclusive). These codes indicate a load operation (i.e., from memory to stack) if the least significant bit of the code is zero, or they indicate a store operation (i.e., from stack to memory) if the least significant bit of the code is set. The memory address used for the load or store is given by:

$$A6.L + A4.L + ((opcode\ AND\ \$FE)\ OR\ \$FF00)$$

Only floating point values may be transferred. A load operation will cause the stack pointer A1 to be decremented by 6 (creating a new TOS). A save operation will cause the stack pointer A1 to be incremented by 6 (NOS will become new TOS).

RI.EXECB   Vector $11E (286)

Execute list of arithmetic operations

Entry parameters: D7   0
                       A1   Pointer to arithmetic stack
                       A3   Pointer to operation list
                       A4   Pointer to base of variable area

Return parameters: A1   Updated stack pointer

Affected registers: A1

Additional errors: OV (-18) arithmetic overflow

Description

This is a SuperBASIC utility. All addresses must be relative to A6.
Also, it is advised that data register D7 be set to zero.

This routine enables a list of operations to be carried out by the
arithmetic package. Any one operation may be as defined under RI.EXEC
(vector $11C). The byte list of operation codes are pointed to by
register A3 on entry to the routine, and the list must be terminated by
a zero byte.

8 LINKING INTO SuperBASIC

There are two major topics within this chapter. One topic is that of SuperBASIC machine code commands (e.g., CALL, SBYTES, etc.), and the second topic is concerned with interfacing machine code procedures and functions into SuperBASIC in order to extend the language. We will, for the present time, look at the theory only. The four chapters in Part 3 present plenty of real examples on how to do things in practice.

8.1   SuperBASIC machine code commands

A total of eight procedures and functions exist within SuperBASIC to enable the assembly language programmer to load, save, and execute machine code routines. Six of the commands are commonly used (i.e., CALL, EXEC, SEXEC, LBYTES, SBYTES, and RESPR). The remaining two (i.e., PEEK and POKE) exist mainly, it is suggested, for completeness. None of the example programs in Part 3 need these last two commands. Peeking and poking, as a discipline on the QL, is discouraged (at least be the author!!). An assembler package should always be used to create, modify, and generate machine code programs.

   Although it may be possible to group the commands into sub-groups, and then look at each sub-group, we will deal with the commands in alphabetical order. This is consistent with the format in previous chapters, and will make future references easier tasks.

CALL

This is a procedure which will accept an address followed by' a maximum of 13 parameters. The general format of the command is:

CALL addr, p1, p2, ... , pn

The address 'addr' is the start address of the machine code to be executed, and the machine code must exist in the resident procedure area (see RESPR). If any parameters are supplied they will be put into the 68000 data and address registers D1 to D7 and A0 to A5, respectively. For example, if one parameter only is supplied, it will be placed into data register D1. If eight parameters are supplied, the first seven will go into data registers D1 to D7 respectively, and the eighth will go into address register A0.

No parameters can be returned from a CALL statement. SuperBASIC will report the error found in register D0 on return from a called routine. If no errors occurred in the machine code program, it is advisable to set D0.L to zero before returning. The CALL procedure is particularly useful for calling the initialisation routine of a machine code package to extend SuperBASIC.

EXEC

This is a procedure which is used to invoke an executable code file, or a sequence of such files. Each executable program will become a separate QDOS job, and will execute within the transient program area. Two forms of the command exist:

$$\text{EXEC job1, job2, job3, ... , jobn}$$

$$\text{EXEC\_W job1, job2, job3, ... , jobn}$$

The first form (i.e., EXEC) will invoke the job and return immediately to SuperBASIC. The second form (i.e., EXEC_W) will invoke the jobs, but not return to SuperBASIC until all the jobs have finished execution. All the example programs in Chapters 9 and 10 are designed to be executable code programs and, therefore, invoked by this EXEC command.

LBYTES

Any file can be loaded into memory, starting at a specified address, using this procedure. The general format of the command is:

$$\text{LBYTES device\_file, addr}$$

The procedure is most obviously used to load machine code extensions to SuperBASIC into the resident procedure area, prior to initialisation and subsequent use. The parameter 'addr' is the base address in memory where the code is to be loaded. Note that this procedure will only load the file, it will not attempt to run the bytes loaded.

PEEK

This is a function which will return the contents of the specified memory location. There are three forms, allowing a choice of data size:

$$\text{value = PEEK addr}$$

$$\text{value = PEEK\_W addr}$$

$$\text{value = PEEK\_L addr}$$

The first of these will return a byte (8-bit) value. The specified address may be any address desired. The last two will return a word (16-bit) and a long-word (32-bit) respectively. Both of these latter two forms require 'addr' to be an even address.

POKE

This is a procedure which will load the specified memory location with the specified data. There are three forms, allowing a choice of data size:

POKE addr, data

POKE_W addr, data

POKE_L addr, data

The first of these will load a byte (8-bit) value. The specified address may be any address desired. The last two will load a word (16-bit) and a long-word (32-bit) respectively. Both of these latter two forms require 'addr' to be an even address. For word operations the memory locations 'addr' and 'addr+1' will be used, with the most significant byte going into 'addr'. Long-word operations will use locations 'addr' to 'addr+3', again with the most significant byte going into 'addr'.

RESPR

This is a function which is used to reserve space in the resident procedure area of memory. It has the general form:

base = RESPR (space)

The function requires one parameter, specifying the amount of memory required. If there is insufficient room in memory to perform the required allocation, the message 'out of memory' will be displayed and the function will abort. The function will also abort, with the error message 'not complete', if any executable programs are in the process of running. On a successful completion, the function will return the base address of the memory area allocated.

Space allocated by RESPR, in the resident procedure area, cannot be reclaimed (normally) without re-booting the machine. It follows that, if two or more RESPR functions are executed without intermediate re-boots, the function will keep extending the resident procedure area until memory is exhausted. This enables more than one block of RAM to be allocated, with each block having its own base address. The blocks will not overlap.

SBYTES

This procedure is the inverse of LBYTES, discussed earlier. The general form of the command is:

SBYTES device_file, addr, length

The area of memory from 'addr' to 'addr+length' will be saved on the specified device, and in the specified file.

SEXEC

This is a procedure which will save an area of memory, on a specified device, in a form suitable for use with the SuperBASIC EXEC (or EXEC_W) procedure. The general form of the statement is:

SEXEC device_file, addr, length, dataspace

It is assumed that the area of memory from 'addr' to 'addr+length' holds a machine code program. The parameter 'dataspace' should specify the size of the data memory (including stack areas) that will be required by the program when it is executed. Note that you do not save, therefore, run-time workspace. You save the code only, and specify the size of run-time workspace required.

8.2   Interfacing to SuperBASIC

When we talk of interfacing to SuperBASIC, we are really talking about extending the SuperBASIC language by the addition of suitably written machine code procedures and functions. Actually making SuperBASIC realise that extra routines (commands or statements) are available is an almost trivial task (see Sec.8.5). Collecting parameters, manipulating SuperBASIC variables and channels, and returning results may not be so easy (though they could not be called onerous).
   In order to interface to SuperBASIC we need to know about such things as the run-time context of our routine (i.e., what pointers exist in which address registers when entry is made to our routine by SuperBASIC), and the structure of the SuperBASIC work area. The rest of this chapter is dedicated to the theory of interfacing to SuperBASIC. Chapters 11 and 12 contain some real examples.

8.3   The SuperBASIC environment

It was shown in Chapter 3 that the whole of the SuperBASIC area can shift dynamically. This being the case, there must be a pointer somewhere that informs SuperBASIC routines where the start of the area is. All references to the actual program, the variable tables, and so on will then be made relative to that (running) pointer. In practice, the pointer is address register A6.

On entry to your machine code extension, register A6 will point to the base of the SuperBASIC work area pointer table (see Fig.8.1). This pointer table holds vital information about the relative positions of distinctly separate SuperBASIC work areas. For example, one of these areas is the program itself! Each pointer is a long-word and its value is itself relative to register A6. In other words, the pointers do not hold absolute location values for the work areas. They contain, instead, relative offsets to the work areas. Let us look at each of these areas in more detail.

BUFFER AREA

This is exactly what the name suggests; a buffer area. A minimum of 128 bytes exist, and routines are free to use the area as they wish. The true length of this area can be determined by subtracting the buffer area base pointer from the pointer held in '$08(A6)', e.g.:

```
     :
     move.l    bv_bfbas(a6),d1      ;get base pointer
     move.l    $08(a6),d2           ;get pointer past top
     subq.l    #1,d2                ;(top)
     sub.l     d1,d2                ;length now in D2
     :
```

A running pointer (BV_BFP) exists for use as required, within this buffer area. It will usually point to the first free location.

SUPERBASIC PROGRAM AREA

This is simply the area where the current SuperBASIC program is held. Pointers BV_PFBAS and BV_PFP point to the base and the byte beyond the end of this area respectively.

NAME TABLE

This table is vitally important. Each reference to a variable in a SuperBASIC program is, internally, a pointer to an entry in the name table. Each entry is eight bytes long, as shown in Fig.8.1.

184

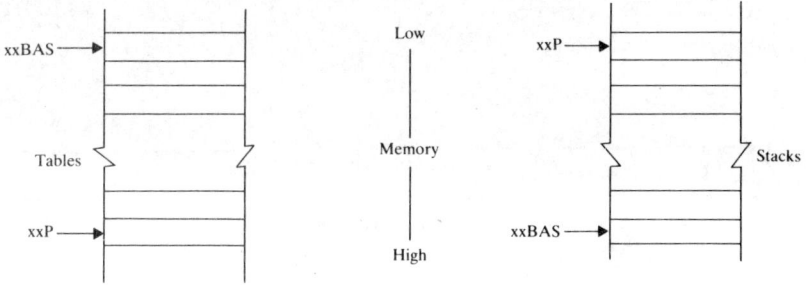

xxBAS →

Tables

xxP →

Low

Memory

High

xxP →

Stacks

xxBAS →

Super BASIC variable
pointer table

$00 (A6)	Buffer base	BV_BFBAS
$04 (A6)	Buffer running pointer	BV_BFP
$08 (A6)		
$10 (A6)	Super BASIC program base	BV_PFBAS
$14 (A6)	Top of Super BASIC program	BV_PFP
$18 (A6)	Name table base	BV_NTBAS
$1C (A6)	Top of name table	BV_NTP
$20 (A6)	Name list base	BV_NLBAS
$24 (A6)	Top of name list	BV_NLP
$28 (A6)	Variable values base	BV_VVBAS
$2C (A6)	Top of variable values	BV_VVP
$30 (A6)	Channel table base	BV_CHBAS
$34 (A6)	Top of channel table	BV_CHP
$58 (A6)	Top of arithmetic stack	BV_RIP
$5C (A6)	Base of arithmetic stack	BV_RIBAS
$60 (A6)	Top of system stack	BV_SSP
$64 (A6)	Base of system stack	BV_SSBAS

Table pointers

Stack pointers

★★ Each pointer is itself
relative to A6

Figure 8.1 SuperBASIC pointer table and work areas

BYTE	USE
0,1	Description of usage of name: 0001 unset string variable 0002 unset floating point variable 0003 unset integer variable 0201 string variable 0202 floating point variable 0203 integer variable 0300 array substring (internal only) 0301 string array 0302 floating point array 0303 integer array 0400 SuperBASIC procedure 0501 SuperBASIC string function 0502 SuperBASIC floating point function 0503 SuperBASIC integer function 0602 REPEAT loop index variable 0702 FOR loop index variable 0800 Machine code procedure 0900 Machine code function
2,3	Name pointer. This is an offset to the name in the name list. A value of -1 signifies that the entry is an expression value for the expression evaluator (in such cases the bytes 0,1 of the name table entry will be 01xx). If the entry is a copy of another entry, the name pointer will be a pointer to that entry.
4-7	Value pointer (long-word). This is an offset to the value of the entry (in the case of variables) or to the descriptor (in the case of arrays), from the base of the variable values area. If the pointer is negative, a value has not been assigned yet. It is also used for the absolute pointer to a procedure or function, or the line number of a SuperBASIC procedure or function.

Note that procedures (SuperBASIC or machine code), and machine code functions, have no 'type'. SuperBASIC functions do have a type, which is defined by the last character of the function name (i.e., none, $, or %).

NAME LIST

This is a list of the actual names themselves. Each name is stored as a byte of data holding the character count, followed by the characters of the name.

VARIABLE VALUES

This area is a heap area with entries allocated in 8-byte blocks. One or more block allocations are used, depending on the type of the variable.

1. An integer is two bytes long. Normal two's complement format is used.

2. A floating point number is stored as a 2-byte offset exponent followed by a 4-byte mantissa. Examples of floating byte codes are:

Exponent	Mantissa		Value
0000	0000	0000	0.0
0801	4000	0000	1.0
0800	8000	0000	−1.0
0804	5000	0000	10.0

3. A string will be stored as a word of data, containing the byte count of the string, followed by the string itself. The actual space taken by a string will be rounded to the nearest even number.

4. Array descriptors have a long-word header that is the offset of the array values from the base of the variable values area. Next, there are the number of dimensions of the array (stored as a word of data), and then there are pairs of data words for each dimension. The first 'dimension word' will specify the maximum index for that dimension, and the second word will be the index multiplier for that dimension. The figure opposite shows the layout of a floating point array. Note that if the dimensioning statement in SuperBASIC was, for example,

DIM A(3,2)

the descriptor would have the format:

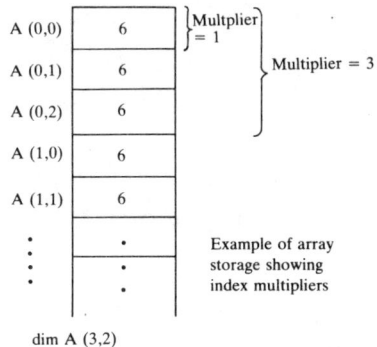

Example of array storage showing index multipliers

dim A (3,2)

base, 2, 3, 3, 2, 1

The storage of floating point arrays and integer arrays is entirely regular. Floating point array elements are six bytes long, and integer array elements are two bytes long.

A string array is regular (i.e., it is an array of standard strings) except for element zero of the last dimension. The last dimension of a string array defines the maximum length of the string. It will always be rounded up to the nearest even number.

CHANNEL TABLE

SuperBASIC channel numbers (#n) are pointers to the channel table. This table is a set of sub-tables, one sub-table for each open channel (see Fig.8.2). A sub-table is 40 ($28) bytes long. The sub-table entry for #n would therefore be located at:

$$\text{BV\_CHBAS(A6)} + (\text{n} \times \text{CH.LENCH})$$

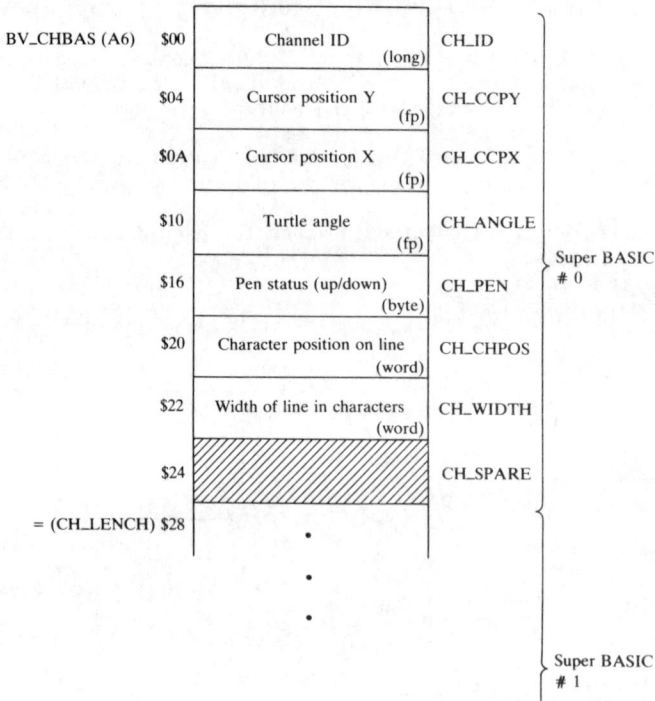

BV_CHBAS (A6)	$00	Channel ID (long)	CH_ID
	$04	Cursor position Y (fp)	CH_CCPY
	$0A	Cursor position X (fp)	CH_CCPX
	$10	Turtle angle (fp)	CH_ANGLE
	$16	Pen status (up/down) (byte)	CH_PEN
	$20	Character position on line (word)	CH_CHPOS
	$22	Width of line in characters (word)	CH_WIDTH
	$24	/////////	CH_SPARE
= (CH_LENCH)	$28	. . .	

Super BASIC # 0

Super BASIC # 1

Figure 8.2 SuperBASIC channel definition table

ARITHMETIC STACK

The arithmetic stack is the working area for expression evaluation. It is also used in evaluating call, and return, parameters. It may also be used as a general working area. Remember that stacks grow downwards (i.e., from high memory to lower memory).

The SuperBASIC interface mechanism automatically tidies up the arithmetic stack after procedure calls, and after errors in functions. On the other hand, a good return from a function must be made with a tidy stack. The return argument must be on the top of the stack (i.e., at the low stack memory end), and no other data must be left below the argument (i.e., at a physically higher stack memory address). See Sec.8.11 also.

SYSTEM STACK

This is the area used when any reference is made (implied or otherwise) to the address register A7. It is, for example, the stack area that will be used to store the return address for a 68000 'BSR' instruction.

8.4   Implementing machine code procedures

There is a simple set of rules that must be obeyed when writing machine code extensions to the SuperBASIC language.

1. It must be remembered that the whole of the SuperBASIC area can move, and therefore all references to this area must be relative to address register A6 (or A7 in the case of stacks). These two address registers should never be saved for future use (obviously!), used in arithmetic or address calculations, or altered (except by pushing and popping on the A7 stack).

2. Not more than 128 bytes may be used on the 'user' stack.

3. Data register D0 must be returned with an error code (long-word).

On entry to the routine, SuperBASIC will have set up, in addition to the above registers, address registers A3 and A5. Any parameters passed over to the routine will have entries created for them in the name table (see Sections 8.3 and 8.6). Register A3 will point to the first parameter entry, and register A5 will point to the end of the last entry (remember that A3 and A5 are relative to A6). The number of parameters passed over will, therefore, be equal to '(A5-A3)/8'. Clearly if A5 equals A3, no parameters were supplied.

Registers D1 to D7, and A0 to A5 may be treated as volatile within the routine itself (though it would be very unwise to destroy A3 or A5 too early!).

8.5   Creating name table entries

A simple mechanism exists for the initialization of RAM based extensions to SuperBASIC. The extensions should be loaded into the resident procedure area by using the SuperBASIC commands RESPR and LBYTES. For simplicity, and the sake of clean source documentation, it is convenient to have the initialization code at the very beginning of the machine code (though this is not essential).

INITIALIZATION CODE

The code, and its corresponding table, for the initialization of extension routines is very simple. Address register A1 should be set to the start of the procedure definition table, and a call made to the utility routine BP.INIT (vector $110):

```
        :
        lea      proc_def(pc),al    ;get table address.
        move.w   $110,a2            ;prepare for BP.INIT and
        jsr      (a2)               ;call it.
        moveq    #0,d0              ;no error.
        rts                         ;finish.
```

More than one extension can exist, and the format of the table is therfore:

Data size	Use
word	number of procedures
	(for each procedure):
word	– pointer to routine
byte	– length of procedure name
characters	– name of procedure
word	0
word	number of functions
	(for each function):
word	– pointer to routine
byte	– length of function name
characters	– name of function
word	0

The number of procedures and/or functions is used purely to reserve internal table space. If the average length of the names exceeds seven, this number needs to be:

```
          (total no. of characters + number of routines + 7)/8
```

The pointers to the routines are relative to the address of the
pointer. All registers (except A1) are preserved by the BP.INIT utility.
No more than 48 bytes are used on the 'user' stack.

8.6   Parameter initialization

When a machine code procedure or function is called, an entry will exist
in the name table for each parameter passed over. At the end of
execution, the parameter entries in the name table will be removed,
together with any temporary entries made in the various tables (e.g.,
the variable values table).

Name table entries, for call parameters, have the various separators
(e.g., hash, comma, semi-colon, and so on) masked into the least
significant byte of the description code (i.e., byte 1, see Sec.8.3).
The full form of this byte is given by the bit pattern:

```
      bit   7 6 5 4   3 2 1 0
            ┌─────────────────┐
            │ h s s s   v v v v │
            └─────────────────┘
```

Bit 7 ('h') will be set if the parameter was preceded by a hash (#).
Bits 4 to 6 specify the separator that follows the parameter:

bit 654	separator
000	no separator
001	comma (,)
010	semi-colon (;)
011	back-slash
100	exclamation (!)
101	the keyword TO

Bits 0 to 3 specify the 'type' of the parameter, as follows:

bit 3210	type
0000	null
0001	string
0010	floating point
0011	integer

Note that if an expression was passed over as an actual parameter to the

191

call, the name pointer in the name table (bytes 2,3 - see Sec.8.3) will be set negative.

8.7   Obtaining arguments

A set of four SuperBASIC utility routines exist which will read an indeterminate number of identical 'type' parameters. They are accessed in the same way as other utilities (i.e., through vectors), and they have the following vector addresses:

$0112	CA.GTINT	Get integers (16–bit)
$0114	CA.GTFP	Get floating point numbers (6 byte)
$0116	CA.GTSTR	Get strings (2+n bytes if even, 3+n bytes if odd)
$0118	CA.GTLIN	Get long integers (32–bit)

If a parameter list contains different 'types', it will be necessary to make multiple calls to appropriate routines in order to collect all of the parameters.

On entry, the utilties require A3 and A5 to be set to the base and the top of the name table parameter entry list respectively. The results will be placed on the arithmetic stack, with the first argument at the lowest physical address pointed to by 'A6,A1.L'. The number of arguments fetched will be returned in register D3 as a word. Register D0 will contain the error code (the status flags will be set also, according to the error return), and registers D1, D2, D4, D6, A0, and A2 are affected. Registers A3 and A5 will be preserved and, therefore, the address register A3 will need to be updated if a further call is required to one of these vectors.

Parameter arguments may, of course, be processed one at a time under the programmer's own control. To do this, you would extract the hash (#) and separator codes, set A5 to be eight bytes above A3, and then call the appropriate utility. It is clearly important, if you adopt this method, to be careful how you manipulate registers A3 and A5 so as not to miss any parameters, nor overrun.

8.8   Returning function values

A function value is returned simply by putting the value on the arithmetic stack (pointed to by 'A6,A1.L'). The value of register A1 must also be in BV_RIP(A6); see Fig.8.1. The 'type' of the return must be placed into register D4 (1=string, 2=floating point, and 3=integer). A long integer (32-bit) must be converted and returned as a floating point value.

8.9 Returning parameter values

Values may be returned through the parameter list of a procedure (or function!) call. As with function value returns, the parameter value should be on the arithmetic stack with BV_RIP(A6) set accordingly. The return value must be integer, string, or floating point, to match the calling parameter. Register A3 must be set to the corresponding parameter entry in the name table, and finally, the utility BP.LET (vector $0120) called.

On returning from BP.LET, register D0 will be set to the error code, and registers D1 to D3 and A0 to A2 will be affected. If the actual parameter initially passed over was in the form of an expression, the return assignment will be made but the value lost.

8.10 Returning strings

The word addressing limitations of the 68000 processor cause some problems when returning strings. Care must be exercised to ensure that the byte counter for the string comes on a word boundary (i.e., an even memory address). In practice, this is achieved by padding out odd length strings by a blank at the end of the string. Note that, for example, a string of length 3, and a string of length 4, will both occupy six bytes on the stack.

8.11 Special note on arithmetic stack handling

The built-in utility routines to fetch arguments will reserve enough space on the arithmetic stack for their own purposes. If a machine code extension requires autonomous use of the arithmetic stack, it also should reserve space by calling the utility BV.CHRIX (vector $011A). The number of bytes required should be in register D1 (as a long-word) on entry. The utility will affect registers D0 and D3.

It is possible that the arithmetic stack will move when this operation is performed. If the procedure has anything on the arithmetic stack before BV.CHRIX is called, the stack pointer (usually register A1) should be saved in BV_RIP(A6), and then retrieved from BV_RIP(A6) afterwards.

8.12 TRAP #4

There is a special TRAP for the SuperBASIC command interpreter, that may be required for use also by machine code procedures. The particular trap call is TRAP #4, and it has the effect of making the addresses passed to the I/O traps (see Chapters 5 and 6) relative to register A6. The call should be made before each and every TRAP #2, or TRAP #3 call, because its effect is cancelled by the latter calls.

For TRAP #2, register A6 is added to A0 on entry. For TRAP #3, register A6 is added to A1 on entry, but removed from it on exit. Note that the TRAP #4 call will not be cancelled by a TRAP #3 call which fails under the error 'not open'.

PART 3 Programming Examples

9 SIMPLE EXECUTABLE PROGRAMS

In this chapter we are going to look at three simple executable programs (i.e., the programs are created as jobs and executed by using the SuperBASIC EXEC command). The three programs are:

1. MESSAGE – Writes a message to the screen

2. CHOICE   – Allows a keyboard input to select a choice of messages to be printed on the screen

3. CLOCKS   – Produces a real-time digital clock display

Each of the programs is listed in full as an assembler output list file, and preceded by a short description. The descriptions tend to rely upon the reader having read and understood previous examples where appropriate. This keeps repetition to a minimum and enables you to get quickly to the new pertinent points. The source code of the programs, and the corresponding '_exec' files, are on one of the two Microdrive cartridges which can accompany this book. The assembler/editor package (described in Part 4) which was used to develop the programs is available on the other Microdrive cartridge.

The full assembly listings will be found to be helpful in a number of ways. First, they act as simple examples of executable file program creation. Second, for those of you who are relatively new to assembly language programming with the 68000, they provide many examples of 68000 opcodes. Third, the hexadecimal opcode listings could be used to enter the machine code directly into memory manually. Although this is long, tedious, and prone to error, it does at least give you the opportunity of trying the programs out without having to purchase an assembler package.

9.1 Example 1 – MESSAGE

This first example of an executable program (see Fig.9.1) illustrates several important points. The first is the amount of code (and junk?) that is required to create even a very simple program. When you write a program in a high-level language, such as SuperBASIC, most of this is hidden. In assembly language it is invariably all too clear.

At the start of the program there are declarations of a number of constants that will be used within the program. These declarations are not absolutely necessary, but the use of the constants within the code, instead of actual values, is usually considered to be that nebulous thing called 'accepted good practice'. Clearly these declarations do not use any space in the program.

The declarations are followed by the job header. When the program is executed (via the SuperBASIC EXEC command), the program counter will be set to the start of the program, so that the first instruction to be executed will be the branch around the header. This is not a mistake! The header is there merely to identify the program. It is not essential and it may be omitted. The 'JOBS' example given in Chapter 11 will, however, produce a more informative output if a job has a header.

The first action of the program, starting at label MESSAGE is to set up a screen (a window without access to the keyboard). The address of the screen definition block is loaded into register A1 (using the LEA - load effective address instruction), and the utility routine UT_SCR is called to open it, set the colours, set the border, and clear it. Note that UT_SCR tests the error code in D0 before returning, so all that is required to be done on return is to branch to the end of the program if the condition codes are non-zero.

Next, the program sets up large characters (just for its own window!). UT_SCR returns the channel ID in register A0, so it is readily available for the TRAP #3 and the call to UT_MTEXT. The call to UT_MTEXT is just like the call to UT_SCR (i.e., the address of the message is loaded into A1 and the routine is called).

At the end of the program, the error code (from UT_SCR or UT_MTEXT) is moved to register D3, and the job is force removed from the QL.

9.2   Example 2 – CHOICE

The second example of a job additionally illustrates the reading of single characters from the keyboard, as well as error reporting. The program (shown in Fig.9.2) must be executed via the SuperBASIC EXEC_W command if the use of CTRL-C to switch input queues is to be avoided. (When there is more than one window that is expecting input, the keyboard can be switched from window to window. If you ever end up without a flashing cursor try typing CTRL-C).

In this program, which starts at label CHOICE, the utility UT_CON is used to open a console (a window with a keyboard queue). Next, a prompt is written to the new console with UT_MTEXT. Note that in early QDOS ROM versions UT_MTEXT does not test its own error return.

The cursor is now enabled. If there is no other console with a cursor enabled, the keyboard will be automatically directed to this console, and a cursor the size of one character will appear in the window.

A further TRAP is now made to read a byte into register D1. The time out is specified as 500 frames (10 seconds on a 50Hz system). If nothing is typed within 10 seconds, the trap will return with the error 'not complete'.

The program now assumes that the user has not typed either 1 or 2 and sets the appropriate error code (ERR_NF - 'not found'). The program then checks that D1 is not less than 1, then whether it is greater than 2.

Following this bit of check code there is some trickery! The program loads the address of the first message (this has an address register as a destination so the condition codes are not changed), then it checks to see if D1 had been less than 2, and, if not, loads the address of the second message.

9.3 Example 3 – CLOCKS

The third example of a simple executable job is a digital clock. This clock is located in the top right-hand side of the command window, wherever that may be.

The first action of the program, which starts at label CLOCK, is to set register A6 to zero. This is done because the program will never need A6, but the date conversion routine uses A6 as a base address. If A6 is zero, then the date conversion will use absolute addresses.

The next action of the job is to set its own priority to 1. This makes it a background job, placing a very low load on the machine. Next, the program opens a window and sets the colours. This is done explicity because, at this point, the program does not know where the window is going to be! Note that UT_SCR would clear the arbitrary window if it were used to open it.

The loop (beginning at the local label 10%) starts off with a TRAP to suspend the job. As the priority of the job is already the lowest possible, this might seem rather irrelevant. In fact, since the job never has to wait for I/O, it would take a higher priority than a job which is always having to wait for I/O. Suspending the job reduces the load on the machine even further.

The next operation in the loop is, perhaps, rather strange. It is a screen driver EXTOP. The purpose of EXTOPs is to allow application programs to add functions to the standard screen driver. In this case, the EXTOP code is a routine called GET_WIND. GET_WIND is written as if it is part of a device driver. Within the routine the register A0 points to the screen definition block for the jobs window (it is no longer the ID) and A6 points to the base of the system variables. The first action in the routine is to find the base address of the channel 0 window. It transfers the X and Y origins to its own definition block, sets the X (dependent on character size) and Y size, and re-calculates the X origin (given as: window_0_X_origin + window_0_width – own_window_width). See Sec.6.3 for a discussion of screen channel definition blocks.

The time is read into register D1 and converted to a standard string by CN_DATE. The standard string format has the byte count in the first word of the string, so this is moved to D2 (the I/O call string length register) before writing the string to the window. Both MT_SUSJB and MT_RCLCK destroy A0, so it is necessary to restore A0 before calling the TRAP #3s.

The last routine in the program is a simple routine to kill the job if the error code is non-zero.

Figure 9.1 MESSAGE – Simple message program

```
Job to write a message          McGraw-Hill(UK) 68000 Ass v1.0A   Page: 0001

                                0001 *H Job to write a message
                                0002 ;
                                0003 ; Copyright (c) 1984 McGraw-Hill(UK)
                                0004 ;
00000000                        0005         ORG   0
                                0006 ;
FFFFFFFF  =                     0007 MYSELF   EQU   -1          ┌─────────────┐
00000005  =                     0008 MT_FRJOB EQU   $05         │ SEXEC       │
0000002D  =                     0009 SD_SETSZ EQU   $2D         │ LEN : 80    │
000000C8  =                     0010 UT_SCR   EQU   $C8         │ DATA: 64    │
000000D0  =                     0011 UT_MTEXT EQU   $D0         └─────────────┘
                                0012 ;
                                0013 ; Header for debuggers etc.
                                0014 ;
00000000 6010                   0015         BRA.S MESSAGE     ;branch to code
00000002 00000000               0016         DEFL  0
00000006 4AFB                   0017         DEFW  $4AFB       ;standard header
00000008 0007                   0018         DEFW  7
0000000A 4D657373616765         0019         DEFB  'Message'
                                0020         ALIGN
                                0021 ;
00000012                        0022 MESSAGE:
00000012 43FA0026               0023         LEA   SCR(PC),A1   ;set up a screen
00000016 387800C8               0024         MOVE.W UT_SCR,A4
0000001A 4E94                   0025         JSR   (A4)
0000001C 6614                   0026         BNE.S SUICIDE      ;check error return
                                0027 ;
0000001E 702D                   0028         MOVEQ #SD_SETSZ,D0 ;set character size
00000020 7203                   0029         MOVEQ #3,D1        ;wide
00000022 7401                   0030         MOVEQ #1,D2        ;tall
00000024 76FF                   0031         MOVEQ #-1,D3       ;no timeout
00000026 4E43                   0032         TRAP  #3
                                0033 ;
00000028 43FA001C               0034         LEA   HALLO(PC),A1 ;write a message
0000002C 387800D0               0035         MOVE.W UT_MTEXT,A4
00000030 4E94                   0036         JSR   (A4)
                                0037 ;
00000032                        0038 SUICIDE:
00000032 2600                   0039         MOVE.L D0,D3       ;notify any error
00000034 7005                   0040         MOVEQ #MT_FRJOB,D0 ;force remove
00000036 72FF                   0041         MOVEQ #MYSELF,D1   ;myself
00000038 4E41                   0042         TRAP  #1
0000003A                        0043 SCR:
0000003A FF                     0044         DEFB  $FF          ;checkerboard border
0000003B 04                     0045         DEFB  $04          ;4 pixels wide
0000003C 04                     0046         DEFB  $04          ;green background
0000003D 00                     0047         DEFB  $00          ;black letters
0000003E 00C8                   0048         DEFW  200          ;200 pixels wide
00000040 0023                   0049         DEFW  35           ;35 high
00000042 009C                   0050         DEFW  156          ;in the middle
00000044 0064                   0051         DEFW  100
00000046                        0052 HALLO:
00000046 0005                   0053         DEFW  5
00000048 48616C6C6F             0054         DEFB  'Hallo'
                                0055 ;
                                0056 END


Symbols:

00000046 HALLO       00000012 MESSAGE     00000005 MT_FRJOB    FFFFFFFF MYSELF      0000003A SCR
0000002D SD_SETSZ    00000032 SUICIDE     000000D0 UT_MTEXT    000000C8 UT_SCR

0000 error(s) detected
6270 bytes free
```

Figure 9.2 CHOICE – Select a message program

```
                            0001 *H Job to write one of 2 messages
                            0002 ;
                            0003 ; Copyright (c) 1984 McGraw-Hill(UK)
                            0004 ;
00000000                    0005         ORG 0
                            0006 ;
FFFFFFFF  =                 0007 MYSELF   EQU   -1
FFFFFFF9  =                 0008 ERR_NF   EQU   -7
00000005  =                 0009 MT_FRJOB EQU   $05
00000001  =                 0010 IO_FBYTE EQU   $01
0000000E  =                 0011 SD_CURE  EQU   $0E
000000C6  =                 0012 UT_CON   EQU   $C6
000000D0  =                 0013 UT_MTEXT EQU   $D0
                            0014 ;
                            0015 ; Header for debuggers etc.
                            0016 ;
00000000 600E               0017         BRA.S  CHOICE          ;branch to code
00000002 00000000           0018         DEFL   0
00000006 4AFB               0019         DEFW   $4AFB           ;standard header
00000008 0006               0020         DEFW   6
0000000A 43686F6365         0021         DEFB   'Choice'
                            0022         ALIGN
                            0023 ;
00000010 43FA004A           0024 CHOICE: LEA    CON(PC),A1      ;set up a screen
00000014 387800C6           0025         MOVE.W UT_CON,A4
00000018 4E94               0026         JSR    (A4)
0000001A 6638               0027         BNE.S  SUICIDE         ;check error return
                            0028 ;
0000001C 43FA004A           0029         LEA    MESSAGE(PC),A1  ;write prompt
00000020 387800D0           0030         MOVE.W UT_MTEXT,A4
00000024 4E94               0031         JSR    (A4)
00000026 4A80               0032         TST.L  D0
00000028 662A               0033         BNE.S  SUICIDE         ;check error return
                            0034 ;
0000002A 700E               0035         MOVEQ  #SD_CURE,D0     ;enable cursor
0000002C 76FF               0036         MOVEQ  #-1,D3
0000002E 4E43               0037         TRAP   #3
                            0038 ;
00000030 7001               0039         MOVEQ  #IO_FBYTE,D0    ;fetch a byte
00000032 363C01F4           0040         MOVE.W #500,D3         ;wait 10s for reply
00000036 4E43               0041         TRAP   #3
00000038 4A80               0042         TST.L  D0              ;check error return
0000003A 6618               0043         BNE.S  SUICIDE
                            0044 ;
0000003C 70F9               0045         MOVEQ  #ERR_NF,D0      ;assume reply is in error
0000003E 04010031           0046         SUB.B  #'1',D1         ;compare against 1
00000042 6D10               0047         BLT.S  SUICIDE         ;... it's too small
00000044 5301               0048         SUBQ.B #1,D1           ;compare against 2
00000046 6E0C               0049         BGT.S  SUICIDE         ;... it's too large
00000048 43FA002E           0050         LEA    MESS1(PC),A1    ;assume message 1
0000004C 6D04               0051         BLT.S  WRITE           ;was it 1?
0000004E 43FA0034           0052         LEA    MESS2(PC),A1    ;no, it is message 2
00000052                    0053 WRITE:
00000052 4E94               0054         JSR    (A4)            ;write message
                            0055 ;
00000054                    0056 SUICIDE:
00000054 2600               0057         MOVE.L D0,D3           ;notify any error
00000056 7005               0058         MOVEQ  #MT_FRJOB,D0    ;force remove
00000058 72FF               0059         MOVEQ  #MYSELF,D1      ;myself
0000005A 4E41               0060         TRAP   #1
                            0061 ;
0000005C 7F                 0062 CON:    DEFB   $7F             ;horizontal stripes
0000005D 04                 0063         DEFB   $04             ;4 pixels wide
0000005E 02                 0064         DEFB   $02             ;red background
0000005F 07                 0065         DEFB   $07             ;white letters
00000060 00C8               0066         DEFW   200             ;200 pixels wide
00000062 0023               0067         DEFW   35              ;35 high
00000064 009C               0068         DEFW   156             ;in the middle
00000066 0064               0069         DEFW   100
                            0070 ;
00000068 000E               0071 MESSAGE:DEFW   14
0000006A 4B657920696E2031206F 0072      DEFB   'Key in 1 or 2'
```

```
┌────────────────┐
│ SEXEC          │
│ LEN : 150      │
│ DATA:   64     │
└────────────────┘
```

```
00000077 0A                        0073            DEFB    $A              ;new line
                                   0074            ALIGN
00000078 000A                      0075 MESS1:     DEFW    10
0000007A 57656C6C20646F6E6521      0076            DEFB    'Well done!'
                                   0077            ALIGN
00000084 000A                      0078 MESS2:     DEFW    10
00000086 5665727920676F6F6421      0079            DEFB    'Very good!'
                                   0080 ;
                                   0081 END
```

Symbols:

```
00000010 CHOICE     0000005C CON       FFFFFFF9 ERR_NF    00000001 IO_FBYTE    00000078 MESS1
00000084 MESS2      00000068 MESSAGE   00000005 MT_FRJOB  FFFFFFFF MYSELF      0000000E SD_CUR
00000054 SUICIDE    000000C6 UT_CON    000000D0 UT_MTEXT  00000052 WRITE
```

0000 error(s) detected
6220 bytes free

+++++++++++++++++++

Figure 9.3 CLOCKS – Real-time digital clock display

```
Clock - clock in window 0      McGraw-Hill(UK) 68000 Ass v1.0A   Page: 0001

                               0001 *H Clock - clock in window 0
                               0002 ;
                               0003 ; Copyright (c) 1984 McGraw-Hill(UK)
                               0004 ;
00000000                       0005          ORG 0
                               0006 ;
FFFFFFFF =                     0007 MYSELF   EQU    -1
00000005 =                     0008 MT_FRJOB EQU    $05
00000008 =                     0009 MT_SUSJB EQU    $08
0000000B =                     0010 MT_PRIOR EQU    $0B
00000013 =                     0011 MT_RCLCK EQU    $13
00000001 =                     0012 IO_OPEN  EQU    $01
00000007 =                     0013 IO_SSTRG EQU    $07
00000009 =                     0014 SD_EXTOP EQU    $09
00000011 =                     0015 SD_TAB   EQU    $11
00000028 =                     0016 SD_SETST EQU    $28
00000029 =                     0017 SD_SETIN EQU    $29
                               0018 ;
00000078 =                     0019 SV_CHBAS EQU    $78
                               0020 ;
00000018 =                     0021 SD_XMIN  EQU    $18
0000001C =                     0022 SD_XSIZE EQU    $1C
0000001E =                     0023 SD_YSIZE EQU    $1E
00000026 =                     0024 SD_XINC  EQU    $26
                               0025 ;
000000EC =                     0026 CN_DATE  EQU    $EC
                               0027 ;
                               0028 ; Insert standard header ID for any debuggers etc.
                               0029 ;
00000000 600E                  0030          BRA.S  CLOCK            ;branch to clock code
00000002 00000000              0031          DEFL   0                ;pad out with 4 bytes
00000006 4AFB                  0032          DEFW   $4AFB            ;standard job flag
00000008 0005                  0033          DEFW   5                ;name is 5 bytes long
0000000A 436C6F636B            0034          DEFB   'Clock'
                               0035          ALIGN
                               0036 ;
00000010 9DCE                  0037 CLOCK:   SUB.L  A6,A6            ;don't need A6 so clear it
00000012 700B                  0038          MOVEQ  #MT_PRIOR,D0     ;set priority
00000014 72FF                  0039          MOVEQ  #MYSELF,D1       ;... of this Job
00000016 7401                  0040          MOVEQ  #1,D2            ;... to 1 (the lowest)
00000018 4E41                  0041          TRAP   #1
                               0042 ;
0000001A 7001                  0043          MOVEQ  #IO_OPEN,D0      ;open window for clock
0000001C 72FF                  0044          MOVEQ  #MYSELF,D1       ;... owned by this Job
0000001E 7600                  0045          MOVEQ  #0,D3            ;... (it's a device)
00000020 41FA0084              0046          LEA    SCR(PC),A0       ;address of name
00000024 4E42                  0047          TRAP   #2
```

```
┌─────────────────┐
│ SEXEC           │
│ LEN : 200       │
│ DATA:  90       │
└─────────────────┘
```

```
00000026 6148      0048         BSR.S   OOPS              ;any errors?
00000028 2848      0049         MOVE.L  A0,A4             ;save channel ID
                   0050 ;
0000002A 7028      0051         MOVEQ   #SD_SETST,D0      ;set strip
0000002C 7210      0052         MOVEQ   #$10,D1           ;... to Burgandy
0000002E 76FF      0053         MOVEQ   #-1,D3
00000030 4E43      0054         TRAP    #3
                   0055 ;
00000032 7029      0056         MOVEQ   #SD_SETIN,D0      ;set ink
00000034 7204      0057         MOVEQ   #$4,D1            ;... to green
00000036 4E43      0058         TRAP    #3
                   0059 ;
00000038 7008      0060 10%:    MOVEQ   #MT_SUSJB,D0      ;suspend
0000003A 72FF      0061         MOVEQ   #MYSELF,D1        ;myself
0000003C 760A      0062         MOVEQ   #10,D3            ;for 1/5 second
0000003E 93C9      0063         SUB.L   A1,A1             ;no flag address
00000040 4E41      0064         TRAP    #1
                   0065 ;
00000042 7009      0066         MOVEQ   #SD_EXTOP,D0      ;find where to put window
00000044 76FF      0067         MOVEQ   #-1,D3            ;wait until complete
00000046 204C      0068         MOVE.L  A4,A0             ;set channel
00000048 45FA0034  0069         LEA     GET_WIND(PC),A2
0000004C 4E43      0070         TRAP    #3
                   0071 ;
0000004E 7011      0072         MOVEQ   #SD_TAB,D0        ;reset to start of line
00000050 7200      0073         MOVEQ   #0,D1
00000052 4E43      0074         TRAP    #3
                   0075 ;
00000054 7013      0076         MOVEQ   #MT_RCLCK,D0      ;now read time into D1
00000056 4E41      0077         TRAP    #1
                   0078 ;
00000058 43FA0068  0079         LEA     BUF_TOP(PC),A1    ;use buffer from top down
0000005C 347800EC  0080         MOVE.W  CN_DATE,A2        ;to convert date into
00000060 4E92      0081         JSR     (A2)
                   0082 ;
00000062 7007      0083         MOVEQ   #IO_SSTRG,D0      ;now send the result
00000064 3419      0084         MOVE.W  (A1)+,D2          ;of 20 characters
00000066 76FF      0085         MOVEQ   #-1,D3            ;... with no timeout
00000068 204C      0086         MOVE.L  A4,A0             ;to our window
0000006A 4E43      0087         TRAP    #3
0000006C 6102      0088         BSR.S   OOPS              ;any errors?
0000006E 60C8      0089         BRA.S   10%
                   0090 ;
                   0091 ; Check for error on IO call
                   0092 ;
00000070 4A80      0093 OOPS:   TST.L   D0                ;has an error occurred
00000072 6708      0094         BEQ.S   OK                ;... no
00000074 2600      0095         MOVE.L  D0,D3             ;... yes - notify it
00000076 7005      0096         MOVEQ   #MT_FRJOB,D0      ;remove Job
00000078 72FF      0097         MOVEQ   #MYSELF,D1        ;... yes, this one
0000007A 4E41      0098         TRAP    #1                ;(we should not get back
                   0099                                  ; from this)
                   0100 ;
0000007C 4E75      0101 OK:     RTS
                   0102 ;
                   0103 ; This routine works out the window required to overlap
                   0104 ; window 0 at top RHS. This code forms part of a device
                   0105 ; driver and is in supervisor mode.
                   0106 ;
0000007E           0107 GET_WIND:
0000007E 246E0078  0108         MOVE.L  SV_CHBAS(A6),A2
00000082 2452      0109         MOVE.L  (A2),A2           ;get origin X,Y
00000084 216A00180018 0110      MOVE.L  SD_XMIN(A2),SD_XMIN(A0)
0000008A 7014      0111         MOVEQ   #20,D0            ;20 characters
0000008C C0E80026  0112         MULU    SD_XINC(A0),D0    ;... of current width
00000090 3140001C  0113         MOVE.W  D0,SD_XSIZE(A0)   ;set size X
00000094 317C000A001E 0114      MOVE.W  #10,SD_YSIZE(A0)  ;... and Y
0000009A 906A001C  0115         SUB.W   SD_XSIZE(A2),D0   ;find X origin
0000009E 91680018  0116         SUB.W   D0,SD_XMIN(A0)    ;... from RHS
000000A2 7000      0117         MOVEQ   #0,D0             ;no error
000000A4 4E75      0118         RTS
                   0119 ;
000000A6 0003      0120 SCR:    DEFW    3                 ;name of output device
000000A8 534352    0121         DEFB    'SCR'
                   0122         ALIGN
000000AC           0123 BUFFER:
                   0124         DEFS    22                ;this is for CN_DATE
000000C2           0125 BUF_TOP:
```

```
                    0126 ;
                    0127 END


    Symbols:

    000000AC BUFFER      000000C2 BUF_TOP     00000010 CLOCK      000000EC CN_DATE    0000007E GET_WIND
    00000001 IO_OPEN     00000007 IO_SSTRG    00000005 MT_FRJOB   0000000B MT_PRIOR   00000013 MT_RCLCK
    00000008 MT_SUSJB    FFFFFFFF MYSELF      0000007C OK         00000070 OOPS       000000A6 SCR
    00000009 SD_EXTOP    00000029 SD_SETIN    00000028 SD_SETST   00000011 SD_TAB     00000026 SD_XINC
    00000018 SD_XMIN     0000001C SD_XSIZE    0000001E SD_YSIZE   00000078 SV_CHBAS

0000 error(s)  detected
6179 bytes free
```

10 GRAPHICS

In this chapter we are going to look at two graphics orientated executable programs (i.e., the programs are graphical in nature and created as jobs and executed by using the SuperBASIC EXEC command). The two programs are:

1. CLOCKF - Produces a real-time analogue clockface display

2. BALL   - Produces a rolling multi-colour ball display

The first example, CLOCKF, is an example of standard graphics. In it we will see how the floating point package may be used to enable straight lines and arcs to be drawn. The second example, BALL, is orientated toward direct screen addressing. This type of graphics programming is the sort that will be found most often in games packages for special figures and moving items.

Each of the programs is listed in full as an assembler output list file, and preceded by a short description. The descriptions tend to rely upon the reader having read and understood previous examples (both in this chapter and the previous chapter), where appropriate. This keeps repetition to a minimum and enables you to get quickly to the new pertinent points. The source code of the programs, and the corresponding '_exec' files, are on one of the two Microdrive cartridges which can accompany this book. The assembler/editor package (described in Part 4) which was used to develop the programs is available on the other Microdrive cartridge.

The hexadecimal opcode listings could be used to enter the machine code directly into memory manually. Although this is long, tedious, and prone to error, it does at least give you the opportunity of trying the programs out without having to purchase an assembler package.

10.1 Screen memory layout

Before going on to look at the examples it is worth making sure that we know how the screen memory is organized. Pixel decoding is performed on a 'word' (i.e., 16-bit) data size system, as shown in Fig.10.1. In four colour mode each word represents eight pixels. In eight colour mode each word represents four pixels.

Overall screen memory layout

Pixel creation

High-res (4 colour)

G	G	G	G	G	G	G	G
R	R	R	R	R	R	R	R

Even byte
Odd byte

Low-res (8 colour)

G	F	G	F	G	F	G	F
R	B	R	B	R	B	R	B

Bit 7   Ø
Single pixel

7   Ø Bit
Single pixel

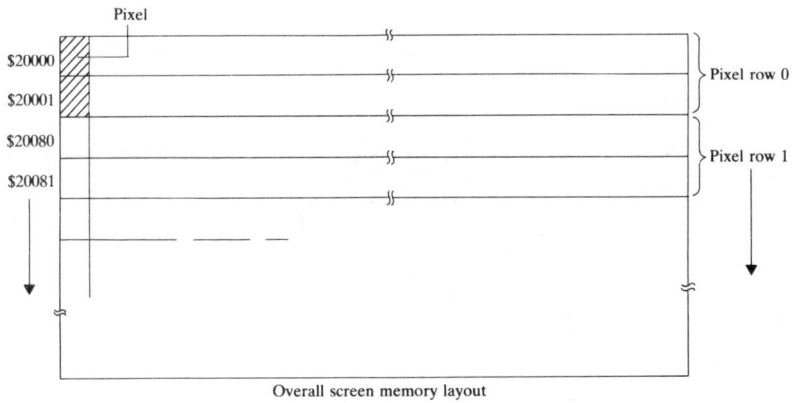

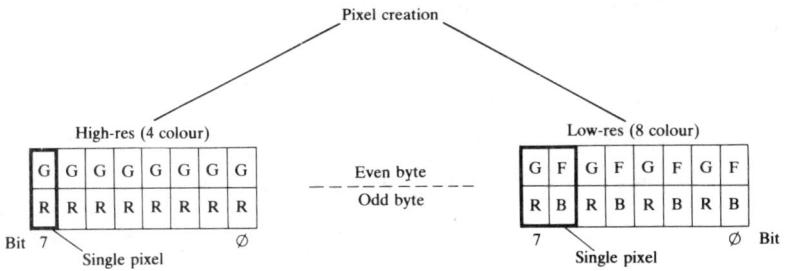

Key: G = green, R = red, B = blue, F = flash

Figure 10.1 Screen memory layout

The screen memory begins at address $20000, and extends for 32K of RAM. The limited colour range in four colour mode means that no flash is available, and turning both green and red bits on will be interpreted by the hardware as white.

Note that 64 words make up any one row of pixels. In high-resolution mode (four colour mode) the screen is, therefore, 512 pixels wide. In low-resolution mode (eight colour mode) the screen is 256 pixels wide. In both modes the screen is 256 pixels high.

10.2   Example 1 – CLOCKF

This first example (see Fig.10.2) of using graphics, within an executable program, draws a simple clock face with hands. It uses the standard screen driver graphics TRAPs, and so requires the information to be presented in floating point format. Extensive use is therefore made of the SuperBASIC floating point arithmetic package.

The program starts in much the same way as the digital clock example (see Chapter 9). The priority is set to the lowest level, and a screen window is opened. Next, the graphics scale is set. This uses a small procedure called CLK_EXEC to put three constants on the arithmetic stack and then to invoke the TRAP #3.

The keys RIS_0, RIS_2PI, RIS_1, etc., are instructions to the arithmetic interpreter to load the constants (or values on the arithmetic stack) onto the top of the arithmetic stack. The values of the keys are the addresses of the constants with respect to register A4.

As the clock will overlap part of the normal working area of the screen, the window of the clock is cleared whenever it is drawn. To avoid continuous flicker, the clock is only re-drawn when the time has changed by two seconds.

To draw the hands, the time is successively divided down to give a remainder which is in turn divided to give a position (in the range 0 to 1) of the appropriate hand. This is multiplied by 2*PI, to give a position in radians, and a line is drawn from (size*SIN,size*COS) to the centre of the window at (0,0). This program will execute quite happily in both four and eight colour modes.

10.3   Example 2 – BALL

This second example (see Fig.10.3) of graphics, within an executable program, accesses the screen directly. This illustrates one of the more complex forms of animation. Each representation of the object is not constrained to be in a limited number of pixel positions, and it can be panned to any position desired.

The bizarre screen organization in eight colour mode, where each pixel is represented by two bits (one bit if you ignore flash) in a byte at an even address, and two bits in the next byte, might appear to make panning an object rather difficult. Fortunately, the MOVEP instruction can be used to read or write alternate bytes! Within the drawing routine, all the green (with flash=0) bits are read into D6 and all the red and blue bits into D7. Each register then holds the pixel information in the same order as it appears on the screen. After panning, masking, or any other operation, the pixels can then be written into the screen using more MOVEP instructions.

To draw the rolling ball, the ball is written to the same word address in the screen four times. Each time, a new rotation of the ball is used (four in total), and the ball is panned within the word by two bits extra each time. When moving to the right, the ball is always panned by at least two bits to ensure that the left-hand side is empty and no part of the ball is left behind.

Figure 10.2 A real-time analogue clockface display

```
                              0001 *H Graphics
                              0002 ;
                              0003 ; CLOCKF - clock face with hands
                              0004 ;
                              0005 ; Copyright (c) 1984 McGraw-Hill(UK)
                              0006 ;
00000000                      0007          ORG 0
                              0008 ;
FFFFFFFF =                    0009 MYSELF    EQU    -1
00000005 =                    0010 MT_FRJOB  EQU    $05
00000008 =                    0011 MT_SUSJB  EQU    $08
0000000B =                    0012 MT_PRIOR  EQU    $0B
00000013 =                    0013 MT_RCLCK  EQU    $13
00000020 =                    0014 SD_CLEAR  EQU    $20
00000029 =                    0015 SD_SETIN  EQU    $29
00000031 =                    0016 SD_LINE   EQU    $31
00000033 =                    0017 SD_ELIPS  EQU    $33
00000034 =                    0018 SD_SCALE  EQU    $34
                              0019 ;
000000C8 =                    0020 UT_SCR    EQU    $C8
000000EC =                    0021 CN_DATE   EQU    $EC
0000011C =                    0022 RI_EXEC   EQU    $11C
0000011E =                    0023 RI_EXECB  EQU    $11E
00000008 =                    0024 RI_FLOAT  EQU    $08
0000000A =                    0025 RI_ADD    EQU    $0A
0000000E =                    0026 RI_MULT   EQU    $0E
00000010 =                    0027 RI_DIV    EQU    $10
00000014 =                    0028 RI_NEG    EQU    $14
00000016 =                    0029 RI_DUP    EQU    $16
00000018 =                    0030 RI_COS    EQU    $18
0000001A =                    0031 RI_SIN    EQU    $1A
                              0032 ;
FFFFFFFA =                    0033 RIS_0     EQU    -6
FFFFFFF4 =                    0034 RIS_2PI   EQU    -12
FFFFFFEE =                    0035 RIS_1     EQU    -18
FFFFFFE8 =                    0036 RIS_SIZE  EQU    -24
FFFFFFE2 =                    0037 RIS_ANG   EQU    -30
                              0038 ;
                              0039 ; Header bytes for debuggers etc.
                              0040 ;
00000000 6012                 0041          BRA.S  CLOCK           ;branch to clock code
00000002 00000000             0042          DEFL   0               ;pad out with 4 bytes
00000006 4AFB                 0043          DEFW   $4AFB           ;standard job flag
00000008 000A                 0044          DEFW   10
0000000A 436C6F636B2066616365 0045          DEFB   'Clock face'
                              0046          ALIGN
                              0047 ;
00000014 9DCE                 0048 CLOCK:   SUB.L  A6,A6           ;set A6 to zero forever
                              0049 ;
00000016 700B                 0050          MOVEQ  #MT_PRIOR,D0    ;set priority
00000018 72FF                 0051          MOVEQ  #MYSELF,D1      ;... of this Job
0000001A 7401                 0052          MOVEQ  #1,D2           ;... to 1 (the lowest)
0000001C 4E41                 0053          TRAP   #1
                              0054 ;
0000001E 347800C8             0055          MOVE.W UT_SCR,A2       ;open window for clock
00000022 43FA008C             0056          LEA    SCR(PC),A1      ;address of definition
00000026 4E92                 0057          JSR    (A2)
00000028 2F08                 0058          MOVE.L A0,-(A7)        ;save channel ID
                              0059 ;
0000002A 43FA01C0             0060          LEA    RIS_CONS(PC),A1 ;RI stack ptr to top of stack
0000002E 47FA00A4             0061          LEA    SET_SCALE(PC),A3;pointer to scale block
00000032 49FA01CA             0062          LEA    RIS_TOP(PC),A4  ;pointer to top of constants
00000036 7E34                 0063          MOVEQ  #SD_SCALE,D7    ;operation to set scale
00000038 6164                 0064          BSR.S  CLK_EXEC        ;set up RI and do graphics
                              0065 ;
0000003A                      0066 CLOCK_LOOP:
0000003A 7008                 0067          MOVEQ  #MT_SUSJB,D0    ;suspend
0000003C 72FF                 0068          MOVEQ  #MYSELF,D1      ;me
0000003E 760A                 0069          MOVEQ  #10,D3          ;for 1/5 seconds
00000040 93C9                 0070          SUB.L  A1,A1           ;no flag
00000042 4E41                 0071          TRAP   #1
```

```
+-------------+
| SEXEC       |
| LEN : 512   |
| DATA: 128   |
+-------------+
```

```
                         0072 ;
00000044 7013           0073          MOVEQ    #MT_RCLCK,D0      ;read time into D1
00000046 4E41           0074          TRAP     #1
00000048 E289           0075          LSR.L    #1,D1             ;in two second units
0000004A B881           0076          CMP.L    D1,D4             ;has the time changed?
0000004C 67EC           0077          BEQ.S    CLOCK_LOOP        ;... no
0000004E 2801           0078          MOVE.L   D1,D4
                         0079 ;
00000050 82FC5460       0080          DIVU     #21600,D1         ;reduce to 12 hour clock
00000054 4841           0081          SWAP     D1
00000056 7C00           0082          MOVEQ    #0,D6
00000058 3C01           0083          MOVE.W   D1,D6             ;in all of D6
                         0084 ;
0000005A 7020           0085          MOVEQ    #SD_CLEAR,D0      ;clear old clock face
0000005C 6148           0086          BSR.S    CLK_TRAP3
                         0087 ;
0000005E 7E33           0088          MOVEQ    #SD_ELIPS,D7      ;draw ellipse
00000060 43FA018A       0089          LEA      RIS_CONS(PC),A1   ;set RI stack ptr
00000064 47FA0075       0090          LEA      SET_CIRC(PC),A3   ;set circle block
00000068 6134           0091          BSR.S    CLK_EXEC
                         0092 ;
0000006A 7A06           0093          MOVEQ    #6,D5             ;start with yellow ink
0000006C 7E31           0094          MOVEQ    #SD_LINE,D7       ;drawing lines
0000006E 47FA0071       0095          LEA      SET_LINE(PC),A3
00000072 4BFA0048       0096          LEA      CLK_DATA(PC),A5
00000076                 0097 CLK_HAND:
00000076 7029           0098          MOVEQ    #SD_SETIN,D0      ;set colour of hands
00000078 3205           0099          MOVE.W   D5,D1
0000007A 612A           0100          BSR.S    CLK_TRAP3
                         0101 ;
0000007C 43FA016E       0102          LEA      RIS_CONS(PC),A1   ;reset RI stack pointer
00000080 4261           0103          CLR.W    -(A1)
00000082 231D           0104          MOVE.L   (A5)+,-(A1)       ;set size of hands
                         0105 ;
00000084 3306           0106          MOVE.W   D6,-(A1)          ;put new position on stack
00000086 7008           0107          MOVEQ    #RI_FLOAT,D0      ;float it
00000088 3478011C       0108          MOVE.W   RI_EXEC,A2
0000008C 4E92           0109          JSR      (A2)
                         0110 ;
0000008E 8CDD           0111          DIVU     (A5)+,D6          ;divide by next divisor
00000090 4246           0112          CLR.W    D6
00000092 4846           0113          SWAP     D6                ;remainder back in D6
                         0114 ;
00000094 331D           0115          MOVE.W   (A5)+,-(A1)       ;put number of seconds
                         0116                                    ;around face on stack
00000096 6106           0117          BSR.S    CLK_EXEC          ;and create the complete
                         0118                                    ;set of call parameters
                         0119 ;
00000098 5545           0120          SUBQ     #2,D5             ;next ink colour
0000009A 6EDA           0121          BGT.S    CLK_HAND
                         0122 ;
0000009C 609C           0123          BRA.S    CLOCK_LOOP
                         0124 ;
0000009E                 0125 CLK_EXEC:
0000009E 3478011E       0126          MOVE.W   RI_EXECB,A2       ;execute instructions
000000A2 4E92           0127          JSR      (A2)
000000A4 2007           0128          MOVE.L   D7,D0             ;set IO key
000000A6                 0129 CLK_TRAP3:
000000A6 76FF           0130          MOVEQ    #-1,D3            ;no timeout
000000A8 206F0004       0131          MOVE.L   4(A7),A0          ;set channel ID
000000AC 4E43           0132          TRAP     #3
000000AE 4E75           0133          RTS
                         0134 ;
000000B0                 0135 SCR:
000000B0 00000000       0136          DEFL     0                 ;no border, black on black
000000B4 003C           0137          DEFW     60                ;3:2 pixel aspect ratio
000000B6 0028           0138          DEFW     40
000000B8 01C4           0139          DEFW     512-60            ;top RHS (512-32-60 for TV mod
000000BA 0000           0140          DEFW     0                 ;       (16 for TV mode)
                         0141 ;
                         0142 ; data for clock face in 2 second units
                         0143 ;
000000BC                 0144 CLK_DATA:
000000BC 08006000       0145          DEFL     $08006000         ;hour hand size = 3/4
000000C0 0708           0146          DEFW     1800              ;1800 units per hour
000000C2 5460           0147          DEFW     21600             ;nr of units around the face
000000C4 08007000       0148          DEFL     $08007000         ;minute hand size = 7/8
000000C8 001E           0149          DEFW     30                ;30 units per minute
```

209

```
000000CA 0708                    0150          DEFW    1800         ;nr of units round the face
000000CC 08014000                0151          DEFL    $08014000    ;second hand size = 1
000000D0 0001                    0152          DEFW    1            ;1 unit per unit
000000D2 001E                    0153          DEFW    30           ;30 units around the face
                                 0154 ;
000000D4                         0155 SET_SCALE:
000000D4 EE                      0156          DEFB    RIS_1        ;stack    1
000000D5 EE                      0157          DEFB    RIS_1        ;         1,1
000000D6 0A                      0158          DEFB    RI_ADD       ;         2
000000D7 EE                      0159          DEFB    RIS_1        ;         2,1
000000D8 14                      0160          DEFB    RI_NEG       ;         2,-1
000000D9 16                      0161          DEFB    RI_DUP       ;         2,-1,-1
000000DA 00                      0162          DEFB    0
000000DB                         0163 SET_CIRC:
000000DB FA                      0164          DEFB    RIS_0        ;stack    0
000000DC FA                      0165          DEFB    RIS_0        ;         0,0
000000DD EE                      0166          DEFB    RIS_1        ;         0,0,1
000000DE EE                      0167          DEFB    RIS_1        ;         0,0,1,1
000000DF FA                      0168          DEFB    RIS_0        ;         0,0,1,1,0
000000E0 00                      0169          DEFB    0
000000E1                         0170 SET_LINE:
000000E1 08                      0171          DEFB    RI_FLOAT     ;stack   size, nr,
                                 0172                               ;    divisor * nr of divs
000000E2 10                      0173          DEFB    RI_DIV       ;        size, position (0 to 1)
000000E3 F4                      0174          DEFB    RIS_2PI      ;        size, position, 2*PI
000000E4 0E                      0175          DEFB    RI_MULT      ;        size, angle
000000E5 E2                      0176          DEFB    RIS_ANG      ;        ...... angle
000000E6 1A                      0177          DEFB    RI_SIN       ;        x0
000000E7 E8                      0178          DEFB    RIS_SIZE     ;        x0, size
000000E8 0E                      0179          DEFB    RI_MULT      ;        x
000000E9 E2                      0180          DEFB    RIS_ANG      ;        x, angle
000000EA 18                      0181          DEFB    RI_COS       ;        x, y0
000000EB E8                      0182          DEFB    RIS_SIZE     ;        x, y0, size
000000EC 0E                      0183          DEFB    RI_MULT      ;        x, y
000000ED FA                      0184          DEFB    RIS_0        ;        x, y, 0
000000EE FA                      0185          DEFB    RIS_0        ;        x, y, 0, 0
000000EF 00                      0186          DEFB    0
                                 0187          ALIGN
                                 0188 ;
000000F0                         0189 RI_STACK:
000000F0 0000000000000000000000  0190          DEFL    0,0,0,0,0,0,0  ;240 bytes plus space
0000010C 0000000000000000000000  0191          DEFL    0,0,0,0,0,0,0,0
0000012C 0000000000000000000000  0192          DEFL    0,0,0,0,0,0,0,0
0000014C 0000000000000000000000  0193          DEFL    0,0,0,0,0,0,0,0
0000016C 0000000000000000000000  0194          DEFL    0,0,0,0,0,0,0,0
0000018C 0000000000000000000000  0195          DEFL    0,0,0,0,0,0,0,0
000001AC 0000000000000000000000  0196          DEFL    0,0,0,0,0,0,0,0
000001CC 0000000000000000000000  0197          DEFL    0,0,0,0,0,0,0,0
                                 0198 ;
000001EC                         0199 RIS_CONS:
000001EC 0801                    0200          DEFW    $0801        ;one
000001EE 40000000                0201          DEFL    $40000000
000001F2 0803                    0202          DEFW    $0803        ;2*PI
000001F4 6487ED51                0203          DEFL    $6487ED51
000001F8 0000                    0204          DEFW    $0000        ;0
000001FA 00000000                0205          DEFL    $00000000
000001FE                         0206 RIS_TOP:
                                 0207 ;
                                 0208 END


Symbols:

000000BC CLK_DATA    0000009E CLK_EXEC    00000076 CLK_HAND    000000A6 CLK_TRAP    00000014 CLOCK
0000003A CLOCK_LO    000000EC CN_DATE     00000005 MT_FRJOB    0000000B MT_PRIOR    00000013 MT_RCLCK
00000008 MT_SUSJB    FFFFFFFF MYSELF      FFFFFFFA RIS_0       FFFFFFEE RIS_1       FFFFFFF4 RIS_2PI
FFFFFFE2 RIS_ANG     000001EC RIS_CONS    FFFFFFE8 RIS_SIZE    000001FE RIS_TOP     0000000A RI_ADD
00000018 RI_COS      00000010 RI_DIV      00000016 RI_DUP      0000011C RI_EXEC     0000011E RI_EXECB
00000008 RI_FLOAT    0000000E RI_MULT     00000014 RI_NEG      0000001A RI_SIN      000000F0 RI_STACK
000000B0 SCR         00000020 SD_CLEAR    00000033 SD_ELIPS    00000031 SD_LINE     00000034 SD_SCALE
00000029 SD_SETIN    000000DB SET_CIRC    000000E1 SET_LINE    000000D4 SET_SCAL    000000C8 UT_SCR

0000 error(s) detected
6080 bytes free
```

Figure 10.3 A rolling multi-colour ball display

```
Rolling ball                        McGraw-Hill(UK) 68000 Ass v1.0A    Page: 0001

                                    0001 *H Rolling ball
                                    0002 ;
                                    0003 ; Copyright (c) 1984 McGraw-Hill(UK)
                                    0004 ;
00000000                            0005          ORG 0
                                    0006 ;                                    ┌─────────────┐
00000008  =                         0007 MT_SUSJB EQU    $08                  │  SEXEC      │
FFFFFFFF  =                         0008 MYSELF   EQU    -1                    │  LEN : 350  │
                                    0009 ;                                    │  DATA:  64  │
                                    0010 ; Header for debuggers etc           └─────────────┘
                                    0011 ;
00000000 600C                       0012          BRA.S  BALL        ;branch to code
00000002 00000000                   0013          DEFL   0
00000006 4AFB                       0014          DEFW   $4AFB       ;standard header
00000008 0004                       0015          DEFW   4
0000000A 42616C6C                   0016          DEFB   'Ball'
                                    0017 ;
0000000E 4BF900020810               0018 BALL:    LEA    $20810,A5   ;start addr of line
                                    0019 ;
                                    0020 ; First we move right (rolling the ball)
                                    0021 ;
00000014 722D                       0022          MOVEQ  #$2D,D1     ;draw 46 complete cycles
00000016 49FA008E                   0023 1%:      LEA    BALL_DATA(PC),A4;start of data for cycle
0000001A 7003                       0024          MOVEQ  #3,D0       ;each cycle is 4 long
0000001C 7802                       0025          MOVEQ  #2,D4       ;initial shift is 2
0000001E 6140                       0026 2%:      BSR.S  DRAW_WAIT   ;wait and draw ball
00000020 5444                       0027          ADDQ   #2,D4       ;shift it right a bit
00000022 51C8FFFA                   0028          DBRA   D0,2%
                                    0029 ;
00000026 544D                       0030          ADDQ   #2,A5       ;move to next word in screen
00000028 51C9FFEC                   0031          DBRA   D1,1%
                                    0032 ;
                                    0033 ; Now we spin a stationary ball
                                    0034 ;
0000002C 7808                       0035          MOVEQ  #8,D4       ;with shift of 8
0000002E 554D                       0036          SUBQ   #2,A5       ;at last position
00000030 7213                       0037          MOVEQ  #$13,D1     ;20 complete cycles
00000032 49FA0072                   0038 3%:      LEA    BALL_DATA(PC),A4;start of data for cycle
00000036 7003                       0039          MOVEQ  #3,D0       ;each cycle is 4 long
00000038 6126                       0040 4%:      BSR.S  DRAW_WAIT   ;wait and draw ball
0000003A 51C8FFFC                   0041          DBRA   D0,4%
0000003E 51C9FFF2                   0042          DBRA   D1,3%
                                    0043 ;
                                    0044 ; Now we move left (rolling the ball backwards)
                                    0045 ;
00000042 722D                       0046          MOVEQ  #$2D,D1
00000044 49FA00E4                   0047 5%:      LEA    BALL_LAST(PC),A4;start of data for cycle
00000048 7003                       0048          MOVEQ  #3,D0       ;each cycle is 4 long
0000004A 7806                       0049          MOVEQ  #6,D4       ;initial shift is 6
0000004C 6112                       0050 6%:      BSR.S  DRAW_WAIT   ;wait and draw ball
0000004E 5544                       0051          SUBQ   #2,D4       ;shift it left a bit
00000050 98FC0058                   0052          SUB.W  #88,A4      ;move back by two objects
00000054 51C8FFF6                   0053          DBRA   D0,6%
                                    0054 ;
00000058 554D                       0055          SUBQ   #2,A5       ;move to previous word in screen
0000005A 51C9FFE8                   0056          DBRA   D1,5%
                                    0057 ;
0000005E 60AE                       0058          BRA.S  BALL        ;keep repeating!!!
                                    0059 ;
                                    0060 ; Wait a while to get smooth movement
                                    0061 ;
00000060                            0062 DRAW_WAIT:
00000060 3F00                       0063          MOVE.W D0,-(A7)    ;save the counters
00000062 3F01                       0064          MOVE.W D1,-(A7)
00000064 7008                       0065          MOVEQ  #MT_SUSJB,D0 ;suspend
00000066 72FF                       0066          MOVEQ  #MYSELF,D1   ;myself
00000068 7602                       0067          MOVEQ  #2,D3        ;for 2 frames
0000006A 93C9                       0068          SUB.L  A1,A1
0000006C 4E41                       0069          TRAP   #1
0000006E 321F                       0070          MOVE.W (A7)+,D1
```

211

```
00000070 301F             0071         MOVE.W  (A7)+,D0
                          0072 ;
                          0073 ; Routine to put an 8*11 pixel object into the screen
                          0074 ;
                          0075 ; (A4) is a block of 11 long words holding the
                          0076 ;       pixels of the object
                          0077 ; (A5) is the top LHS of the object in the screen
                          0078 ;       which is shifted right by D4 (512 mode) pixels
                          0079 ;
                          0080 ;   A4 is updated by 11 on each call
                          0081 ;   D5 to D7 are scratch
                          0082 ;
00000072                  0083 DRAW_8X11:
00000072 2FOD             0084         MOVE.L  A5,-(A7)        ;preserve screen address
00000074 7A0A             0085         MOVEQ   #10,D5          ;draw 11 lines
00000076                  0086 DRAW_LOOP:
00000076 7C00             0087         MOVEQ   #0,D6           ;clear (top ends of)
00000078 7E00             0088         MOVEQ   #0,D7           ;       working registers
0000007A 0D0C0000         0089         MOVEP.W 0(A4),D6        ;move green and flash into D6
0000007E 0F0C0001         0090         MOVEP.W 1(A4),D7        ;and red and blue into D7
00000082 E8BE             0091         ROR.L   D4,D6           ;move object round
00000084 E8BF             0092         ROR.L   D4,D7
00000086 0D8D0000         0093         MOVEP.W D6,0(A5)        ;and put it into the screen
0000008A 0F8D0001         0094         MOVEP.W D7,1(A5)
0000008E E19E             0095         ROL.L   #8,D6           ;move the missing bit of the
00000090 E19F             0096         ROL.L   #8,D7           ;object back
00000092 584D             0097         ADDQ    #4,A5
00000094 1AC6             0098         MOVE.B  D6,(A5)+        ;and put it into the screen
00000096 1A87             0099         MOVE.B  D7,(A5)         ;as well
                          0100 ;
00000098 584C             0101         ADDQ    #4,A4           ;move to next line of the object
0000009A DAFC007B         0102         ADD.W   #$80-5,A5       ;and of the screen
0000009E 51CDFFD6         0103         DBRA    D5,DRAW_LOOP
                          0104 ;
000000A2 2A5F             0105         MOVE.L  (A7)+,A5        ;restore the screen address
000000A4 4E75             0106         RTS
                          0107 ;
000000A6                  0108 BALL_DATA:
000000A6 000AA0F0         0109         DEFL    $000AA0F0
000000AA 203AA0F8         0110         DEFL    $203AA0F8
000000AE 283E80E8         0111         DEFL    $283E80E8
000000B2 28BE82EB         0112         DEFL    $28BE82EB
000000B6 02AB2ABF         0113         DEFL    $02AB2ABF
000000BA 22BB22BB         0114         DEFL    $22BB22BB
000000BE A8FE80EA         0115         DEFL    $A8FE80EA
000000C2 82EB28BE         0116         DEFL    $82EB28BE
000000C6 022B28BC         0117         DEFL    $022B28BC
000000CA 0A2F08AC         0118         DEFL    $0A2F08AC
000000CE 0A0F00A0         0119         DEFL    $0A0F00A0
                          0120 ;
000000D2 080E20B0         0121         DEFL    $080E20B0
000000D6 283E28BC         0122         DEFL    $283E28BC
000000DA 082E20B8         0123         DEFL    $082E20B8
000000DE 02AB80EA         0124         DEFL    $02AB80EA
000000E2 A2FB8AEF         0125         DEFL    $A2FB8AEF
000000E6 A8FE2ABF         0126         DEFL    $A8FE2ABF
000000EA A2FB8AEF         0127         DEFL    $A2FB8AEF
000000EE 02AB80EA         0128         DEFL    $02AB80EA
000000F2 082E20B8         0129         DEFL    $082E20B8
000000F6 283E28BC         0130         DEFL    $283E28BC
000000FA 080E20B0         0131         DEFL    $080E20B0
                          0132 ;
000000FE 0A0F00A0         0133         DEFL    $0A0F00A0
00000102 0A2F08AC         0134         DEFL    $0A2F08AC
00000106 022B28BC         0135         DEFL    $022B28BC
0000010A 82EB28BE         0136         DEFL    $82EB28BE
0000010E A8FE80EA         0137         DEFL    $A8FE80EA
00000112 88EE88EE         0138         DEFL    $88EE88EE
00000116 02AB2ABF         0139         DEFL    $02AB2ABF
0000011A 28BE82EB         0140         DEFL    $28BE82EB
0000011E 283E80E8         0141         DEFL    $283E80E8
00000122 203AA0F8         0142         DEFL    $203AA0F8
00000126 000AA0F0         0143         DEFL    $000AA0F0
0000012A                  0144 BALL_LAST:
0000012A 020B80E0         0145         DEFL    $020B80E0
0000012E 022B80E8         0146         DEFL    $022B80E8
00000132 223B88EC         0147         DEFL    $223B88EC
00000136 A8FE2ABF         0148         DEFL    $A8FE2ABF
```

212

```
0000013A 08AE20BA          0149        DEFL    $08AE20BA
0000013E 02AB80EA          0150        DEFL    $02AB80EA
00000142 08AE20BA          0151        DEFL    $08AE20BA
00000146 A8FE2ABF          0152        DEFL    $A8FE2ABF
0000014A 223B88EC          0153        DEFL    $223B88EC
0000014E 022B80E8          0154        DEFL    $022B80E8
00000152 020B80E0          0155        DEFL    $020B80E0
                           0156 ;
                           0157 END
```

Symbols:

```
0000000E BALL       000000A6 BALL_DAT   0000012A BALL_LAS   00000072 DRAW_8X1   00000076 DRAW_LOO
00000060 DRAW_WAI   00000008 MT_SUSJB   FFFFFFFF MYSELF
```

0000 error(s) detected
6256 bytes free

11 EXTENDING SUPERBASIC

In this chapter we are going to look at four programs, each of which extend the SuperBASIC language in some manner. Each of the programs is listed in full as an assembler output list file, and preceded by a short description. The descriptions tend to rely upon the reader having read and understood previous examples, where appropriate. This keeps repetition to a minimum and enables you to get quickly to the new pertinent points. The source code of the programs, and the corresponding '_code' files, are on one of the two Microdrive cartridges which can accompany this book. The assembler/editor package (described in Part 4) which was used to develop the programs is available on the other Microdrive cartridge.

The full assembly listings will be found to be helpful in a number of ways. First, they act as simple examples of SuperBASIC extension-file creation. Second, the hexadecimal opcode listings could be used to enter the machine code directly into memory manually. Although this is long, tedious, and prone to error, it does at least give you the opportunity of trying the programs out without having to purchase an assembler package.

11.1 Using the programs

The procedures and functions within the four programs have to be initialized in order to inform SuperBASIC that they exist. The routine for doing this is demonstrated in the four programs, and discussed in Secs. 8.4 and 8.5. To physically link the procedures from SuperBASIC, a BOOT file could be created with commands in it of the form:

```
100 base=RESPR(size)
110 LBYTES filename,base
120 CALL base
130 NEW
```

This first sets up a suitably sized slice of RAM in the resident procedure area. The '_code' file is then loaded into this area and CALLed. This will cause a jump to the start of the procedure file, which in turn simply executes the short initialization routine.

11.2   Example 1 – CURSOR

This file contains two extension procedures, CURSEN and CURDIS. The short initialization routine is at the very beginning, starting at label EXTEN. The procedure definition table follows this, starting at label PROC_DEF.

The function INKEY$, within the QL ROM, does not enable the cursor. It is possible that an application program written in SuperBASIC may require the cursor to be enabled while polling the keyboard using INKEY$. CURSEN will perform just this very easily! First, set register D0 to SD_CURE, then set D3 to -1 and A0 to the appropriate channel ID, and, finally, perform a TRAP #3. The procedure CURDIS disables the cursor.

Unfortunately, though the principle is easy, life itself is harder than it should be. Owing to one of those inexplicable oversights that occur in new software, the routine in the QL ROM for finding the ID of a SuperBASIC channel is not vectored, and so you have to write it yourself! The complete routine, which will be required for any SuperBASIC function or procedure that uses channels, starts at CHANNEL. Sec.6.3 describes the channel structure.

Note how the channel is checked for being open in the code starting at CHAN_LOOK (just before CHAN_EXIT). First, the channel ID is placed into register A0 (because that is where it is needed!). Second, the least significant word of A0 is copied into a dummy register in order to set the flags. A closed or unopened channel is marked as -1 (long-word). The least significant word should be checked to be greater than or equal to zero for an open channel. The most significant word is, of course, the tag, and for an open channel it could take any value.

11.3   Example 2 – UTILS

Not all procedures are used purely for performing actions. Often they will find or calculate values to be returned. Usually this will be done by a function call to return one value, but, occasionally, more than one value will be required. In this latter case it becomes convenient to return the values through a procedure parameter list. The file in this example contains two functions (MEAN and NHEX$), and one procedure (TIME).

The MEAN function takes one (or more) values, coerced to floating point, and adds them together in a loop using the arithmetic routine RI_ADD. At this point the arithmetic stack has only one floating point number left on it. The number of values is then put on the stack, floated, and divided into the sum. Finally, the return argument address and type are set (D0 is set by the arithmetic routines) and the function returns.

The NHEX$ function is slightly more complex in that, when returning an odd length string, the start of the string must be aligned on a word boundary. First, the two arguments are fetched (in long integer form so there can be eight hex digits). The routine is a little bit careless in allocating the arithmetic stack, because CA_GTLIN will have taken at least 10 bytes to create the two long integers on the stack. Next, the second long integer is converted (in place!) to eight hex digits. If an odd number of digits is required the characters are moved down by one (note that auto increment cannot be used as all references within the SuperBASIC area must be based on A6). Finally, the word holding the length of the string is put before the string and the return argument address and type are set.

The TIME procedure returns two values giving the time of day in hours and minutes. The critical part of the procedure is the TIME_SET routine. This returns an integer value into either a floating point variable or an integer variable. It will not return a value to a REPeat or FOR identifier. The first part of TIME_SET puts the integer on the arithmetic stack, and then checks if the parameter is either unset, or a variable. Next, it decides whether the integer on the stack needs to be converted into floating point. Finally, the value is assigned using BP_LET.

11.4 Example 3 – ARRAY

Arrays have a pre-defined allocation. Individual elements of an array may be set using BP_LET, but it is very easy to write procedures to modify complete arrays. The examples given here move part of an array (or sub-array) filling the space left behind with zeros. The procedure MAKE_ROOM creates room for extra entries in an array, and TAKE_ROOM removes entries.

The ROOM_SET routine first finds the amount of space to make (or take). It then works its way through the array pointers, finding the base address of the array, the length of each of the most significant elements (e.g., for the array A(20,3) the length is (3+1)*6 bytes), and the number of the elements which require moving.

The rest of the code in the MAKE_ROOM and TAKE_ROOM procedures simply perform block copying and block clearing, with all addressing being based on register A6.

To see the effect of, for example, the MAKE_ROOM routine, try the following (extended) SuperBASIC program:

```
DIM array(9,4)
FOR i=0 to 9
  FOR j=0 to 4
    array(i,j)=10*i+j
  END FOR j
END FOR i

PRINT array,
MAKE_ROOM array(3 to 8),2
PRINT array,
```

Now try a similar test, but this time use a string array.

11.5   Example 4 – JOBS

The final example of adding procedures to SuperBASIC is a set of job
control procedures. There is one procedure to write out a list of all
the jobs in the QL (JOBS), and there are four procedures to control jobs
(SJOB, KJOB, RJOB, and PJOB). These latter four are very similar, the
first (or only) two arguments are the job number and the job tag. The
number is the index into the table of jobs, and the tag is the job's own
identifier. These are combined to form the complete job ID required by
QDOS calls.

   The JOBS procedure to write a list of jobs has no parameters (except
possibly a channel number) and the loop that scans the job tree is
simple enough. After the jobs loop there is our old friend CHANNEL and
finally the routine to format and write out the job information
(JOB_INF).

   The output is formatted by filling a buffer with the characters to be
sent, then the line is sent to the required channel. The buffer used is
the SuperBASIC interpreter's own buffer, which is at least 128 bytes
long. The first two bytes are used to hold the integers which are to be
added to the buffer. To add a number, the next integer is put in
register D1, and the pointer to the end of the field is put in register
A5. JOB_NUM puts the number in the start of the buffer and CN_ITOD is
used to convert it to characters in the buffer. JOB_NUM then fills (with
at least one space) up to A5.

   Finally, the start of the job is checked for a standard header, and,
if found, the characters of the program identification are copied into
the buffer. Note the difference in handling the data in the jobs header
(at an absolute address) and the interpreter buffer (address based on
A6).

Figure 11.1 Cursor enable/disable extensions

```
                              0001 *H Extensions to BASIC
                              0002 ;
                              0003 ; Copyright (c) 1984 McGraw-Hill(UK)
                              0004 ;
                              0005 ; This program contains the following extensions:
                              0006 ;
                              0007 ; CURSEN   enables the cursor
                              0008 ; CURDIS   disables the cursor
                              0009 ;
00000000                      0010          ORG   0
                              0011 ;
FFFFFFFC =                    0012 ERR_OR   EQU   -4
FFFFFFFA =                    0013 ERR_NO   EQU   -6
FFFFFFF1 =                    0014 ERR_BP   EQU   -15
0000000E =                    0015 SD_CURE  EQU   $E
0000000F =                    0016 SD_CURS  EQU   $F
00000110 =                    0017 BP_INIT  EQU   $110
00000112 =                    0018 CA_GTINT EQU   $112
00000028 =                    0019 BV_VVBAS EQU   $28
00000030 =                    0020 BV_CHBAS EQU   $30
00000034 =                    0021 BV_CHP   EQU   $34
                              0022 ;
                              0023 ; Entry point for initialisation
                              0024 ;
00000000 43FAOOOC             0025 EXTEN:   LEA   PROC_DEF(PC),A1 ;get definitions
00000004 34780110             0026          MOVE.W BP_INIT,A2
00000008 4E92                 0027          JSR   (A2)
0000000A 7000                 0028          MOVEQ #0,DO          ;no errors
0000000C 4E75                 0029          RTS                  ;back to SuperBASIC
                              0030 ;
0000000E                      0031 PROC_DEF:
0000000E 0002                 0032          DEFW  2              ;2 procedures
00000010 001A                 0033 1%:      DEFW  CURSEN-1%      ;offset to entry
00000012 0643555253454E       0034          DEFB  6,'CURSEN'     ;6 characters in name
                              0035          ALIGN
0000001A 0014                 0036 2%:      DEFW  CURDIS-2%
0000001C 06435552444953       0037          DEFB  6,'CURDIS'
                              0038          ALIGN
00000024 0000                 0039          DEFW  0              ;end of procedures
00000026 0000                 0040          DEFW  0              ;0 functions
00000028 0000                 0041          DEFW  0              ;end of functions
                              0042 ;
                              0043 ; Enable the cursor
                              0044 ;
0000002A 780E                 0045 CURSEN:  MOVEQ #SD_CURE,D4    ;set cursor enable key
0000002C 6002                 0046          BRA.S CUR_COM
                              0047 ;
                              0048 ; Disable the cursor
                              0049 ;
0000002E 780F                 0050 CURDIS:  MOVEQ #SD_CURS,D4    ;set cursor disable key
                              0051 ;
00000030                      0052 CUR_COM:
00000030 6114                 0053          BSR.S CHANNEL        ;use routine for ID in AO
00000032 660C                 0054          BNE.S CUR_EXIT       ;... OK?
00000034 BBCB                 0055          CMP.L A3,A5          ;should be no parameters
00000036 660A                 0056          BNE.S ERRR_BP
00000038 1004                 0057          MOVE.B D4,DO         ;set key in DO
0000003A 363CFFFF             0058          MOVE.W #-1,D3        ;set timeout
0000003E 4E43                 0059          TRAP  #3             ;(sets DO to error code)
00000040                      0060 CUR_EXIT:
00000040 4E75                 0061          RTS
00000042                      0062 ERRR_BP:
00000042 70F1                 0063          MOVEQ #ERR_BP,DO     ;bad parameter
00000044 4E75                 0064          RTS
                              0065 ;
                              0066 ; Set default or given channel
                              0067 ; Call parameters   : A3 and A5 standard pointers to name
                              0068 ;                     table for parameters
                              0069 ; Return parameters : D6 pointer to channel table
                              0070 ;                     AO channel ID
                              0071 ;
```

```
┌─────────────────┐
│ SBYTES          │
│ LEN : 140       │
│ RESPR : 256     │
└─────────────────┘
```

```
00000046                      0072 CHANNEL:
00000046 7C01                 0073         MOVEQ  #1,D6             ;default is channel #1
00000048 BBCB                 0074         CMP.L  A3,A5             ;any parameters?
0000004A 6720                 0075         BEQ.S  CHAN_LOOK         ;... no
                              0076 ;
0000004C 08360007B801         0077         BTST   #7,1(A6,A3.L)     ;has 1st parameter a hash?
00000052 6718                 0078         BEQ.S  CHAN_LOOK         ;... no
                              0079 ;
00000054 2F0D                 0080         MOVE.L A5,-(A7)          ;save top parameter pointer
00000056 2A4B                 0081         MOVE.L A3,A5             ;set new top
00000058 504D                 0082         ADDQ   #8,A5             ;   to 8 bytes above bottom
0000005A 2F0D                 0083         MOVE.L A5,-(A7)          ;   (it will be new bottom)
0000005C 34780112             0084         MOVE.W CA_GTINT,A2       ;get an integer
00000060 4E92                 0085         JSR    (A2)
00000062 265F                 0086         MOVE.L (A7)+,A3          ;restore the pointers
00000064 2A5F                 0087         MOVE.L (A7)+,A5          ;(doesn't affect cond codes)
00000066 661C                 0088         BNE.S  CHAN_EXIT         ;was it OK?
00000068 3C369800             0089         MOVE.W 0(A6,A1.L),D6     ;get value in D6
                              0090 ;
0000006C                      0091 CHAN_LOOK:
0000006C CCFC0028             0092         MULU   #$28,D6           ;make D6 (long) pointer to
00000070 DCAE0030             0093         ADD.L  BV_CHBAS(A6),D6   ;channel table
00000074 BCAE0034             0094         CMP.L  BV_CHP(A6),D6     ;is it within the table?
00000078 6C0C                 0095         BGE.S  ERR_NO            ;... no
0000007A 20766800             0096         MOVE.L 0(A6,D6.L),A0     ;set channel ID
0000007E 3008                 0097         MOVE.W A0,D0             ;is it open?
00000080 6B04                 0098         BMI.S  ERR_NO            ;... no
00000082 7000                 0099         MOVEQ  #0,D0             ;no error
00000084                      0100 CHAN_EXIT:
00000084 4E75                 0101         RTS
                              0102 ;
00000086                      0103 ERR_NO:
00000086 70FA                 0104         MOVEQ  #ERR_NO,D0        ;channel not open
00000088 4E75                 0105         RTS
                              0106 ;
                              0107 END
```

```
Symbols:

00000110 BP_INIT     00000030 BV_CHBAS    00000034 BV_CHP     00000028 BV_VVBAS    00000112 CA_GTINT
00000046 CHANNEL     00000084 CHAN_EXI    0000006C CHAN_LOO   0000002E CURDIS      0000002A CURSEN
00000030 CUR_COM     00000040 CUR_EXIT    00000042 ERRR_BP    FFFFFFF1 ERR_BP      FFFFFFFA ERR_NO
FFFFFFFC ERR_OR      00000086 ERR_NO      00000000 EXTEN      0000000E PROC_DEF    0000000E SD_CURE
0000000F SD_CURS
```

0000 error(s) detected
61A2 bytes free

+++++++++++++++++++++

Figure 11.2 General function/procedure parameter passing extensions

```
Extra BASIC functions        McGraw-Hill(UK) 68000 Ass v1.0A   Page: 0001

                             0001 *H Extra BASIC functions
                             0002 ;
                             0003 ; Copyright (c) 1984 McGraw-Hill(UK)
                             0004 ;
                             0005 ; x=MEAN (value[,value])   returns the arithmetic
                             0006 ;                          mean of all the parameters
                             0007 ; x=NHEX$ (number of hex digits,number)
                             0008 ;                          converts number to hex string
                             0009 ;
                             0010 ; TIME hours,minutes       returns time of day (12 hr clock)
                             0011 ;
00000000                     0012         ORG 0
                             0013 ;
00000013  =                  0014 MT_RCLCK EQU   $13
000000FE  =                  0015 CN_ITOHL EQU   $FE
00000110  =                  0016 BP_INIT  EQU   $110
00000114  =                  0017 CA_GTFP  EQU   $114
00000118  =                  0018 CA_GTLIN EQU   $118
```

```
┌─────────────────┐
│ SBYTES          │
│ LEN : 300       │
│ RESPR : 512     │
└─────────────────┘
```

```
0000011A  =              0019 BV_CHRIX EQU   $11A
0000011C  =              0020 RI_EXEC  EQU   $11C
00000120  =              0021 BP_LET   EQU   $120
00000008  =              0022 RI_FLOAT EQU   $08
0000000A  =              0023 RI_ADD   EQU   $0A
00000010  =              0024 RI_DIV   EQU   $10
                         0025 ;
00000058  =              0026 BV_RIP   EQU   $58
                         0027 ;
FFFFFFF1  =              0028 ERR_BP   EQU   -15
                         0029 ;
                         0030 ;Initialisation
                         0031 ;
00000000 43FA000C        0032          LEA   PROC_TAB(PC),A1 ;procedure definition table
00000004 34780110        0033          MOVE.W BP_INIT,A2      ;add to BASIC's table
00000008 4E92            0034          JSR   (A2)
0000000A 7000            0035          MOVEQ #0,D0            ;no - error
0000000C 4E75            0036          RTS
                         0037 ;
0000000E                 0038 PROC_TAB:
0000000E 0001            0039          DEFW  1               ;1 procedure
00000010 00A2            0040 1%:      DEFW  TIME-1%         ;offset
00000012 0454494D45      0041          DEFB  4,'TIME'
                         0042          ALIGN
00000018 0000            0043          DEFW  0               ;end of procedures
0000001A 0002            0044          DEFW  2               ;two functions
0000001C 0012            0045 2%:      DEFW  MEAN-2%
0000001E 044D45414E      0046          DEFB  4,'MEAN'
                         0047          ALIGN
00000024 0042            0048 3%:      DEFW  NHEX-3%
00000026 054E48455824    0049          DEFB  5,'NHEX$'
                         0050          ALIGN
0000002C 0000            0051          DEFW  0               ;end of functions
                         0052 ;
                         0053 ; MEAN function
                         0054 ;
0000002E 34780114        0055 MEAN:    MOVE.W CA_GTFP,A2      ;get floating point numbers
00000032 4E92            0056          JSR   (A2)
00000034 662A            0057          BNE.S MEAN_RTS        ;... oops
00000036 3803            0058          MOVE.W D3,D4          ;save number of parameters
00000038 6728            0059          BEQ.S ERRR_BP         ;... there were not any
0000003A 5543            0060          SUBQ.W #2,D3          ;n-1 adds (adjust for DBRA)
0000003C 6D1C            0061          BLT.S MEAN_SET        ;only one number - return it
0000003E 3478011C        0062          MOVE.W RI_EXEC,A2     ;now use arithmetic package
00000042                 0063 ADD_LOOP:
00000042 700A            0064          MOVEQ #RI_ADD,D0       ;add
00000044 4E92            0065          JSR   (A2)
00000046 6618            0066          BNE.S MEAN_RTS        ;... oops
00000048 51CBFFF8        0067          DBRA  D3,ADD_LOOP     ;... and do another one
                         0068 ;
0000004C 5549            0069          SUBQ  #2,A1           ;number of parameters on stack
0000004E 3D849800        0070          MOVE.W D4,0(A6,A1.L)
00000052 7008            0071          MOVEQ #RI_FLOAT,D0     ;float it
00000054 4E92            0072          JSR   (A2)
00000056 7010            0073          MOVEQ #RI_DIV,D0       ;and divide by it
00000058 4E92            0074          JSR   (A2)
0000005A                 0075 MEAN_SET:
0000005A 2D490058        0076          MOVE.L A1,BV_RIP(A6)   ;set return argument address
0000005E 7802            0077          MOVEQ #2,D4            ;and type
00000060                 0078 MEAN_RTS:
00000060 4E75            0079          RTS
00000062                 0080 ERRR_BP:
00000062 70F1            0081          MOVEQ #ERR_BP,D0
00000064 4E75            0082          RTS
                         0083 ;
                         0084 ; Hex conversion
                         0085 ;
00000066 34780118        0086 NHEX:    MOVE.W CA_GTLIN,A2     ;get two long integers
0000006A 4E92            0087          JSR   (A2)
0000006C 6642            0088          BNE.S NHEX_RTS        ;oops
0000006E 5543            0089          SUBQ.W #2,D3          ;we wanted two arguments
00000070 66F0            0090          BNE.S ERRR_BP         ;sorry it wasn't 2
00000072 28369800        0091          MOVE.L 0(A6,A1.L),D4  ;number of digits required
00000076 67EA            0092          BEQ.S ERRR_BP         ;... what none!!
00000078 0C440008        0093          CMP.W #8,D4           ;we can't do more than 8
0000007C 62E4            0094          BHI.S ERRR_BP         ;(unsigned greater than)
                         0095 ;
0000007E 2049            0096          MOVE.L A1,A0           ;2 long's, so room for 8 chars
```

220

```
00000080 5849        0097         ADDQ     #4,A1                ;now only 1 long word there
00000082 347800FE    0098         MOVE.W   CN_ITOHL,A2          ;convert to 8 hex digits
00000086 4E92        0099         JSR      (A2)
                     0100                                       ;now the problems!!
00000088 08040000    0101         BTST     #0,D4                ;is it an odd length string
0000008C 6712        0102         BEQ.S    NHEX_SET_LEN         ;... no
0000008E 3204        0103         MOVE.W   D4,D1                ;yes, so have to move it
00000090 92C1        0104         SUB.W    D1,A1                ;move the pointer
00000092             0105 10%:                                  ;move a digit
00000092 1DB6980098FF 0106        MOVE.B   0(A6,A1.L),0-1(A6,A1.L)
00000098 5249        0107         ADDQ     #1,A1
0000009A 51C9FFF6    0108         DBRA     D1,10%               ;this moves D1+1 characters
0000009E 5549        0109         SUBQ     #2,A1                ;add 1 to A1, + 1 'cos it's moved
000000A0             0110 NHEX_SET_LEN:
000000A0 92C4        0111         SUB.W    D4,A1                ;move A1 to start of string
000000A2 5549        0112         SUBQ     #2,A1                ;... and a word further on
000000A4 3D849800    0113         MOVE.W   D4,0(A6,A1.L)        ;then put string length in
000000A8 2D490058    0114         MOVE.L   A1,BV_RIP(A6)        ;set arithmetic stack pointer
000000AC 7801        0115         MOVEQ    #1,D4                ;... and type string
000000AE 7000        0116         MOVEQ    #0,D0
000000B0             0117 NHEX_RTS:
000000B0 4E75        0118         RTS
                     0119 ;
                     0120 ; Procedure to return the time of day
                     0121 ;
000000B2 7010        0122 TIME:   MOVEQ    #16,D0               ;two parameters?
000000B4 D08B        0123         ADD.L    A3,D0
000000B6 908D        0124         SUB.L    A5,D0
000000B8 6662        0125         BNE.S    ERRR_BP1             ;... no
                     0126 ;
000000BA 720C        0127         MOVEQ    #12,D1               ;space for 2 floating points
000000BC 3478011A    0128         MOVE.W   BV_CHRIX,A2          ;(not going to be very tidy)
000000C0 4E92        0129         JSR      (A2)
                     0130 ;
000000C2 7013        0131         MOVEQ    #MT_RCLCK,D0         ;read clock
000000C4 4E41        0132         TRAP     #1
000000C6 82FCA8C0    0133         DIVU     #43200,D1            ;get half a day of seconds
000000CA 4241        0134         CLR.W    D1                   ;... without the days
000000CC 4841        0135         SWAP     D1
000000CE 82FC003C    0136         DIVU     #60,D1               ;then half a day of minutes
000000D2 48C1        0137         EXT.L    D1                   ;... without the seconds
000000D4 82FC003C    0138         DIVU     #60,D1               ;split into hours and minutes
000000D8 2801        0139         MOVE.L   D1,D4                ;save minutes (top end of D4)
                     0140 ;
000000DA 6108        0141         BSR.S    TIME_SET             ;set one return parameter
000000DC 6640        0142         BNE.S    TIME_RTS             ;... oops
000000DE 504B        0143         ADDQ     #8,A3                ;move param. ptr to next
000000E0 4844        0144         SWAP     D4
000000E2 3204        0145         MOVE.W   D4,D1                ;set other return parameter
000000E4             0146 TIME_SET:
000000E4 226E0058    0147         MOVE.L   BV_RIP(A6),A1
000000E8 92FC0002    0148         SUB.W    #2,A1                ;put it on the RI stack
000000EC 3D819800    0149         MOVE.W   D1,0(A6,A1.L)
                     0150 ;
000000F0 4B36B800    0151         TST.B    0(A6,A3.L)           ;is parameter unset?
000000F4 6708        0152         BEQ.S    TIME_TYPE            ;... yes, that's alright
000000F6 0C360002B800 0153        CMP.B    #2,0(A6,A3.L)        ;is it a variable?
000000FC 661E        0154         BNE.S    ERRR_BP1             ;... no, cannot set
000000FE             0155 TIME_TYPE:
000000FE 720F        0156         MOVEQ    #$F,D1               ;mask out separators
00000100 C236B801    0157         AND.B    1(A6,A3.L),D1
00000104 5501        0158         SUBQ.B   #2,D1                ;see what type it is
00000106 6D14        0159         BLT.S    ERRR_BP1             ;null or string
00000108 6E08        0160         BGT.S    TIME_LET             ;integer - no conversion
0000010A 7008        0161         MOVEQ    #RI_FLOAT,D0         ;floating point - float it
0000010C 3478011C    0162         MOVE.W   RI_EXEC,A2
00000110 4E92        0163         JSR      (A2)
00000112             0164 TIME_LET:
00000112 2D490058    0165         MOVE.L   A1,BV_RIP(A6)        ;RI stack ptr to value
00000116 34780120    0166         MOVE.W   BP_LET,A2            ;set value in data structure
0000011A 4ED2        0167         JMP      (A2)
0000011C             0168 ERRR_BP1:
0000011C 70F1        0169         MOVEQ    #ERR_BP,D0
0000011E             0170 TIME_RTS:
0000011E 4E75        0171         RTS
                     0172 ;
                     0173 END
```

00000042 ADD_LOOP	00000110 BP_INIT	00000120 BP_LET	0000011A BV_CHRIX	00000058 BV_RIP
00000114 CA_GTFP	00000118 CA_GTLIN	000000FE CN_ITOHL	00000062 ERRR_BP	0000011C ERRR_BP1
FFFFFFF1 ERR_BP	0000002E MEAN	00000060 MEAN_RTS	0000005A MEAN_SET	00000013 MT_RCLCK
00000066 NHEX	000000B0 NHEX_RTS	000000A0 NHEX_SET	0000000E PROC_TAB	0000000A RI_ADD
00000010 RI_DIV	0000011C RI_EXEC	00000008 RI_FLOAT	000000B2 TIME	00000112 TIME_LET
0000011E TIME_RTS	000000E4 TIME_SET	000000FE TIME_TYP		

0000 error(s) detected
6124 bytes free

++++++++++++++++++++

Figure 11.3 Array manipulation procedures

```
Extensions to BASIC              McGraw-Hill(UK) 68000 Ass v1.0A    Page: 0001

                                 0001 *H Extensions to BASIC
                                 0002 ;
                                 0003 ; Copyright (c) 1984 McGraw-Hill(UK)
                                 0004 ;
                                 0005 ; This file contains the following extensions
                                 0006 ;
                                 0007 ; MAKE_ROOM array,n      makes room for n extra entries
                                 0008 ;                         in an array
                                 0009 ; TAKE_ROOM array,n      takes n entries out of an array
                                 0010 ;
00000000                         0011        ORG 0
                                 0012 ;
FFFFFFFC  =                      0013 ERR_OR    EQU   -4
FFFFFFFA  =                      0014 ERR_NO    EQU   -6
FFFFFFF1  =                      0015 ERR_BP    EQU   -15
0000000E  =                      0016 SD_CURE   EQU   $E
0000000F  =                      0017 SD_CURS   EQU   $F
00000110  =                      0018 BP_INIT   EQU   $110
00000112  =                      0019 CA_GTINT  EQU   $112
00000028  =                      0020 BV_VVBAS  EQU   $28
00000030  =                      0021 BV_CHBAS  EQU   $30
00000034  =                      0022 BV_CHP    EQU   $34
                                 0023 ;
                                 0024 ; entry point for initialisation
                                 0025 ;
00000000 43FA000C                0026 EXTEN:  LEA    PROC_DEF(PC),A1 ;get procedure table
00000004 34780110                0027         MOVE.W BP_INIT,A2
00000008 4E92                    0028         JSR    (A2)
0000000A 7000                    0029         MOVEQ  #0,D0           ;no errors
0000000C 4E75                    0030         RTS                   ;back to BASIC
                                 0031 ;
0000000E                         0032 PROC_DEF:
0000000E 0004                    0033         DEFW   4               ;2 only - but long names
00000010 001E                    0034 1%:     DEFW   MAKE_ROOM-1%    ;offset to code
00000012 094D414B455F524F4F4D    0035         DEFB   9,'MAKE_ROOM'   ;name
                                 0036         ALIGN
0000001C 0038                    0037 2%:     DEFW   TAKE_ROOM-2%
0000001E 095441454B455F524F4F4D  0038         DEFB   9,'TAKE_ROOM'
00000028 0000                    0039         DEFW   0               ;end of procedures
0000002A 0000                    0040         DEFW   0               ;0 functions
0000002C 0000                    0041         DEFW   0               ;end of functions
                                 0042 ;
                                 0043 ;
                                 0044 ; Array manipulation procedures
                                 0045 ;
0000002E                         0046 MAKE_ROOM:
0000002E 6146                    0047         BSR.S  ROOM_SET        ;set pointers to array
00000030 6620                    0048         BNE.S  MAKE_RTS
00000032 4BF55800                0049         LEA    0(A5,D5.L),A5   ;make space - from top down
00000036 49F54800                0050         LEA    0(A5,D4.L),A4   ;set destination pointer
0000003A                         0051 MAKE_MOVE:
0000003A 554C                    0052         SUBQ   #2,A4           ;predecrement
0000003C 554D                    0053         SUBQ   #2,A5           ;and move up
0000003E 3DB6D800C800            0054         MOVE.W 0(A6,A5.L),0(A6,A4.L)
```

SBYTES
LEN : 210
RESPR : 256

```
00000044 5545          0055        SUBQ    #2,D5
00000046 62F2          0056        BHI.S   MAKE_MOVE
00000048               0057 MAKE_CLEAR:
00000048 554C          0058        SUBQ    #2,A4              ;predecrement
0000004A 4276C800      0059        CLR.W   O(A6,A4.L)         ;and clear the left over bit
0000004E 5544          0060        SUBQ    #2,D4
00000050 62F6          0061        BHI.S   MAKE_CLEAR
00000052               0062 MAKE_RTS:
00000052 4E75          0063        RTS
                       0064 ;
00000054               0065 TAKE_ROOM:
00000054 6120          0066        BSR.S   ROOM_SET           ;set pointers to array
00000056 661C          0067        BNE.S   TAKE_RTS
00000058 49F54800      0068        LEA     O(A5,D4.L),A4      ;set source pointer
0000005C               0069 TAKE_MOVE:                       ;move down
0000005C 3DB6C800D800  0070        MOVE.W  O(A6,A4.L),O(A6,A5.L)
00000062 544C          0071        ADDQ    #2,A4              ;and postincrement
00000064 544D          0072        ADDQ    #2,A5
00000066 5545          0073        SUBQ    #2,D5
00000068 62F2          0074        BHI.S   TAKE_MOVE
0000006A               0075 TAKE_CLEAR:
0000006A 4276D800      0076        CLR.W   O(A6,A5.L)         ;clear bit at the top
0000006E 544D          0077        ADDQ    #2,A5              ;and postincrement
00000070 5544          0078        SUBQ    #2,D4
00000072 62F6          0079        BHI.S   TAKE_CLEAR
00000074               0080 TAKE_RTS:
00000074 4E75          0081        RTS
                       0082 ;
                       0083 ; General setup for room routines
                       0084 ; returns D4 distance to move
                       0085 ;         D5 amount to move
                       0086 ;         A5 base address of array
                       0087 ;
00000076               0088 ROOM_SET:
00000076 504B          0089        ADDQ    #8,A3              ;ignore array for moment
00000078 BBCB          0090        CMP.L   A3,A5              ;any arguments left?
0000007A 6F56          0091        BLE.S   ERR__BP1
0000007C 34780112      0092        MOVE.W  CA_CTINT,A2        ;we need one integer
00000080 4E92          0093        JSR     (A2)
00000082 6648          0094        BNE.S   ROOM_RTS           ;oops
00000084 5343          0095        SUBQ.W  #1,D3              ;just one
00000086 664A          0096        BNE.S   ERR__BP1           ;oops
00000088 38369800      0097        MOVE.W  O(A6,A1.L),D4      ;set distance to move
0000008C 6F40          0098        BLE.S   ERR__OR            ;oops
                       0099 ;
0000008E 514B          0100        SUBQ    #8,A3
00000090 0C36003B800   0101        CMP.B   #3,O(A6,A3.L)      ;it must be an array
00000096 663A          0102        BNE.S   ERR__BP1
00000098 720F          0103        MOVEQ   #$F,D1             ;mask out separators
0000009A C236B801      0104        AND.B   1(A6,A3.L),D1      ;when we get array type
                       0105 ;
0000009E 2A6E0028      0106        MOVE.L  BV_VVBAS(A6),A5    ;get base of VV area
000000A2 2876B804      0107        MOVE.L  4(A6,A3.L),A4
000000A6 D9CD          0108        ADD.L   A5,A4              ;and so base of descriptor
000000A8 DBF6C800      0109        ADD.L   O(A6,A4.L),A5      ;... and base of array
                       0110 ;
000000AC 3C36C808      0111        MOVE.W  8(A6,A4.L),D6      ;get element length
000000B0 5501          0112        SUBQ.B  #2,D1              ;adjust for array type
000000B2 6D08          0113        BLT.S   ROOM_SIZE          ;nothing for strings
000000B4 6E04          0114        BGT.S   ROOM_BY_2          ;*2 for integers
000000B6 CCFC0003      0115        MULU    #3,D6              ;*6 for floating point
000000BA               0116 ROOM_BY_2:
000000BA DC46          0117        ADD.W   D6,D6              ;assume element length < 64k
000000BC               0118 ROOM_SIZE:
000000BC 3A36C806      0119        MOVE.W  6(A6,A4.L),D5      ;get total nr of elements
000000C0 5245          0120        ADDQ.W  #1,D5              ;max. dimension +1
000000C2 9A44          0121        SUB.W   D4,D5              ;thus nr of elements to move
000000C4 6F08          0122        BLE.S   ERR__OR
000000C6 C8C6          0123        MULU    D6,D4              ;conv. dist. to move to bytes
000000C8 CAC6          0124        MULU    D6,D5              ;and number of bytes to move
                       0125 ;
000000CA 7000          0126        MOVEQ   #O,DO
000000CC               0127 ROOM_RTS:
000000CC 4E75          0128        RTS
000000CE               0129 ERR__OR:
000000CE 70FC          0130        MOVEQ   #ERR_OR,DO
000000D0 4E75          0131        RTS
000000D2               0132 ERR__BP1:
```

```
        000000D2 70F1          0133              MOVEQ    #ERR_BP,D0
        000000D4 4E75          0134              RTS
                               0135 ;
                               0136 END


Symbols:

   00000110 BP_INIT    00000030 BV_CHBAS   00000034 BV_CHP    00000028 BV_VVBAS   00000112 CA_GTII
   FFFFFFF1 ERR_BP     FFFFFFFA ERR_NO     FFFFFFFC ERR_OR    000000D2 ERR__BP1   000000CE ERR__O:
   00000000 EXTEN      00000048 MAKE_CLE   0000003A MAKE_MOV  0000002E MAKE_ROO   00000052 MAKE_R'
   0000000E PROC_DEF   000000BA ROOM_BY_   000000CC ROOM_RTS  00000076 ROOM_SET   000000BC ROOM_S
   0000000E SD_CURE    0000000F SD_CURS    0000006A TAKE_CLE  0000005C TAKE_MOV   00000054 TAKE_R'
   00000074 TAKE_RTS

0000 error(s) detected
6152 bytes free
```

++++++++++++++++++++

Figure 11.4 Job control/display procedures

```
    Job control for BASIC          McGraw-Hill(UK) 68000 Ass v1.0A   Page: 0001

                                 0001 *H Job control for BASIC
                                 0002 ;
                                 0003 ; Copyright (c) 1984 McGraw-Hill
                                 0004 ;
                                 0005 ; This file contains the following extensions:
                                 0006 ;
                                 0007 ; JOBS [#n]                    lists the current jobs
                                 0008 ; SJOB nr,tag,time             suppresses a job
                                 0009 ; KJOB nr,tag                  kills a job
                                 0010 ; RJOB nr,tag                  releases a job
                                 0011 ; PJOB nr,tag,priority         sets a job's priority
                                 0012 ;
    00000000                     0013              ORG 0
                                 0014 ;
    FFFFFFFA =                   0015 ERR_NO    EQU    -6
    FFFFFFF1 =                   0016 ERR_BP    EQU    -15              ┌─────────────────────┐
    00000002 =                   0017 MT_JINF   EQU    $02              │ SBYTES              │
    00000005 =                   0018 MT_FRJOB  EQU    $05              │                     │
    00000008 =                   0019 MT_SUSJB  EQU    $08              │ LEN : 400           │
    00000009 =                   0020 MT_RELJB  EQU    $09              │ RESPR : 512         │
    0000000B =                   0021 MT_PRIOR  EQU    $0B              └─────────────────────┘
    000000F2 =                   0022 CN_ITOD   EQU    $F2
    00000110 =                   0023 BP_INIT   EQU    $110
    00000112 =                   0024 CA_GTINT  EQU    $112
    00000000 =                   0025 BV_BFBAS  EQU    $00
    00000030 =                   0026 BV_CHBAS  EQU    $30
    00000034 =                   0027 BV_CHP    EQU    $34
    00000007 =                   0028 IO_SSTRG  EQU    $07
                                 0029 ;
                                 0030 ; Entry point for initialisation
                                 0031 ;
    00000000 43FA000C            0032 JOB:      LEA     PROC_DEF(PC),A1 ;get table pointer
    00000004 34780110            0033           MOVE.W  BP_INIT,A2
    00000008 4E92                0034           JSR     (A2)
    0000000A 7000                0035           MOVEQ   #0,D0           ;no errors
    0000000C 4E75                0036           RTS                     ;back to SuperBASIC
                                 0037 ;
    0000000E                     0038 PROC_DEF:
    0000000E 0005                0039           DEFW    5               ;5 procedures
    00000010 0064                0040 1%:       DEFW    JOBS-1%         ;offset to entry
    00000012 044A4F4253          0041           DEFB    4,'JOBS'        ;4 character name
                                 0042           ALIGN
    00000018 0026                0043 2%:       DEFW    SJOB-2%
    0000001A 04534A4F42          0044           DEFB    4,'SJOB'
                                 0045           ALIGN
    00000020 0024                0046 3%:       DEFW    KJOB-3%
    00000022 044B4A4F42          0047           DEFB    4,'KJOB'
```

```
00000028 0022        0048           ALIGN
0000002A 04524A4F42  0049 4%:       DEFW      RJOB-4%
                     0050           DEFB      4,'RJOB'
                     0051           ALIGN
00000030 0020        0052 5%:       DEFW      PJOB-5%
00000032 04504A4F42  0053           DEFB      4,'PJOB'
                     0054           ALIGN
00000038 0000        0055           DEFW      0                  ;end of procedures
0000003A 0000        0056           DEFW      0                  ;0 functions
0000003C 0000        0057           DEFW      0                  ;end of functions
                     0058 ;
0000003E 7808        0059 SJOB:     MOVEQ     #MT_SUSJB,D4       ;suspend job
00000040 7A03        0060           MOVEQ     #3,D5              ;get 3 parameters
00000042 6010        0061           BRA.S     JOB_COMMON
00000044 7805        0062 KJOB:     MOVEQ     #MT_FRJOB,D4       ;force remove job
00000046 7A02        0063           MOVEQ     #2,D5              ;get 2 parameters
00000048 600A        0064           BRA.S     JOB_COMMON
0000004A 7809        0065 RJOB:     MOVEQ     #MT_RELJB,D4       ;release job
0000004C 7A02        0066           MOVEQ     #2,D5              ;get 2 parameters
0000004E 6004        0067           BRA.S     JOB_COMMON
00000050 780B        0068 PJOB:     MOVEQ     #MT_PRIOR,D4       ;set job priority
00000052 7A03        0069           MOVEQ     #3,D5              ;get 3 parameters
                     0070 ;
00000054             0071 JOB_COMMON:
00000054 34780112    0072           MOVE.W    CA_GTINT,A2        ;get some integers
00000058 4E92        0073           JSR       (A2)
0000005A 6644        0074           BNE.S     JOB_EXIT
0000005C B645        0075           CMP.W     D5,D3              ;got the right number?
0000005E 6642        0076           BNE.S     ERRR_BP
00000060 22369800    0077           MOVE.L    0(A6,A1.L),D1      ;get job ID and tag
00000064 4841        0078           SWAP      D1                 ;(in the right order)
00000066 36369804    0079           MOVE.W    4(A6,A1.L),D3      ;get timeout (SJOB)
0000006A 3403        0080           MOVE.W    D3,D2              ;or priority (PJOB)
0000006C 2004        0081           MOVE.L    D4,D0              ;set operation key
0000006E 93C9        0082           SUB.L     A1,A1              ;flag address (SJOB) = 0
00000070 4E41        0083           TRAP      #1
00000072 4E75        0084           RTS
                     0085 ;
                     0086 ; Write a list of jobs to selected or default channel
                     0087 ;
00000074 6130        0088 JOBS:     BSR.S     CHANNEL
00000076 6628        0089           BNE.S     JOB_EXIT           ;... OK?
00000078 BBCB        0090           CMP.L     A3,A5              ;should be no parameters
0000007A 6626        0091           BNE.S     ERRR_BP
0000007C 2848        0092           MOVE.L    A0,A4              ;save channel ID
0000007E 43FA00F0    0093           LEA       JOB_HEAD(PC),A1    ;write out a header
00000082 3419        0094           MOVE.W    (A1)+,D2           ;... set length
00000084 610000C4    0095           BSR       JOB_WRITE
00000088 7200        0096           MOVEQ     #0,D1              ;start at job 0
                     0097 ;
0000008A 2801        0098 1%:       MOVE.L    D1,D4              ;save this job ID
0000008C 7002        0099           MOVEQ     #MT_JINF,D0        ;get job information
0000008E 7400        0100           MOVEQ     #0,D2              ;scan the whole tree
00000090 4E41        0101           TRAP      #1
00000092 4A80        0102           TST.L     D0                 ;give up if an error
00000094 660A        0103           BNE.S     JOB_EXIT
00000096 2A01        0104           MOVE.L    D1,D5              ;save next job ID
00000098 6150        0105           BSR.S     JOB_INF            ;output information on job
0000009A 6604        0106           BNE.S     JOB_EXIT
0000009C 2205        0107           MOVE.L    D5,D1              ;if next job is not
0000009E 66EA        0108           BNE.S     1%                 ;zero, carry on
                     0109 ;
000000A0             0110 JOB_EXIT:
000000A0 4E75        0111           RTS
                     0112 ;
000000A2             0113 ERRR_BP:
000000A2 70F1        0114           MOVEQ     #ERR_BP,D0         ;bad parameter
000000A4 4E75        0115           RTS
                     0116 ;
                     0117 ; Set default or given channel
                     0118 ; Call parameters   : A3 and A5 standard pointers to name
                     0119 ;                      table for parameters
                     0120 ; Return parameters : D6 pointer to channel table
                     0121 ;                      A0 channel ID
                     0122 ;
000000A6             0123 CHANNEL:
000000A6 7C01        0124           MOVEQ     #1,D6              ;default is channel #1
000000A8 BBCB        0125           CMP.L     A3,A5              ;any parameters?
```

225

```
000000AA 6720          0126          BEQ.S      CHAN_LOOK       ;... no
                       0127 ;
000000AC 08360007B801  0128          BTST       #7,1(A6,A3.L)   ;has 1st parameter a hash?
000000B2 6718          0129          BEQ.S      CHAN_LOOK       ;... no
                       0130 ;
000000B4 2F0D          0131          MOVE.L     A5,-(A7)        ;save top parameter pointer
000000B6 2A4B          0132          MOVE.L     A3,A5           ;set new top
000000B8 504D          0133          ADDQ       #8,A5           ;   to 8 bytes above bottom
000000BA 2F0D          0134          MOVE.L     A5,-(A7)        ;  (it will be new bottom)
000000BC 34780112      0135          MOVE.W     CA_GTINT,A2     ;get an integer
000000C0 4E92          0136          JSR        (A2)
000000C2 265F          0137          MOVE.L     (A7)+,A3        ;restore the pointers
000000C4 2A5F          0138          MOVE.L     (A7)+,A5        ;(doesn't affect cond codes)
000000C6 661C          0139          BNE.S      CHAN_EXIT       ;was it OK?
000000C8 3C369800      0140          MOVE.W     0(A6,A1.L),D6   ;get value in D6
                       0141 ;
000000CC               0142 CHAN_LOOK:
000000CC CCFC0028      0143          MULU       #$28,D6         ;make D6 (long) pointer to
000000D0 DCAE0030      0144          ADD.L      BV_CHBAS(A6),D6 ;channel table
000000D4 BCAE0034      0145          CMP.L      BV_CHP(A6),D6   ;is it within the table?
000000D8 6C0C          0146          BGE.S      ERRR_NO         ;... no
000000DA 20766800      0147          MOVE.L     0(A6,D6.L),A0   ;set channel ID
000000DE 3008          0148          MOVE.W     A0,D0           ;is channel open?
000000E0 6B04          0149          BMI.S      ERRR_NO         ;... no
000000E2 7000          0150          MOVEQ      #0,D0           ;no error
000000E4               0151 CHAN_EXIT:
000000E4 4E75          0152          RTS
                       0153 ;
000000E6               0154 ERRR_NO:
000000E6 70FA          0155          MOVEQ      #ERR_NO,D0      ;channel not open
000000E8 4E75          0156          RTS
                       0157 ;
                       0158 ; Routine to format and write out job information
                       0159 ;
000000EA               0160 JOB_INF:
000000EA 2C02          0161          MOVE.L     D2,D6           ;we are about to smash
000000EC 2E03          0162          MOVE.L     D3,D7           ;the registers,
000000EE 2F08          0163          MOVE.L     A0,-(A7)        ;and the job address
                       0164 ;
000000F0 206E0000      0165          MOVE.L     BV_BFBAS(A6),A0 ;use the BASIC buffer
000000F4 5448          0166          ADDQ       #2,A0           ;leave room at bottom for
000000F6 2248          0167          MOVE.L     A0,A1           ;a RI stack for 1 integer
000000F8 2A48          0168          MOVE.L     A0,A5           ;and set our field pointer
                       0169 ;
000000FA 3204          0170          MOVE.W     D4,D1           ;first the job number
000000FC 584D          0171          ADDQ       #4,A5           ;in field of 4 characters
000000FE 6156          0172          BSR.S      JOB_NUM
00000100 2204          0173          MOVE.L     D4,D1           ;now the job tag
00000102 4841          0174          SWAP       D1              ;which is in the msw
00000104 5E4D          0175          ADDQ       #7,A5           ;in a field of 7
00000106 614E          0176          BSR.S      JOB_NUM
00000108 3206          0177          MOVE.W     D6,D1           ;now the owner number
0000010A 5C4D          0178          ADDQ       #6,A5           ;in a field of 5+1
0000010C 6148          0179          BSR.S      JOB_NUM
0000010E 4A87          0180          TST.L      D7              ;now check if suspended
00000110 6A06          0181          BPL.S      JOB_W_PR
00000112 1DBC005388FF  0182          MOVE.B     #'S',-1(A6,A0.L);yes, put in S flag
00000118               0183 JOB_W_PR:
00000118 7200          0184          MOVEQ      #0,D1
0000011A 1207          0185          MOVE.B     D7,D1           ;now priority (byte)
0000011C 584D          0186          ADDQ       #4,A5           ;in a field of 4
0000011E 6136          0187          BSR.S      JOB_NUM
                       0188 ;
                       0189 ; All the numbers are in - now check for a name
                       0190 ; (max 60 characters)
                       0191 ;
00000120 7416          0192          MOVEQ      #22,D2          ;21 chars are in buffer (+LF)
00000122 245F          0193          MOVE.L     (A7)+,A2        ;restore job base address
00000124 5C4A          0194          ADDQ       #6,A2           ;check bytes 6 and 7
00000126 0C5A4AFB      0195          CMP.W      #$4AFB,(A2)+    ;... for flag
0000012A 6616          0196          BNE.S      JOB_INF_DONE    ;no flag
0000012C 321A          0197          MOVE.W     (A2)+,D1        ;get length
0000012E 0C41003C      0198          CMP.W      #60,D1          ;is it too long?
00000132 620E          0199          BHI.S      JOB_INF_DONE    ;... yes, forget it
00000134 D441          0200          ADD.W      D1,D2           ;now we've some more
00000136 6006          0201          BRA.S      2%              ;characters to go in.
00000138 1D9A8800      0202 1%:      MOVE.B     (A2)+,0(A6,A0.L);copy characters of name
0000013C 5248          0203          ADDQ       #1,A0
```

226

```
0000013E 51C9FFF8          0204 2%:     DBRA     D1,1%
                           0205 ;
00000142                   0206 JOB_INF_DONE:
00000142 1DBC000A8800      0207 •      MOVE.B   #$A,0(A6,A0.L)  ;put <LF> at end
00000148 4E44              0208        TRAP     #4              ;A1 is relative to A6
0000014A                   0209 JOB_WRITE:
0000014A 7007              0210        MOVEQ    #IO_SSTRG,D0    ;send string
0000014C 76FF              0211        MOVEQ    #-1,D3          ;no timeout
0000014E 204C              0212        MOVE.L   A4,A0           ;restore channel ID
00000150 4E43              0213        TRAP     #3
00000152 4A80              0214        TST.L    D0              ;check error
00000154 4E75              0215        RTS
                           0216 ;
                           0217 ; Put an integer into a line and space along to end of field
                           0218 ;    (A6,A1.L) points to base of buffer, A1 is preserved
                           0219 ;    (A6,A0.L) points to buffer
                           0220 ;    (A6,A5.L) points to end of field
                           0221 ;
00000156                   0222 JOB_NUM:
00000156 5549              0223        SUBQ     #2,A1           ;make room for integer
00000158 3D819800          0224        MOVE.W   D1,0(A6,A1.L)   ;and put integer in
0000015C 347800F2          0225        MOVE.W   CN_ITOD,A2      ;convert integer to decimal
00000160 4E92              0226        JSR      (A2)
00000162                   0227 JOB_N_LOOP:
00000162 1DBC00208800      0228        MOVE.B   #' ',0(A6,A0.L) ;move a space in
00000168 5248              0229        ADDQ     #1,A0           ;and move buffer pointer on
0000016A BBC8              0230        CMP.L    A0,A5           ;have we filled field yet?
0000016C 62F4              0231        BHI.S    JOB_N_LOOP      ;try again
0000016E 4E75              0232        RTS
                           0233 ;
                           0234 ; JOBS heading line
                           0235 ;
00000170                   0236 JOB_HEAD:
00000170 001A              0237        DEFW     26
00000172 4A6F6220746167202020 0238    DEFB     'Job tag   owner priority',$A
                           0239 ;
                           0240 END
```

Symbols:

```
00000110 BP_INIT      00000000 BV_BFBAS     00000030 BV_CHBAS     00000034 BV_CHP       00000112 CA_GTINT
000000A6 CHANNEL      000000E4 CHAN_EXI     000000CC CHAN_LOO     000000F2 CN_ITOD      000000A2 ERRR_BP
000000E6 ERRR_NO      FFFFFFF1 ERR_BP       FFFFFFFA ERR_NO       00000007 IO_SSTRG     00000000 JOB
00000074 JOBS         00000054 JOB_COMM     000000A0 JOB_EXIT     00000170 JOB_HEAD     000000EA JOB_INF
00000142 JOB_INF_     00000156 JOB_NUM      00000162 JOB_N_LO     0000014A JOB_WRIT     00000118 JOB_W_PR
00000044 KJOB         00000005 MT_FRJOB     00000002 MT_JINF      0000000B MT_PRIOR     00000009 MT_RELJB
00000008 MT_SUSJB     00000050 PJOB         0000000E PROC_DEF     0000004A RJOB         0000003E SJOB
```

0000 error(s) detected
6098 bytes free

12 FILE HANDLING

In this chapter we are going to look at one, rather larger program, which extends the SuperBASIC language to cater for direct file handling. The program is listed in full as an assembler output list file, and is preceded by a short description. The description tends to rely upon the reader having read and understood the previous examples (in Chapter 11 especially). This keeps repetition to a minimum and enables you to get quickly to the new pertinent points. The source code of the program, and the corresponding '_code' file, are on one of the two Microdrive cartridges which can accompany this book. The assembler/editor package (described in Part 4) which was used to develop the programs is available on the other Microdrive cartridge.

12.1 Using the program

The procedures and functions within the program have to be initialized in order to inform SuperBASIC that they exist. The routine for doing this is demonstrated in the program, and discussed in Secs. 8.4 and 8.5. To physically link the procedures from SuperBASIC, a BOOT file could be created with commands in it of the form:

```
100 base=RESPR(size)
110 LBYTES mdvn_filer_code,base
120 CALL base
130 NEW
```

This first sets up a suitably sized slice of RAM in the resident procedure area. The '_code' file is then loaded into this area and CALLed. This will cause a jump to the start of the procedure file, which in turn simply executes the short initialization routine.

12.2 Example – FILER

In many systems, direct access file handling is made complex by the need to fit data into fixed length record structures. On the QL there is no such problem. It is possible to read or write any amount of data from anywhere in a file. It follows that it is easy to write procedures to handle fixed length records, but, as these would be primarily of historical interest, that is not performed here.

Procedures are defined to GET from and PUT onto files a list of arbitrary type values, to GET and PUT single bytes, and to position the file pointer. One function is defined to return the current file pointer. With these routines it is possible to set up sequential, indexed or linked list file structures. The file slaving algorithms in the QL mean that widely separated parts of a file may be accessed at the same time, and that the file positioning call can be used to pre-fetch parts of a file to increase the efficiency even further.

GET, PUT, BGET, and BPUT are purely re-directable, and will work with any I/O device (such as the NETwork or the SERial ports). BGET and BPUT can be emulated with the QL ROM procedures:

BGET #n,x   is the same as   x=CODE(INKEY$(#n,-1))
BPUT #n,x   is the same as   PRINT #n,CHR$(X);

The subsidiary routines in this group of procedures are the most important. There is, of course, the old faithful CHANNEL. FSTRG and SSTRG reduce the code size slightly by taking out the common part of getting and putting strings from and to a file. PUT_ON_A1 is a general purpose routine for fetching the value of a parameter of known type, and putting it on the arithmetic stack. SET_TYPE is used to check the parameters one at a time to ensure that each is actually a variable. It also sets up a type flag so that, for example, PUT can put two bytes on a file for an integer parameter, six bytes for a floating point, and '2+n' for a string.

The code would be considerably smaller if some tricks were used to convert the long branches into short branches. But the only tricks used in this code are to do with the stack (A7) handling. In some cases exits are made directly out of routines by just removing the return address by incrementing A7. This can save both code and time.

In the case of SET_POS and POS, the TRAPs are made with immediate return and both the 'not complete' and 'end of file' errors are suppressed. File positioning is always done immediately, and 'not complete' indicates that the required block of the file is, therefore, not yet in RAM.

There is one problem with POS, and that is it returns a long integer. There are no long integers in SuperBASIC! The long integer can be stored in a floating point form without loss of precision, and in this form it must be normalized. The normalization routine used here is fairly slow but simple. The number is simply shifted up until it overflows, and then it is shifted back by one. A faster normalize would be to try shifting by 16 places, then 8, 4, 2, and 1.

Figure 12.1 Direct file access procedures and functions

```
                                     0001 *H FILER
                                     0002 ;
                                     0003 ; Copyright (c) 1984 McGraw-Hill(UK)
                                     0004 ;
                                     0005 ; Direct access file handling
                                     0006 ;
                                     0007 ; This file contains the following extensions
                                     0008 ;
                                     0009 ; GET   #n (,variable}   get value(s) from file
                                     0010 ; BGET #n (,variable}    get byte(s) from file
                                     0011 ; PUT   #n (,value}      put values(s) on file
                                     0012 ; BPUT #n (,value}       put byte(s) on file
                                     0013 ; SET_POS #n,value       set file pointer
                                     0014 ; POS  (#n)              function to find current
                                     0015 ;                        file pointer
                                     0016 ;
                                     0017 ;
          00000000                   0018          ORG 0
                                     0019 ;
          FFFFFFFF =                 0020 ERR_NC    EQU   -1
          FFFFFFFA =                 0021 ERR_NO    EQU   -6
          FFFFFFF6 =                 0022 ERR_EF    EQU   -10
          FFFFFFF1 =                 0023 ERR_BP    EQU   -15
          FFFFFFEE =                 0024 ERR_OV    EQU   -18
          00000001 =                 0025 IO_FBYTE EQU    $01
          00000003 =                 0026 IO_FSTRG EQU    $03
          00000005 =                 0027 IO_SBYTE EQU    $05
          00000007 =                 0028 IO_SSTRG EQU    $07
          00000042 =                 0029 FS_POSAB EQU    $42
          00000043 =                 0030 FS_POSRE EQU    $43
          00000110 =                 0031 BP_INIT   EQU   $110
          00000112 =                 0032 CA_GTINT EQU    $112
          00000114 =                 0033 CA_GTFP   EQU   $114
          00000116 =                 0034 CA_GTSTR EQU    $116
          00000118 =                 0035 CA_GTLIN EQU    $118
          0000011A =                 0036 BV_CHRIX EQU    $11A
          0000011C =                 0037 RI_EXEC   EQU   $11C
          00000120 =                 0038 BP_LET    EQU   $120
          00000008 =                 0039 RI_FLOAT EQU    $08
          00000030 =                 0040 BV_CHBAS EQU    $30
          00000034 =                 0041 BV_CHP    EQU   $34
          00000058 =                 0042 BV_RIP    EQU   $58
                                     0043 ;
                                     0044 ; Entry point for initialization
                                     0045 ;
          00000000 43FA000C          0046 FILES:    LEA   PROC_DEF(PC),A1 ;ptr to proc defs
          00000004 34780110          0047          MOVE.W BP_INIT,A2
          00000008 4E92              0048          JSR   (A2)
          0000000A 7000              0049          MOVEQ #0,D0           ;no errors
          0000000C 4E75              0050          RTS                  ;back to BASIC
                                     0051 ;
          0000000E                   0052 PROC_DEF:
          0000000E 0005              0053          DEFW   5             ;5 procedures
          00000010 0032              0054 1%:       DEFW   GET-1%       ;offset to entry
          00000012 03474554          0055          DEFB   3,'GET'
                                     0056          ALIGN
          00000016 0088              0057 2%:       DEFW   BGET-2%
          00000018 0442474554        0058          DEFB   4,'BGET'
                                     0059          ALIGN
          0000001E 00BC              0060 3%:       DEFW   PUT-3%
          00000020 03505554          0061          DEFB   3,'PUT'
                                     0062          ALIGN
          00000024 00EE              0063 4%:       DEFW   BPUT-4%
          00000026 0442505554        0064          DEFB   4,'BPUT'
                                     0065          ALIGN
          0000002C 010E              0066 5%:       DEFW   SET_POS-5%
          0000002E 075345545F504F53  0067          DEFB   7,'SET_POS'
                                     0068          ALIGN
          00000036 0000              0069          DEFW   0             ;end of procedures
          00000038 0001              0070          DEFW   1             ;1 function
          0000003A 011C              0071 6%:       DEFW   FPOS-6%
          0000003C 03504F53          0072          DEFB   3,'POS'
```

```
┌─────────────────────┐
│  SBYTES             │
│  LEN : 620          │
│  RESPR : 1024       │
└─────────────────────┘
```

```
00000040 0000          0073          DEFW    0                  ;end of functions
                       0074 ;
                       0075 ; Get items from a file
                       0076 ;
00000042 6100018C      0077 GET:      BSR     CHAN_SET
00000046               0078 GET_LOOP:
00000046 61000198      0079          BSR     CHK_RI6            ;check for room on RI stack
0000004A 610001A2      0080          BSR     TYPE_SET           ;get type of next
0000004E 6E32          0081          BGT.S   GET_INT            ;... integer
00000050 6734          0082          BEQ.S   GET_FP             ;... floating point
                       0083 ;
00000052 7402          0084          MOVEQ   #2,D2              ;get length of string
00000054 61000160      0085          BSR     FSTRG_PUSH
00000058 6600014C      0086          BNE     EXIT_8             ;oops
0000005C 38369800      0087          MOVE.W  O(A6,A1.L),D4      ;save it
00000060 7200          0088          MOVEQ   #0,D1
00000062 3204          0089          MOVE.W  D4,D1              ;round up to even byte
00000064 5241          0090          ADDQ.W  #1,D1
00000066 08810000      0091          BCLR    #0,D1
0000006A 2A01          0092          MOVE.L  D1,D5              ;save rounded value
0000006C 61000174      0093          BSR     CHK_RI             ;check for room for string
00000070 92C5          0094          SUB.W   D5,A1              ;move stack pointer down
00000072 3D849800      0095          MOVE.W  D4,O(A6,A1.L)      ;and put length in
00000076 5449          0096          ADDQ    #2,A1
00000078 3404          0097          MOVE.W  D4,D2              ;fetch characters of string
0000007A 6100013C      0098          BSR     FSTRG
0000007E 5549          0099          SUBQ    #2,A1              ;and include string length
00000080 600A          0100          BRA.S   GET_LET            ;in return value.
                       0101 ;
00000082 7402          0102 GET_INT:MOVEQ    #2,D2              ;get two bytes
00000084 6002          0103          BRA.S   GET_BYTES
00000086 7406          0104 GET_FP:  MOVEQ   #6,D2              ;get six bytes
                       0105 ;
00000088               0106 GET_BYTES:
00000088 6100012C      0107          BSR     FSTRG_PUSH         ;push bytes onto A1
0000008C               0108 GET_LET:
0000008C 66000118      0109          BNE     EXIT_8             ;was there a read error
00000090 2D490058      0110          MOVE.L  A1,BV_RIP(A6)      ;set stack pointer
00000094 34780120      0111          MOVE.W  BP_LET,A2          ;and assign value
00000098 4E92          0112          JSR     (A2)
0000009A 504B          0113          ADDQ    #8,A3              ;move to next parameter
0000009C 60A8          0114          BRA.S   GET_LOOP           ;carry on
                       0115 ;
                       0116 ; Get a byte (and convert to FP if necessary)
                       0117 ;
0000009E 61000130      0118 BGET:     BSR     CHAN_SET           ;set up channel ID etc.
000000A2               0119 BGET_LOOP:
000000A2 6100013C      0120          BSR     CHK_RI6            ;check for room for 1 FP
000000A6 61000146      0121          BSR     TYPE_SET           ;find type
000000AA 6D0000F8      0122          BLT     ERRR_BP            ;... won't do string
000000AE 1C01          0123          MOVE.B  D1,D6              ;save type flag
000000B0 7401          0124          MOVEQ   #1,D2              ;get one byte
000000B2 61000102      0125          BSR     FSTRG_PUSH
000000B6 660000EE      0126          BNE     EXIT_8             ;oops
000000BA 5349          0127          SUBQ    #1,A1              ;put zero byte on stack
000000BC 42369800      0128          CLR.B   O(A6,A1.L)
000000C0 4A06          0129          TST.B   D6                 ;was FP required?
000000C2 6E08          0130          BGT.S   BGET_LET           ;... no
000000C4 7008          0131          MOVEQ   #RI_FLOAT,D0       ;... yes, float it
000000C6 3478011C      0132          MOVE.W  RI_EXEC,A2
000000CA 4E92          0133          JSR     (A2)
000000CC               0134 BGET_LET:
000000CC 2D490058      0135          MOVE.L  A1,BV_RIP(A6)      ;set arithmetic SP
000000D0 34780120      0136          MOVE.W  BP_LET,A2          ;assign value
000000D4 4E92          0137          JSR     (A2)
000000D6 504B          0138          ADDQ    #8,A3              ;move to next parameter
000000D8 60C8          0139          BRA.S   BGET_LOOP
                       0140 ;
                       0141 ; Put data onto file
                       0142 ;
000000DA 610000F4      0143 PUT:      BSR     CHAN_SET           ;set up the channel ID etc.
000000DE               0144 PUT_LOOP:
000000DE 6100010E      0145          BSR     TYPE_SET           ;find the type
000000E2 6712          0146          BEQ.S   PUT_FP             ;floating point
000000E4 6E1C          0147          BGT.S   PUT_INT            ;integer
                       0148 ;
000000E6 34780116      0149          MOVE.W  CA_GTSTR,A2        ;get a string
000000EA 610000BE      0150          BSR     PUT_ON_A1          ;just one
000000EE 34369800      0151          MOVE.W  O(A6,A1.L),D2      ;find length
```

231

```
000000F2 5442        0152         ADDQ.W    #2,D2              ;put length/string on file
000000F4 6016        0153         BRA.S     PUT_FILE
000000F6             0154 PUT_FP:
000000F6 34780114    0155         MOVE.W    CA_GTFP,A2         ;get a floating point
000000FA 610000AE    0156         BSR       PUT_ON_A1          ; just one
000000FE 7406        0157         MOVEQ     #6,D2              ;and put 6 bytes on file
00000100 600A        0158         BRA.S     PUT_FILE
00000102             0159 PUT_INT:
00000102 34780112    0160         MOVE.W    CA_GTINT,A2        ;get an integer
00000106 610000A2    0161         BSR       PUT_ON_A1          ; just one
0000010A 7402        0162         MOVEQ     #2,D2              ;and put 2 bytes on file
0000010C             0163 PUT_FILE:
0000010C 610000AE    0164         BSR       SSTRG              ;put bytes on file
00000110 60CC        0165         BRA.S     PUT_LOOP           ;carry on
                     0166 ;
                     0167 ; Put a byte on the file
                     0168 ;
00000112 610000BC    0169 BPUT:    BSR      CHAN_SET           ;set up channel ID etc.
00000116             0170 BPUT_LOOP:
00000116 B7EF0004    0171         CMP.L     4(A7),A3           ;end of list?
0000011A 6700008A    0172         BEQ       EXIT_8             ;yes (DO already set)
0000011E 34780112    0173         MOVE.W    CA_GTINT,A2        ;get an integer
00000122 61000086    0174         BSR       PUT_ON_A1          ; just one
00000126 4A369800    0175         TST.B     O(A6,A1.L)         ;MSByte must be zero
0000012A 6704        0176         BEQ.S     BPUT_FILE          ;good
0000012C 70EE        0177         MOVEQ     #ERR_OV,DO         ;no, call it overflow
0000012E 6076        0178         BRA.S     EXIT_8
00000130             0179 BPUT_FILE:
00000130 5249        0180         ADDQ      #1,A1              ; just the LSByte
00000132 7401        0181         MOVEQ     #1,D2
00000134 61000086    0182         BSR       SSTRG              ;onto the file
00000138 60DC        0183         BRA.S     BPUT_LOOP
                     0184 ;
                     0185 ; Set the file pointer
                     0186 ;
0000013A             0187 SET_POS:
0000013A 61000094    0188         BSR       CHAN_SET           ;set up channel ID etc.
0000013E 34780118    0189         MOVE.W    CA_GTLIN,A2        ;and get a long integer
00000142 4E92        0190         JSR       (A2)
00000144 5343        0191         SUBQ.W    #1,D3              ; just one
00000146 665C        0192         BNE.S     ERRR_BP
00000148 22369800    0193         MOVE.L    O(A6,A1.L),D1      ;set file pointer
0000014C 7042        0194         MOVEQ     #FS_POSAB,DO       ;position file absolute
0000014E 7600        0195         MOVEQ     #0,D3              ;return immediately
00000150 2057        0196         MOVE.L    (A7),A0            ;set channel ID
00000152 4E43        0197         TRAP      #3
00000154 603A        0198         BRA.S     POS_DO             ;check for valid DO return
                     0199 ;
                     0200 ; Get file pointer
                     0201 ;
00000156 6178        0202 FPOS:    BSR.S    CHAN_SET           ;set up channel ID etc
00000158 BBCB        0203         CMP.L     A3,A5              ;should be no other parameters
0000015A 6648        0204         BNE.S     ERRR_BP
0000015C 61000082    0205         BSR       CHK_RI6            ;make room for return value (FP)
00000160 2849        0206         MOVE.L    A1,A4              ;save RI stack pointer
00000162 7043        0207         MOVEQ     #FS_POSRE,DO       ;position file relative
00000164 7200        0208         MOVEQ     #0,D1              ;by no bytes
00000166 7600        0209         MOVEQ     #0,D3              ;and return immediately
00000168 2057        0210         MOVE.L    (A7),A0            ;set channel ID
0000016A 4E43        0211         TRAP      #3
0000016C 224C        0212         MOVE.L    A4,A1              ;restore RI stack pointer
0000016E 5D49        0213         SUBQ      #6,A1              ;put
00000170 42769800    0214         CLR.W     O(A6,A1.L)         ;zero exponent on
00000174 383C0820    0215         MOVE.W    #$0820,D4          ;set unnormalised exponent (+1)
00000178             0216 POS_NORM:
00000178 5344        0217         SUBQ.W    #1,D4              ;reduce exponent
0000017A E381        0218         ASL.L     #1,D1              ;and multiply mantissa by 2
0000017C 6708        0219         BEQ.S     POS_MANT           ;... if zero do not carry on
0000017E 68F8        0220         BVC.S     POS_NORM           ;if not overflowed, try again
00000180 E291        0221         ROXR.L    #1,D1              ;restore mantissa to non overflowed
00000182 3D849800    0222         MOVE.W    D4,O(A6,A1.L)      ;put actual exponent on RI stack
00000186             0223 POS_MANT:
00000186 2D819802    0224         MOVE.L    D1,2(A6,A1.L)      ;and mantissa
0000018A 2D490058    0225         MOVE.L    A1,BV_RIP(A6)      ;set RI stack pointer
0000018E 7802        0226         MOVEQ     #2,D4              ;and return type
                     0227 ;
                     0228 ; Test DO return from file position calls
                     0229 ;
00000190 4A80        0230 POS_DO:  TST.L    DO                 ;OK?
```

232

```
00000192 6712      0231          BEQ.S    EXIT_8           ;yes
00000194 72FF      0232          MOVEQ    #ERR_NC,D1       ;not complete is quite normal
00000196 B081      0233          CMP.L    D1,D0
00000198 6706      0234          BEQ.S    EXIT_OK8
0000019A 72F6      0235          MOVEQ    #ERR_EF,D1       ;end of file is still OK
0000019C B081      0236          CMP.L    D1,D0
0000019E 6606      0237          BNE.S    EXIT_8           ;no, it is not end of file
000001A0           0238 EXIT_OK8:
000001A0 7000      0239          MOVEQ    #0,D0            ;yes, set no error
000001A2 6002      0240          BRA.S    EXIT_8
                   0241 ;
000001A4           0242 ERRR_BP:
000001A4 70F1      0243          MOVEQ    #ERR_BP,D0       ;bad parameter
000001A6           0244 EXIT_8:
000001A6 504F      0245          ADDQ     #8,A7            ;remove channel ID and top of
000001A8 4E75      0246          RTS                       ;parameter list
                   0247 ;
                   0248 ; Put next item on the A1 stack (A2 set to CA_GT...)
                   0249 ;
000001AA           0250 PUT_ON_A1:
000001AA 4BEB0008  0251          LEA      8(A3),A5         ;get just one item
000001AE 4E92      0252          JSR      (A2)             ;call appropriate type
000001B0 264D      0253          MOVE.L   A5,A3            ;move onto next item
000001B2 6642      0254          BNE.S    EXIT_12          ;remove return and channel ID
000001B4 4E75      0255          RTS                       ;and saved A5
                   0256 ;
                   0257 ; Fetch bytes
                   0258 ;
000001B6           0259 FSTRG_PUSH:
000001B6 92C2      0260          SUB.W    D2,A1            ;make room on A1 stack
000001B8 7003      0261 FSTRG:   MOVEQ    #IO_FSTRG,D0     ;fetch known number of bytes
000001BA 6002      0262          BRA.S    TRAP4_3
                   0263 ;
                   0264 ; Send bytes
                   0265 ;
000001BC 7007      0266 SSTRG:   MOVEQ    #IO_SSTRG,D0     ;send known number of bytes
                   0267 ;
000001BE           0268 TRAP4_3:
000001BE 4E44      0269          TRAP     #4               ;A1 relative to A6
000001C0 76FF      0270          MOVEQ    #-1,D3           ;no timeout
000001C2 206F0004  0271          MOVE.L   4(A7),A0         ;set channel ID
000001C6 4E43      0272          TRAP     #3
000001C8 92C1      0273          SUB.W    D1,A1            ;restore A1 to original
000001CA 4A80      0274          TST.L    D0               ;check error return
000001CC 6628      0275          BNE.S    EXIT_12
000001CE 4E75      0276          RTS
                   0277 ;
                   0278 ; Set up and save channel ID and top of parameter list
                   0279 ;
000001D0           0280 CHAN_SET:
000001D0 6144      0281          BSR.S    CHANNEL          ;get channel ID
000001D2 6608      0282          BNE.S    GET_OUT          ;return directly
000001D4 2257      0283          MOVE.L   (A7),A1          ;get return address
000001D6 2E8D      0284          MOVE.L   A5,(A7)          ;save top of parameter list
000001D8 2F08      0285          MOVE.L   A0,-(A7)         ;and channel ID
000001DA 4ED1      0286          JMP      (A1)             ;and return
                   0287 ;
000001DC           0288 GET_OUT:
000001DC 584F      0289          ADDQ     #4,A7            ;remove one return address
000001DE 4E75      0290          RTS                       ;and return to BASIC
                   0291 ;
                   0292 ; Check for room for 6 or D1 bytes on RI stack
                   0293 ;
000001E0           0294 CHK_RI6:
000001E0 7206      0295          MOVEQ    #6,D1            ;check for 6 bytes
000001E2           0296 CHK_RI:
000001E2 3478011A  0297          MOVE.W   BV_CHRIX,A2      ;check for room on RI stack
000001E6 4E92      0298          JSR      (A2)
000001E8 226E0058  0299          MOVE.L   BV_RIP(A6),A1    ;set RI stack pointer
000001EC 4E75      0300          RTS
                   0301 ;
                   0302 ; Set up type of next parameter
                   0303 ;
000001EE           0304 TYPE_SET:
000001EE B7EF0008  0305          CMP.L    8(A7),A3         ;end of parameter list?
000001F2 6D06      0306          BLT.S    TYPE_VAR         ;... no
000001F4 7000      0307          MOVEQ    #0,D0            ;... yes, OK
000001F6           0308 EXIT_12:
000001F6 584F      0309          ADDQ     #4,A7            ;remove return
```

233

```
000001F8 60AC          0310          BRA.S    EXIT_8        ;and exit
000001FA               0311 TYPE_VAR:
000001FA 1236B800      0312          MOVE.B   0(A6,A3.L),D1 ;get name type
000001FE 343C00C5      0313          MOVE.W   #$C5,D2       ;mask of acceptable types
00000202 0302          0314          BTST     D1,D2
00000204 670C          0315          BEQ.S    TYPE_BP       ;not permissable
00000206 720F          0316          MOVEQ    #$F,D1        ;mask out separators
00000208 C236B801      0317          AND.B    1(A6,A3.L),D1
0000020C 6704          0318          BEQ.S    TYPE_BP       ;it is null
0000020E 5501          0319          SUBQ.B   #2,D1         ;set -ve for string, 0 for FP,
00000210 4E75          0320          RTS                    ;+ve for integer
00000212               0321 TYPE_BP:
00000212 584F          0322          ADDQ     #4,A7         ;remove return
00000214 608E          0323          BRA.S    ERRR_BP       ;and bad parameter
                       0324 ;
                       0325 ; Set default or given channel
                       0326 ; Call parameters   : A3 and A5 standard pointers to name
                       0327 ;                      table for parameters
                       0328 ; Return parameters : D6 pointer to channel table
                       0329 ;                      A0 channel ID
                       0330 ;
00000216               0331 CHANNEL:
00000216 7C01          0332          MOVEQ    #1,D6         ;default is channel #1
00000218 BBCB          0333          CMP.L    A3,A5         ;are there any parameters?
0000021A 6720          0334          BEQ.S    CHAN_LOOK     ;... no
                       0335 ;
0000021C 08360007B801  0336          BTST     #7,1(A6,A3.L) ;has first parameter a hash?
00000222 6718          0337          BEQ.S    CHAN_LOOK     ;... no
                       0338 ;
00000224 2F0D          0339          MOVE.L   A5,-(A7)      ;save top parameter pointer
00000226 2A4B          0340          MOVE.L   A3,A5         ;set new top
00000228 504D          0341          ADDQ     #8,A5         ;to 8 bytes above bottom
0000022A 2F0D          0342          MOVE.L   A5,-(A7)      ;(when done, it's new bottom)
0000022C 34780112      0343          MOVE.W   CA_GTINT,A2   ;get an integer
00000230 4E92          0344          JSR      (A2)
00000232 265F          0345          MOVE.L   (A7)+,A3      ;restore parameter pointers
00000234 2A5F          0346          MOVE.L   (A7)+,A5      ;(doesn't affect cond codes)
00000236 661C          0347          BNE.S    CHAN_EXIT     ;was it OK?
00000238 3C369800      0348          MOVE.W   0(A6,A1.L),D6 ;D6 to replace the default
                       0349 ;
0000023C               0350 CHAN_LOOK:
0000023C CCFC0028      0351          MULU     #$28,D6       ;D6 (long) ptr to chan table
00000240 DCAE0030      0352          ADD.L    BV_CHBAS(A6),D6
00000244 BCAE0034      0353          CMP.L    BV_CHP(A6),D6 ;is it within the table?
00000248 6C0C          0354          BGE.S    ERRR_NO       ;... no
0000024A 20766800      0355          MOVE.L   0(A6,D6.L),A0 ;set channel ID
0000024E 3008          0356          MOVE.W   A0,D0         ;is it open?
00000250 6B04          0357          BMI.S    ERRR_NO       ;... no
00000252 7000          0358          MOVEQ    #0,D0         ;no error
00000254               0359 CHAN_EXIT:
00000254 4E75          0360          RTS
00000256               0361 ERRR_NO:
00000256 70FA          0362          MOVEQ    #ERR_NO,D0    ;channel not open
00000258 4E75          0363          RTS
                       0364 ;
                       0365 END
```

Symbols:

```
0000009E BGET        000000CC BGET_LET    000000A2 BGET_LOO    00000112 BPUT       00000130 BPUT_FIL
00000116 BPUT_LOO    00000110 BP_INIT     00000120 BP_LET      00000030 BV_CHBAS   00000034 BV_CHP
0000011A BV_CHRIX    00000058 BV_RIP      00000114 CA_GTFP     00000112 CA_GTINT   00000118 CA_GTLIN
000001E2 CA_GTSTR    00000216 CHANNEL     00000254 CHAN_EXI    0000023C CHAN_LOO   000001D0 CHAN_SET
000001E2 CHK_RI      000001E0 CHK_R16     000001A4 ERRR_BP     00000256 ERRR_NO    FFFFFFF1 ERR_BP
FFFFFFF6 ERR_EF      FFFFFFFF ERR_NC      FFFFFFFA ERR_NO      FFFFFFEE ERR_OV     000001F6 EXIT_12
000001A6 EXIT_8      000001A0 EXIT_OK8    00000000 FILES       00000156 FPOS       000001B8 FSTRG
000001B6 FSTRG_PU    00000042 FS_POSAB    00000043 FS_POSRE    00000042 GET        00000088 GET_BYTE
00000086 GET_FP      00000082 GET_INT     0000008C GET_LET     00000046 GET_LOOP   000001DC GET_OUT
00000001 IO_FBYTE    00000003 IO_FSTRG    00000005 IO_SBYTE    00000007 IO_SSTRG   00000190 POS_DO
00000186 POS_MANT    00000178 POS_NORM    0000000E PROC_DEF    000000DE PUT_LOOP   0000010C PUT_FILE
000000F6 PUT_FP      00000102 PUT_INT     000000DA PUT         000001AA PUT_ON_A   0000011C RI_EXEC
00000008 RI_FLOAT    0000013A SET_POS     000001BC SSTRG       000001BE TRAP4_3    00000212 TYPE_BP
000001EE TYPE_SET    000001FA TYPE_VAR
```

0000 error(s) detected
5EA6 bytes free

PART 4 The Assembler/Editor

13 USING THE EDITOR

The full screen editor developed for this text is simple to operate and yet powerful enough to enable assembler source code to be quickly and efficiently edited. All the example subroutines and programs given in the previous chapters have been prepared using this editor (and then assembled using the assembler described in the following chapter). In practice it is important to use this editor and not, for example, the word-processor package 'Quill', because the latter does not produce pure ASCII text files on the Microdrives. Pure text files are the only type of file which the complementary assembler can parse.

The editor is designed specifically for the creation of source (textual) programs. It allows up to 400 lines to be edited at any one time, with 72 characters per line. This is more than adequate for two major reasons. First, the size of program developed, at least in the early stages, is not likely to exceed this length, and second, the assembler will permit the inclusion of external 'library' files. If a large program is to be developed it is a simple case of creating one central program that will include as many external source file modules as it takes to produce the entire code.

13.1   Editor windows

On entry, the editor screen will appear as shown in Fig.13.1. Four windows exist in the display. Going from the top of the screen to the bottom the function of the windows is as follows.

At the very top there is a 'status' window. The contents of this window will show, in a continuous manner, the cursor line position, the total number of lines used, and the line position of a special marker which can be employed during an edit session.

Below the status window there is a 'tabulation ruler'. This particular window will never change. The tabulation ruler shows that nine tab-stops are available and that these exist at every eighth column position along a line. Each time the TABULATE key on the keyboard is pressed, the text cursor will move across to the next tab-stop. These tabulation positions are important in that the assembler, described in the next chapter, will tabulate its list-file in an identical way.

The third window in the display is the actual 'text window'. This is truly a window! It is a window with a view into your text. At any one time you can look at up to 17 lines of your program. The flashing cursor within the window enables you to edit your text program easily. When the editor is initially entered the text cursor will be in the top left-hand corner of the text window, corresponding to column 1, line 0. Any text left in the editor buffer from a previous editing session will be displayed.

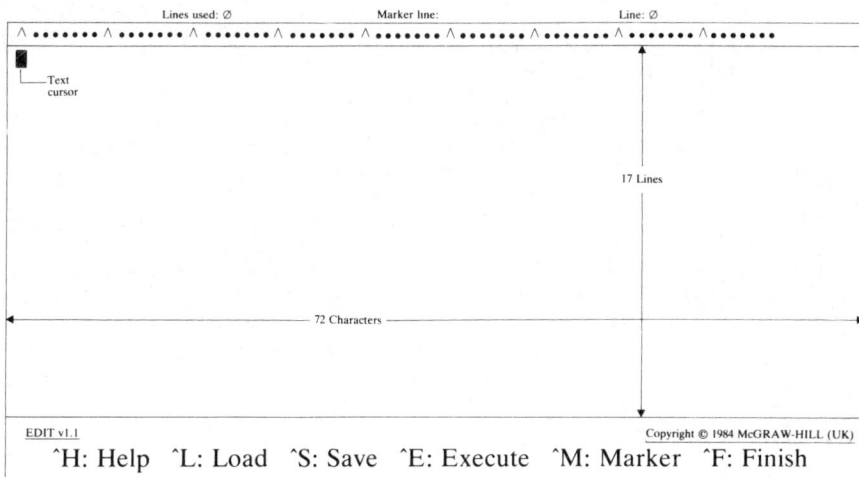

Lines used: ∅   Marker line: Line: ∅

Text cursor

17 Lines

72 Characters

EDIT v1.1   Copyright © 1984 McGRAW-HILL (UK)

^H: Help   ^L: Load   ^S: Save   ^E: Execute   ^M: Marker   ^F: Finish

Figure 13.1 Editor screen layout

The last window, at the very bottom of the screen, is used as a message and prompt window. There will be a number of occasions when the contents of this window change. For example, when you request help, the 'help' message will appear in this bottom window.

13.2   Editor modes

When the editor is initially entered it will be in its command/edit mode. In this mode there are two major operations available. First, one of six top-level commands (listed in the bottom message window) may be executed. They are all control commands and are therefore entered by typing the appropriate control character (to do this hold the CTRL key down while typing the desired command character). Second, text may be entered and edited simply by typing the required characters, cursor control commands, and text deletion commands.

At first sight it may seem that there are a lot of options to learn. In practice, however, the editor is very simple to use and you can obtain a useful 'help' message, which lists all the cursor control and text deletion commands, should you need it!

13.3 Getting help

The editor has three basic groups of commands and a facility exists to enable you to view a list of the commands in each group, together with their function. The three groups are:

1. Top-level commands (e.g., load-file)
2. Cursor control commands (e.g., cursor-down-a-line)
3. Text deletion commands (e.g., delete-character-left)

The message window at the bottom of the screen normally displays the six top-level commands. One of these commands is the 'help' command, entered by typing ^H (short for CTRL-H). This will produce a 'help' message in the bottom window showing the 12 cursor control commands, and the four text deletion commands that are available.

Typing a second ^H will cause the original message display to be regained. In this way, one control command is used to toggle between two command group lists. Note that this means the editor is totally self-documenting in terms of its command availability.

13.4 Entering text

Text is entered simply by typing in the characters required. On any one line a maximum of 72 characters may be entered. To move on to the next line press the ENTER key, and then continue as before. At any time, except at the very end of a line, the TABULATE key can be pressed, and the cursor will move to the next available tab-stop on the current line.

The real power of the editor is, of course, in the ability to change text, either because it is wrong or because you wish to delete some lines or add extra lines. To do this we need to be able to move the cursor to the appropriate place in the text, and then delete or enter text accordingly.

13.5 Moving the cursor

A total of 12 'immediate' cursor control commands exist. They are entered by using one of the four cursor control keys (up, down, left, or right) in one of three ways:

1. **NORMAL** – the keys are used on their own.
2. **SHIFT** – the keys are entered as 'shift' keys (i.e., the SHIFT key is held down while the cursor control key is pressed).
3. **ALTMODE** – the keys are entered as 'altmode' keys (i.e., the ALT key is held down while the cursor control key is pressed).

The cursor may be moved left or right along a line in a variety of ways. The cursor may also be moved up and down the text. You will notice if you type in more than eight lines that the cursor will stay in the middle of the text window and the text will scroll around it. If, at

some later stage, you position the cursor within the first eight lines
you will again notice that the cursor moves up and down and the text
stays still. This cursor operation is purpose designed to enable you to
see the current cursor line in its true context. This in turn makes
editing the text much easier. The function of each of the cursor control
commands is as follows:

1. **UP**   – The cursor will move up one line. If the cursor is
                   at the beginning of the text no action will be
                   taken. If the line moved to is shorter than the
                   current line, the cursor will be positioned at the
                   end of the new line.

2. **DOWN**   – The cursor will move down one line. If the cursor
                   is at the end of the text no action will be taken.
                   If the line moved to is shorter than the current
                   line, the cursor will be positioned at the end of
                   the new line.

3. **LEFT**   – The cursor will move one character to the left. If
                   the cursor is at the beginning of a line no action
                   will be taken.

4. **RIGHT**   . – The cursor will move one character to the right.
                   If the cursor is at the end of a line no action will
                   be taken.

5. **SHIFT–UP**   – The cursor will move up one page, equivalent to 16
                   lines. Notice that, as the text window is 17 lines
                   deep, there will always be an overlap of one line.
                   This feature will help you to scan the text more
                   easily. The cursor will always be positioned at the
                   beginning of the new line.

6. **SHIFT–DOWN**   – The cursor will move down one page, equivalent to
                   16 lines. Notice that, as the text window is 17
                   lines deep, there will always be an overlap of one
                   line. This feature will help you to scan the text
                   more easily. The cursor will always be positioned at
                   the beginning of the new line.

7. **SHIFT–LEFT**   – The cursor will move one word to the left. If the
                   cursor is at the beginning of a line no action will
                   be taken.

8. **SHIFT–RIGHT**   – The cursor will move one word to the right. If the
                   cursor is at the end of a line no action will be
                   taken.

9. **ALTMODE–UP**   – The cursor will move to the beginning of the text.
10. **ALTMODE–DOWN** – The cursor will move to the end of the text.
11. **ALTMODE–LEFT** – The cursor will move to the beginning of the
                   current line.
12. **ALTMODE–RIGHT** – The cursor will move to the end of the current
                   line.

If the cursor is moved to a position within a line, and then text
entered in the usual way, the characters will be inserted immediately
prior to the character under the cursor. The rest of the line will be

seen to pan to the right.

13.6   Deleting text

Only four immediate text deletion commands exist, and these in turn only
provide three functions (because two of the commands perform the same
task). The commands are entered by using the normal cursor control keys
(up, down, left, and right) together with the CTRL key. The function of
the commands are as follows:

1. **CTRL–UP**   – The current cursor line will be deleted. The
                       command will not be executed if a marker line exists.
2. **CTRL–DOWN**   – (Same as CTRL–UP).
3. **CTRL–LEFT**   – The character immediately to the left of the cursor
                       will be deleted. The rest of the line will pan to the
                       left. No action will be taken if the cursor is at the
                       beginning of a line. If the character to be deleted
                       is a space (single or as part of a tabulation) then
                       spaces will continue to be deleted until the entire
                       gap to the left of the cursor is erased.
4. **CTRL–RIGHT**   – The character under the cursor will be deleted. The
                       rest of the line will pan to the left. No action will
                       be taken if the cursor is at the end of a line. If
                       the character to be deleted is a space (single or as
                       part of a tabulation) then spaces will continue to be
                       deleted until the entire gap to the right of the
                       cursor is erased.

The above commands enable local text to be deleted. It is often useful
to delete whole blocks of program text, and this can be done by using
one of the editor 'execute' command options.

13.7   The ENTER key

When you have entered a reasonable number of program lines into the
editor and moved the cursor around the text, you will undoubtedly notice
that the ENTER key performs different functions at different times. Its
functions may be defined as follows.
    If the cursor is at the very end of the text then the ENTER key will
move the cursor to the beginning of a newly created line, directly after
the previous line. This makes the initial entry of text, and the
appending of text, very simple. If the cursor is at the beginning of a
line, but that line is not the last line of the text, then the ENTER key
will create a new blank line at that point and move the rest of the text
down. This enables new lines to be inserted within some current text
very easily. If the cursor is within a line then the ENTER key will
simply move the cursor down to the beginning of the next line.

240

13.8   Editor 'execute' command options

These commands are entered initially by using the top-level command ^E (CTRL-E). Four commands are available and they will be listed in the bottom message display window when the ^E command is given. To execute any one of the options simply press the character key corresponding to the first letter of the option. For example, to execute the 'find string' option you would simply enter F. The operation of the commands is as follows.

FIND STRING COMMAND

A prompt will be given in the bottom window asking for the textual string to search for. Simply type in your search string and press the ENTER key. The editor will search for the string, beginning at the start of the current cursor line. If the string is found then the cursor will be moved to the beginning of the string, and the text window updated accordingly.

If the search string is not within the text searched, the cursor will remain in its previous position. Note that the case of the text is not relevant. For example, 'This' is exactly the same as 'this', as far as the editor search option is concerned.

It may be that the editor search option places the cursor at a match, which is not the particular one you were looking for. If this is so then remember to move the cursor down to the beginning of the next line, or the search option will simply find the same one again.

DELETE BLOCK COMMAND

This is the one command that requires the use of the special marker, so let us look at this first. A marker symbol (shown as a right-sided comilla - double angled bracket character) can be entered, by using the ^M (CTRL-M) top-level command, to mark any particular line in the text. The marker will always be entered and shown at the beginning of the current line, regardless of the current cursor position, and the cursor moved to the first character in the line. It is not possible to mark a line which is completely full, and neither is it possible to mark more than one line.

Assuming a marked line is available, the 'delete-block' command will delete all lines between the marked line and the current cursor line inclusive. The command will issue an error message if no marker is present (type any character to continue after the error message is printed).

MOVE TO LINE COMMAND

This command lets you move to an absolute line within the text. A prompt will be given requesting the number of the line to which you wish to move. Enter the appropriate number and press the ENTER key. The cursor will be moved to the beginning of the corresponding line and the text window updated.

If a line number less than zero is entered, the cursor will be moved to the beginning of the text. Conversely, if a line number greater than the total number of lines available is entered, the cursor will be moved to the end of the text.

INCLUDE FILE COMMAND

When editing program text it is very useful to be able to merge in other bits of program text from another file. This command will enable a text file (produced by this editor) to be included in the current source text at the current cursor position. A prompt will be given for the device and file name of the external file, which must be on a Microdrive. Simply enter the appropriate information and the file will be included in the current text. While the text inclusion is taking place a series of '+' markers will be displayed in the bottom window to act as an indicator. Without such an indicator the editor could appear to lock-up, whereas in fact it is simply doing some internal shuffling.

Care must be taken over this operation. If the requested file does not exist, the editor will report a fatal error and cease running! You are advised to save a copy of your current text on a Microdrive before executing this command. The command will issue an error message if a marker line is present (type any character to continue after the error message is printed). An error message will also be given if the editor runs out of storage in the process of trying to merge in the external file.

When specifying the device and file name of the external file, the extension may or may not be given. If it is left off, the default extension '_ASM' will be used.

13.9 Loading a text file

A new source file can be loaded into the editor from a Microdrive by using the ^L (CTRL-L) top-level command. The file must have been created previously using the editor. Any current text will be erased from the memory of the editor and the cursor will be returned to the beginning of the new text.

When specifying the device and file name of the file, the extension may or may not be given. If it is left off, the default extension '_ASM' will be used.

13.10 Saving the current text

The current contents of the editor buffer can be saved on to a Microdrive by using the ^S (CTRL-S) top-level command. The contents of the editor will not be erased and therefore the 'save' command can be used any number of times during an editing session for safety backup purposes.

When specifying the device and file name of the file, the extension may or may not be given. If it is left off, the default extension '_ASM' will be used. It is not possible to save text which has a marker line in it, and under such a condition an error message will be issued (type any character to continue after the error message is printed).

14 ASSEMBLER OPERATION

The 68000 assembler described here is a full implementation with many features normally only found in expensive cross-assemblers running on minicomputer equipment. It is purpose designed for use with the Microdrive cartridges and standard QL serial-printer interfaces. Its specification includes:

1. full 2-pass assembly
2. output streaming to screen, printer or Microdrive
3. pseudo-operations (e.g., ORG, COND)
4. assembler directives (e.g., *HEADING)
5. simple expression parsing
6. long label names and local labels
7. alternative mnemonics, and
8. external library file inclusion.

Note that this chapter describes the facilities available within the assembler only. It does not attempt to discuss 68000 instructions.

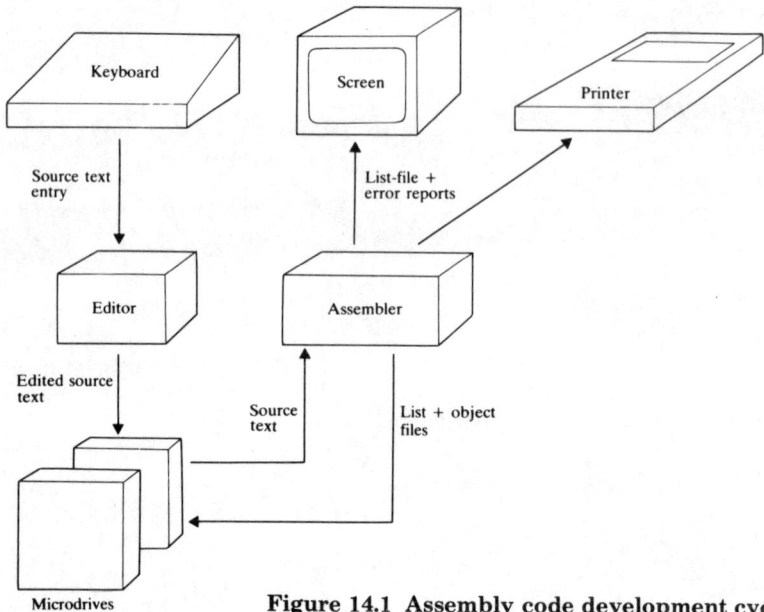

Figure 14.1 Assembly code development cycle

14.1 Assembler operation

The assembler lies at the heart of the assembly language system. It takes its input from a Microdrive file (or some other suitable mass storage medium), and can direct its output either to the screen, a printer, or the mass storage medium. Figure 14.1 illustrates the development cycle. The editor is used first in order to create the source program. This source is then fed to the assembler which creates its various output files. These output files, and in particular the object (binary) file, can then be manipulated in a number of ways. For example, the binary file may be left as it is and accessed by SuperBASIC's LBYTES command. Alternatively its contents could be loaded into memory and then re-saved in the form of an executable file for use with SuperBASIC's EXEC command.

The user manual, which comes with the assembler package, describes in detail the command options available for the assembler, and how the assembler interacts with the editor described in the previous chapter.

14.2 Assembler line syntax

The source input lines for the assembler are single statement lines. Given here is the general syntax of these lines, more detailed explanations being given later under the appropriate headings.

Assembler source input consists of a series of text lines of maximum length 80 characters, created by the editor described in the previous chapter. Each line is of the form:

LABEL: OPERATOR ARGUMENT ;COMMENT

Any of the four parts - label, operator, argument, or comment - may be omitted where this is appropriate. (Clearly a blank line would contain none of these, and a pure comment line would contain just the fourth element). Items are separated by one or more blanks (spaces or tab characters), the colon following a label, or the semi-colon preceding the comment.

LABELS

Each label name must start with a letter but thereafter may contain any combination of characters, underscores, or digits. No account is taken of case, everything of importance being converted into upper-case internally. Additionally a temporary label may be given (see Sec.14.4).

OPERATORS AND ARGUMENTS

Operators can be 68000 mnemonics (e.g., ADDX, ROR), assembler pseudo-operators (e.g., DEFB, COND), or an assembler directive (e.g., *INCLUDE). The format of the argument parameter will depend upon the operator that precedes it.

COMMENTS

Any line may have a comment appended to aid source documentation. A comment must be preceded by a semi-colon (;). Anything after this comment delimiter will be ignored by the assembler.

THE 'END' PSEUDO-OPERATOR

Assembler source text can optionally be terminated with the END assembler pseudo-operator. If it is not used then the natural end-of-file will be taken as the end of the source text.

14.3   Symbols

Symbols, acting as constants for the duration of the assembly operation, can be defined either from within the source, or dynamically as boolean (true/false) constants at assembly time.

DEFINITION FROM SOURCE (EQU)

Alphanumeric symbols may be defined using the assembler pseudo-operator EQU (or simply an '=' sign):

For example: LETA   EQU $41   ;'A'
                 LETB   =   LETA+1   ;'B'

The argument following the EQU can be any valid simple expression (as defined later). If an attempt is made to redefine a symbol, an assembler 'M' (Multiple definition) error will ensue – during pass 1 only. If such an error occurs it would be sensible to halt assembly by pressing the ESC key as there may be many future errors, particularly if temporary labels are also being used (which will normally be the case). Upper and lower case are treated as being the same within symbol definitions:

For example: LETC   EQU   letb+1   ;'C'
                 letd   EQU   letc+1   ;'D'
                 LETE   EQU   LETD+1   ;'E'

Symbols are distinct only within the first eight alphanumeric characters and they must start with an alpha character (A..Z, a..z). If the latter rule is violated an 'L' (Label format) error will ensue.

For example: DELAYforTimer1 = 64
                 Timer2Delay   = DELAYfor shl 2

DEFINITION AT ASSEMBLY TIME (QRY)

If a symbol is defined with the QRY pseudo-operator, the value may be given as either zero (false) by entering N at the keyboard, or as minus one (true) by entering Y. The prompt for the keyboard entry is given at assembly time (during pass 1), as defined by the QRY argument. For example:

FLIST QRY Full listing required

will prompt with 'Full listing required?' and expect either a Y or an N as the response. The keyboard entry is immediate (no ENTER required) and the assembler will echo either Y or N as appropriate. Note that keying any letter other than Y will effect an N response. This facility is extremely useful when conditional assembly is being used as it allows the programmer to specify flag values at assembly time, and therefore the source does not have to be edited.

14.4   Labels

There are two types of label which can be used. Alphanumeric labels may be defined which will have a scope of the entire program. Temporary or local numeric labels may also be defined, which will have a scope limited to the area between the two standard labels in which they are defined.

STANDARD LABELS

A normal alphanumeric label is a special kind of symbol. It is declared by ending it with a colon (:), and it will be given the value of the location counter for the current statement. The label itself must obey the same rules as for symbols (i.e., must be alphanumeric, must start with an alpha character, and be significant in its first eight characters).

TEMPORARY (LOCAL) LABELS

Temporary or local variables have a number of important attributes. Each label takes up only one third of the symbol table space required for normal symbols. They do not appear in the symbol table and therefore the table will refer only to important locations, and they may be re-used within different scope blocks thereby greatly reducing the possibility of multi-defined labels.

A local label is defined by the label form '1%' to '255%' and may optionally be followed by a colon (:). A local label may only exist after a normal label has been declared, and its scope of existence is limited up to the next normal label:

```
nlab1:   moveq    #0,d0
         moveq    #delay,d1
1%:      cmp.b    d0,d1
         beq.s    2%
         addq.b   #1,d0
         bra      1%
2%:      rts
;
nlab2:   bra      1%              ;1% is undefined here
2%:      nop
nlab3:
```

During pass two a 'U' (Undeclared symbol) error will ensue if a local label does not exist within its defined scope.

14.5 Expressions

The assembler will accept any non-prioritized simple expression consisting of:

1. symbols
2. normal/local labels
3. denary/hexadecimal numbers
4. single character strings
   (Up-arrow facility, see Sec.14.6, is neither
   required nor permitted)
5) the operators:

+	Unary plus / Add
–	Unary minus / Subtract
*	Unsigned 16-bit Multiply
/	Unsigned 16-bit Divide
SHR	Shift right ('n' places)
SHL	Shift left ('n' places)
OR	Logical OR
AND	Logical AND
NOT	One's complement

NUMBERS

Numeric values may be defined either in denary or in hexadecimal. If hexadecimal is being used the number must be preceded by an ampersand (&) or a dollar sign ($):

For example: defb 12,45,&3A
               defw $E2,$3AB0

If the first digit following a $ or & hexadecimal delimiter is not a valid hexadecimal digit then an 'N' (Number format), or 'S' (Syntax), error will ensue.

SIMPLE EXPRESSIONS

A simple non-prioritized expression is defined in this case to mean any expression of the general form:

<+/-> <operand> (<operator> <operand>)

A unary minus or plus may precede the first operand. Further operator-operand pairs may be used if desired. Expression evaluation is strictly from left to right. The NOT operator is a special case in that only one operand may exist, and this operand must be a symbol or a normal label. An 'I' (Illegal expression) error will ensue if the assembler cannot pass the expression in its context. In most cases this will also be followed by an 'S' (Syntax) error. Some valid examples are:

```
true      = -1
false     = not true
days      = 5
;
prog:     moveq  #true and &FF,d0
          moveq  #name and 255,d2
          moveq  #name shr 8,d3
          moveq  #'A',d0
          moveq  #'z'+1,d0
;
          moveq  #''',d0        ;Up-arrow (see 14.6)
          moveq  #'^',d0        ;equivalents, ie:
          moveq  #'A'+$80,d0    ;short form is used.
;
          moveq  #name/256+1,d2
          moveq  #days*24,d3
;
1%:       defb   0             ;Data store
;
          move.w store,a0
;
store:    defb   0,0
;
mask      = true shl 8 + 1
mask2     = mask or $2020
```

Expression values will take on an 8-bit, 16-bit, or 32-bit value depending upon the context of the expression. Assembler 'O' (Overflow) or 'R' (Range) errors will ensue if it seems that an assignment is out of context (e.g., if a 16-bit value is being used in an 8-bit context). Some assemblers will simply assign the least significant bytes in such cases, which greatly increases the amount of debugging time required when you find out that your program does not work as you intended. For the purposes of conditional assembly, the expression will be deemed true if the most significant bit of the result is set (e.g., -1), or false if this bit is unset (e.g., 0).

14.6 Data definition

Data may be defined by using the following assembler pseudo-operators:

>**DEFB**   –   Define byte / char (8-bit)
>**DEFW**   –   Define word (16-bit)
>**DEFL**   –   Define long-word (32-bit)

Alternatively data storage space may be allocated (but not defined) by using the pseudo-operator:

>**DEFS**   –   Define space (n bytes)

The four data pseudo-operators available enable any form of static data storage to be defined, and may be used in the following ways.

DEFB

This pseudo-operator is used to define byte values and character strings. A free integration of both types is permitted in any one definition line:

```
defb 13,'This is a message',13,0
defb 'ABCDEF'
defb 0,1,2,3,4,5,6,7,8,9
```

Each element of the definition line is separated from the next by a comma (,). If the first character of an element is a single quote, a string of characters is assumed to exist up to, but not including, the next single quote ('). In the context of string definitions the following is also applicable:

1. an up-arrow followed by a single quote will assemble as a single quote: defb '^''
2. an up-arrow followed by an up-arrow will assemble as a single up-arrow: defb '^^'
3. an up-arrow followed by any other character will force the most significant bit of that character to be set: defb '^A'

These special cases may exist anywhere with a string definition:

```
defb 'A^BC'
defb '^'up^''          ;'up' (with quotes)
defb 'A^^2'
```

DEFW AND DEFL

These pseudo-operators force numeric definitions to occupy 16-bits (in the case of DEFW) or 32-bits (in the case of DEFL) whether or not the actual value could reside in an 8-bit location.

```
defw 34,$56
defl 900,$4B330,2
```

Strings (as defined under DEFB) may not be defined using these pseudo-operators. Each element in the definition line must be separated from the next by a comma (,).

DEFS

If an area of memory is to be allocated to some use, but the initial values within this area do not need to be specified (e.g., heap storage space), this pseudo-operator may be used. The single argument which must follow this operator will specify the number of bytes to reserve.

14.7   Origin setting

The memory address where the assembled code is to start is defined by the ORG pseudo-operation:

```
ORG $2A000
```

More than one ORG statement may exist within a program although it would be unwise to define an origin which was lower in memory than the current assembly address. Previously declared labels or symbols may be used within an expression as an argument to ORG. For example, it would be possible to force an ensuing piece of code to reside at a clean page boundary:

```
current:
;
            ORG current+256 and $FFFFFF00
;
ncode:
```

It is common practice when writing executable code programs and extensions to SuperBASIC, to omit the ORG statement altogether. Assembly will then be based at address zero.

WARNING: Labels and symbols used in ORG expressions **must** be pre-defined. If this is not the case, different origins will exist during pass 1 and pass 2. In such cases the code will fail to assemble properly.

14.8   Conditional assembly

Individual blocks of code may be conditionally assembled using the COND, ELSE, and ENDC pseudo-operators. The operator COND expects an expression as an argument. If the most significant bit of the result is set, the value is deemed true and the following code will be assembled.

Conditional assembly (or non-assembly) of code will continue up until the next ELSE or ENDC operator. If an ELSE operator is found, the condition for assembly is reversed, and the appropriate assembly continued up until the next ENDC operator. The particular level of conditional assembly is terminated on reaching the corresponding ENDC operator.

Conditional assembly may be nested. If pass 1 is completed, but nesting levels for conditional assembly have not been completely matched, a fatal 'Assembler error' will ensue and assembly will cease (i.e., pass 2 will not be entered). A 'C' error will ensue if an ELSE or an ENDC operator is encountered before a corresponding COND operator. Examples of this nesting are as follows:

```
          yes_please    = -1
          no_thank_you  = not yes_please

     1.   cond yes_please
             subx   d2,d0          ;assembled
          else
             subx   d0,d2          ;not-assembled
          endc

     2.   addx   d1,d2             ;level 0
          cond no_thank_you
             addx   d2,d3          ;level 1a
             cond true
               addx   d3,d4        ;level 2a
             else
               subx   d4,d3        ;level 2b
             endc
          else                     ;level 1b
             subx   d3,d2
          endc
          nop                      ;Back to level 0
```

Note that the QRY form of defining symbol values as true or false (described in Sec.14.3), is an extremely useful mechanism for conditional assembly, for example, in cases where slightly different code needs to be generated depending on whether or not the code is to run in ROM. The actual source code need never be changed — it would simply be a matter of entering the appropriate responses at assembly time.

14.9 Directives

The assembler supports a number of assembly directives, invoked by using an asterisk (*) as the first non-blank character in a statement line. The following are supported:

1.   *Eject
2.   *Heading <string>
3.   *List   <on/off>
4.   *Number <on/off>
5.   *Include <filespec>

All of these may be abbreviated to just their first character (for example, *E is the same as *EJECT).

*EJECT AND *HEADING

*Eject causes a form-feed to occur in the list file, and the page number to be increased by one. Any heading, which had previously been defined, remains.

*Heading allows a heading message to be defined which will be used to document page headings in the list file. A form-feed will also occur automatically (as with *E). The maximum length of a heading is 35 characters. Headings longer than this will be truncated.

If one of these two directives is not given before a form-feed is due on a list file (in order to skip over pages in perforated listing paper), then the assembler will force a page throw as and when necessary (normally after 56 lines of assembly listing).

*LIST

*List is used to turn the listing on and off. If the word ON follows the directive then the listing will be turned on. If the word OFF follows the directive then the listing will be turned off. Note that the directive *L ON will have no effect if the list-file device, specified in the original command line, was coded as null (Z). The directive is particularly useful for conditionally listing parts of a large source file. The symbol table is always produced if the list-file is active and therefore one way of getting just a symbol table as the list output is to (conditionally) set the list directive off at the beginning of the source:

```
     FLST QRY Full listing required
     ;
          cond not FLST
     *L off
          endc
     ;
      <Symbol table produced anyway!>
```

*NUMBER

*Number has the same syntax requirements as *List. The directive enables the generation and printing of line numbers within the list file to be switched on and off. The normal state is for line numbers to be given.

*INCLUDE

*Include requires a full file specification as its argument. The specified file will be included in the source input stream at that point in the assembly. This feature enables a suite of library sources to be kept on a Microdrive cartridge and included in a program as and when required.

Only one level of inclusion is allowed and a file will fail to be included if its *I directive is within an already included file. In such cases an 'F' (File inclusion) error will ensue and assembly will continue at the next line in the current source file.

If a file cannot be opened because, for example, the file specification is incomplete or wrong, an error message will be given and assembly will stop. Note that the file specification must be the same as that which would be given to access a Microdrive under SuperBASIC. There are no restrictions on extensions, as is the case within command line specifications.

It is normal practice with large source documents to have one (short) main module which *Includes all other external modules that are required.

14.10 Alternative mnemonics

A set of alternative mnemonics exist within the assembler to aid the programmer both in terms of style and readability. First is the mnemonic for 'exclusive-or' operations. There are two widely used mnemonics for this instruction and both are supported:

Standard	Alternative
EOR	XOR

Second, there is the common confusion, especially with processors which cater for signed and unsigned arithmetic, as to the true interpretation of the 'carry-clear' and 'carry-set' conditional statements. As such the assembler provides the following:

Standard	Alternative
BCC, BCS	BHS, BLO
DBCC, DBCS	DBHS, DBLO
SCC, SCS	SHS, SLO

The mnemonic part 'HS' stands for 'higher or same', and 'LO' stands for 'lower'. They differ from the 'greater or equal' (GE) and 'less than' (LT) mnemonics in that they refer to conditions set after an unsigned operation.

14.11 Error messages

The assembler performs many checks while running and a number of errors and list-file error codes will occur if the source is illegal in some way. The error codes and messages which exist are as follows:

N> Number format error. A hexadecimal number is illegal.

L> Label format error. The format of a normal or local label is incorrect.

S> Syntax error. A catch-all message for lines which contain some form of illegal syntax.

M> Multiple definition. An attempt is being made to redefine a label or symbol during pass 1.

I> Illegal expression. The arithmetic or logical expression is illegal within the context given.

U> Undeclared identifier. During pass 2 a symbol or label is being referenced which was not defined during pass 1.

O> Overflow / Branch out of range error. A 16-bit value is being assigned to an 8-bit location, or a relative branch is out of range.

C> Conditional assembly error. An ELSE or ENDC operator was found before a corresponding COND.

F> File inclusion error. More than one level of file inclusion is being attempted.

R> Range error. An out-of-limits range is being specified within a particular instruction.

GENERAL ERROR MESSAGES

A few other errors may occur, usually fatal in effect. If a file cannot be opened or a Microdrive cartridge error occurs, an appropriate message is displayed and assembly will cease. If bad conditional assembly exists in pass 1, an error message is displayed and pass 2 is not entered. In all these fatal cases the error message will indicate the nature of the fault.

14.12   Word boundary alignment (ALIGN)

The 68000 processor will always require a word or long-word of data to begin on a word boundary (i.e., an even memory address). This implies that any instruction opcode must also be on a word boundary. When the assembler DEFB or DEFS pseudo-operators are used, the location counter could point to an odd address at the end of the definition line. If a 68000 instruction, DEFW line, or DEFL line immediately follows the definition, the resultant object code will not execute as expected. The 68000 will enter an error type exception process when an attempt is made to access any instruction or word of data at an odd address.

To stop you from having to count byte definitions, in order to make sure there are an even number of bytes defined (and getting it wrong!), the assembler pseudo-operator ALIGN is provided. This operator should follow any byte definition line that must, because of what follows, leave the location counter at an even address. For example:

```
        :
dat1:       defb 6,'FREEIT'
            align
dat2:       defw first,last,max,min
        :
```

If the location counter is incremented internally, to produce alignment, the byte skipped over will be set to zero by the assembler.

Appendices

Appendix A – 68000 INSTRUCTION SET SUMMARY

A.1 Addressing modes

Six basic addressing modes in the 68000 give rise to 14 actual modes. The modes of addressing are shown in Fig.A.1, together with the appropriate assembler syntax.

MODE	SYNTAX
Implied	
Register	SR, CCR, USP, PC
Immediate	
Immediate	#n
Quick immediate	#b
Absolute	
Short	a16
Long	a32
Register Direct	
Data register	Dn
Address register direct	An
Register Indirect	
Address register	(An)
Postincrement	(An)+
Predecrement	-(An)
Address register with offset	d16(An)
Register with index and offset	d8(An,i)
Program Counter Relative	
Address register with offset	d16(PC)
Register with index and offset	d8(PC,i)

Notes:
```
    b = 3, 4 or 8 bits      i   = An or Dn
    n = 8,16, or 32 bits    An  = address register
   d8 = 8 bit offset        Dn  = data register
  d16 = 16 bit offset       PC  = current location
  a16 = 16 bit address      SR  = status register
  a32 = 32 bit address      CCR = condition codes
                            USP = user stack ptr
```

Figure A.1 68000 addressing modes

A.2 Condition codes

There are three instructions (Bcc, DBcc, and Scc) which use a set of conditional tests. The tests are given 'one/two character' mnemonics and the full instruction mnemonic consists of the above names with 'cc' replaced by the test mnemonic (e.g., BHI, BF, DBEQ, SNE, and so on). Each test produces a true or false result depending on the state of given condition flags in the 68000 CCR register.

In the table below, the alternative mnemonics are given in parenthesis after the standard mnemonic.

Mnemonic	Test	Interpretation
T	1	true (always)
F	0	false (always)
HI	not(C).not(Z)	higher (unsigned)
LS	C+Z	less than or same (unsigned)
CC (HS)	not(C)	carry clear (unsigned)
CS (LO)	C	carry set (unsigned)
NE	not(Z)	not equal
EQ	Z	equal
VC	not(V)	overflow clear
VS	V	overflow set
PL	not(N)	plus
MI	N	minus
GE	not(N xor V)	greater than or equal (signed)
LT	N xor V	less than (signed)
GT	not(Z+(N xor V))	greater than
LE	Z+(N xor V)	less than or equal

A.3 68000 instruction set summary

In Fig.A.2 (below) the instruction set of the 68000 MPU is given in alphabetic order. The effect of each instruction on the CCR flags is supplied, together with an indication of whether or not the instruction is privileged (i.e., can only be executed while the 68000 is in supervisor mode). Within the condition code list, the following key is used:

x : flag is affected
u : flag is undefined
— : flag is unaffected
0 : flag is reset to zero
1 : flag is set to one

The privileged instruction column (P) uses the following key:

    n : not a privileged instruction
    y : privileged instruction
    ? : privileged under certain conditions

If a '?' does appear in the 'P' column, reference should be made to Chap.2 in order to determine which special cases can occur.

		X N Z V C	P
ABCD	Add decimal with extend	x u x u x	n
ADD	Add	x x x x x	n
	(When destination is 'An')	- - - - -	n
ADDQ	Add quick	x x x x x	n
ADDX	Add with extend	x x x x x	n
AND	Logical AND	- x x 0 0	?
ASL	Arithmetic shift left	x x x x x	n
ASR	Arithmetic shift right	x x x x x	n
Bcc	Branch conditionally	- - - - -	n
BCHG	Bit test and change	- - x - -	n
BCLR	Bit test and clear	- - x - -	n
BRA	Branch always	- - - - -	n
BSET	Bit test and set	- - x - -	n
BSR	Branch to subroutine	- - - - -	n
BTST	Bit test	- - x - -	n
CHK	Check reg. against bounds	- x u u u	n
CLR	Clear operand	- 0 1 0 0	n
CMP	Compare	- x x x x	n
CMPM	Compare memory	- x x x x	n
DBcc	Dec. and branch cond.	- - - - -	n
DBRA	Decrement and branch always	- - - - -	n
DIVS	Signed divide	- x x x 0	n
DIVU	Unsigned divide	- x x x 0	n
EOR	Exclusive OR	- x x 0 0	?
EXG	Exchange registers	- - - - -	n
EXT	Sign extend	- x x 0 0	n
JMP	Jump	- - - - -	n
JSR	Jump to subroutine	- - - - -	n
LEA	Load effective address	- - - - -	n
LINK	Link stack	- - - - -	n
LSL	Logical shift left	x x x 0 x	n
LSR	Logical shift right	x x x 0 x	n
MOVE	Move	- x x 0 0	n
	(When dest. is 'An')	- - - - -	n
	(When dest. is 'CCR')	x x x x x	n
	(When src. is 'SR')	- - - - -	n
	(When dest. is 'SR')	x x x x x	y
	(When 'USP' used)	- - - - -	y
MOVEM	Move multiple registers	- - - - -	n

		X	N	Z	V	C	P
MOVEP	Move peripheral data	–	–	–	–	–	n
MOVEQ	Move quick	–	x	x	0	0	n
MULS	Signed multiply	–	x	x	0	0	n
MULU	Unsigned multiply	–	x	x	0	0	n
NBCD	Negate decimal with extend	x	u	x	u	x	n
NEG	Negate	x	x	x	x	x	n
NEGX	Negate with extend	x	x	x	x	x	n
NOP	No operation	–	–	–	–	–	n
NOT	One's complement	–	x	x	0	0	n
OR	Logical OR	–	x	x	0	0	?
PEA	Push effective address	–	–	–	–	–	n
RESET	Reset external devices	–	–	–	–	–	y
ROL	Rotate left	–	x	x	0	x	n
ROR	Rotate right	–	x	x	0	x	n
ROXL	Rotate left through extend	x	x	x	0	x	n
ROXR	Rotate right through extend	x	x	x	0	x	n
RTE	Return from exception	x	x	x	x	x	y
RTR	Return and restore CCR	x	x	x	x	x	n
RTS	Return from subroutine	–	–	–	–	–	n
SBCD	Subtract decimal with extend	x	u	x	u	x	n
Scc	Set conditional	–	–	–	–	–	n
STOP	Stop	x	x	x	x	x	y
SUB	Subtract	x	x	x	x	x	n
	(When destination is 'An')	–	–	–	–	–	n
SUBQ	Subtract quick	x	x	x	x	x	n
SUBX	Subtract with extend	x	x	x	x	x	n
SWAP	Swap data register halves	–	x	x	0	0	n
TAS	Test and set bit 7	–	x	x	0	0	n
TRAP	Trap	–	–	–	–	–	n
TRAPV	Trap on overflow	–	–	–	–	–	n
TST	Test	–	x	x	0	0	n
UNLK	Unlink	–	–	–	–	–	n

Figure A.2 68000 instruction set summary

Appendix B – QL SYSTEM CALL SUMMARY

Given here is a list of all the QDOS system 'TRAP#n' calls, and 'vectored' utility calls, described in detail in Chapters 4 to 7. The trap code for trap calls #1 to #3 are passed in register 'DO'. There are a number of other calls and utilities available which are of use when, for example, writing device drivers for external I/O (on extension cards). These have not been previously discussed and are not listed below, as they are outside the scope of this text.

		TRAP #1 MACHINE RESOURCE MANAGEMENT	
MNEMONIC	CODE (hex.)	CODE (den.)	DESCRIPTION
MT.INF	0	0	Get system information
MT.CJOB	1	1	Create a job in TPA
MT.JINF	2	2	Get job information
MT.RJOB	4	4	Remove inactive job from TPA
MT.FRJOB	5	5	Force remove job(s) from TPA
MT.FREE	6	6	Length of largest space in TPA
MT.TRAPV	7	7	Set job trap vector pointer
MT.SUSJB	8	8	Suspend a job
MT.RELJB	9	9	Release a job & re-schedule
MT.ACTIV	A	10	Activate a job
MT.PRIOR	B	11	Change job priority
MT.ALRES	E	14	Allocate resident procedure area
MT.RERES	F	15	Release resident procedure area
MT.DMODE	10	16	Set/read display mode
MT.IPCOM	11	17	IPC command (kbd row scan, sound)
MT.BAUD	12	18	Set baud rate
MT.RCLCK	13	19	Read real-time clock
MT.SCLCK	14	20	Set real-time clock
MT.ACLCK	15	21	Adjust real-time clock
MT.ALCHP	18	24	Allocate common heap area
MT.RECHP	19	25	Release common heap area

TRAP #2 INPUT/OUTPUT ALLOCATION			
MNEMONIC	CODE (hex.)	CODE (den.)	DESCRIPTION
IO.OPEN	1	1	Open a channel
IO.CLOSE	2	2	Close a channel
IO.FORMT	3	3	Format a sectored medium
IO.DELET	4	4	Delete a file

TRAP #3 INPUT/OUTPUT OPERATIONS			
MNEMONIC	CODE (hex.)	CODE (den.)	DESCRIPTION
IO.PEND	0	0	Check for pending input
IO.FBYTE	1	1	Fetch a byte
IO.FLINE	2	2	Fetch a line (terminator LF)
IO.FSTRG	3	3	Fetch a string of bytes
IO.EDLIN	4	4	Edit a line (console only)
IO.SBYTE	5	5	Send a byte
IO.SSTRG	7	7	Send a string of bytes
IO.EXTOP	9	9	Call an extended operation
SD.PXENQ	A	10	Return window size & cursor position in pixel coords.
SD.CHENQ	B	11	Return window size & cursor position in character coords.
SD.BORDR	C	12	Set border width & colour
SD.WDEF	D	13	Define window
SD.CURE	E	14	Enable cursor
SD.CURS	F	15	Suppress cursor
SD.POS	10	16	Move cursor absolute (char.)
SD.TAB	11	17	Tabulate
SD.NL	12	18	Newline
SD.PCOL	13	19	Cursor back
SD.NCOL	14	20	Cursor forward
SD.PROW	15	21	Cursor up
SD.NROW	16	22	Cursor down
SD.PIXP	17	23	Move cursor absolute (pixel)
SD.SCROL	18	24	Scroll entire window
SD.SCRTP	19	25	Scroll top of window
SD.SCRBT	1A	26	Scroll bottom of window
SD.PAN	1B	27	Pan entire window
SD.PANLN	1E	30	Pan cursor line
SD.PANRT	1F	31	Pan RHS of cursor line
SD.CLEAR	20	32	Clear entire window
SD.CLRTP	21	33	Clear top of window
SD.CLRBT	22	34	Clear bottom of window
SD.CLRLN	23	35	Clear cursor line

SD.CLRRT	24	36	Clear RHS of cursor line
SD.FONT	25	37	Set/reset character font
SD.RECOL	26	38	Re-colour a window
SD.SETPA	27	39	Set paper colour
SD.SETST	28	40	Set strip colour
SD.SETIN	29	41	Set ink colour
SD.SETFL	2A	42	Set/reset flash
SD.SETUL	2B	43	Set/reset underscore
SD.SETMD	2C	44	Set writing/plotting mode
SD.SETSZ	2D	45	Set character size
SD.FILL	2E	46	Fill rectangle
SD.POINT	30	48	Plot a point
SD.LINE	31	49	Plot a line
SD.ARC	32	50	Plot an arc
SD.ELIPS	33	51	Plot an ellipse
SD.SCALE	34	52	Set scale
SD.FLOOD	35	53	Set/reset area flood
SD.GCUR	36	54	Set graphic cursor position
FS.CHECK	40	64	Check pending file operations
FS.FLUSH	41	65	Flush file buffers
FS.POSAB	42	66	Set file pointer absolute
FS.POSRE	43	67	Set file pointer relative
FS.MDINF	45	69	Get medium information
FS.HEADS	46	70	Set file header
FS.HEADR	47	71	Read file header
FS.LOAD	48	72	Load a file
FS.SAVE	49	73	Save a file

VECTORED UTILITY ROUTINES			
MNEMONIC	VECTOR (hex.)	VECTOR (den.)	DESCRIPTION
UT.WINDW	C4	196	Set window using name
UT.CON	C6	198	Set up console window
UT.SCR	C8	200	Set up screen window
UT.ERRO	CA	202	Write error message to channel 0
UT.ERR	CC	204	Write error message to channel n
UT.MINT	CE	206	Convert integer to ASCII and write it to channel n.
UT.MTEXT	D0	208	Send message to channel n
UT.CSTR	E6	230	Compare two strings
CN.DATE	EC	236	Get date and time
CN.DAY	EE	238	Get day of week
CN.FTOD	F0	240	Convert floating point to ASCII
CN.ITOD	F2	242	Convert integer to ASCII
CN.ITOBB	F4	244	Convert byte to ASCII
CN.ITOBW	F6	246	Convert word to ASCII
CN.ITOBL	F8	248	Convert long-word to ASCII
CN.ITOHB	FA	250	Convert byte to hex. ASCII

CN.ITOHW	FC	252	Convert word to hex. ASCII
CN.ITOHL	FE	254	Convert long-word to hex. ASCII
CN.DTOF	100	256	Convert ASCII to floating point
CN.DTOI	102	258	Convert ASCII to integer
CN.BTOIB	104	260	Convert ASCII to byte
CN.BTOIW	106	262	Convert ASCII to word
CN.BTOIL	108	264	Convert ASCII to long-word
CN.HTOIB	10A	266	Convert hex. ASCII to byte
CN.HTOIW	10C	268	Convert hex. ASCII to word
CN.HTOIL	10E	270	Convert hex. ASCII to long-word
RI.EXEC	11C	284	Execute single arithmetic op.
RI.EXECB	11E	286	Execute list of arithmetic ops.

The four Microdrive support utilities mentioned at the end of Chapter 3 are not included here, as they are outside the scope of this book. They would normally be used for direct sector reading, writing, and verification.

Appendix C – 'QDOS' SYSTEM ERROR CODES

The QDOS system recognises 21 standard error conditions. These error conditions may occur (and be reported) either from within a SuperBASIC program or an assembly language program. In the latter case the error code is returned in register 'DO', as shown in Chapters 4 to 7 of Part 2 (QL System Procedures). All error codes are 'long words' (i.e., 32 bits). The system errors are:

MNEMONIC	VALUE	DESCRIPTION
ERR.NC	-1	Operation not complete
ERR.NJ	-2	Not a valid job
ERR.OM	-3	Out of memory
ERR.OR	-4	Out of range
ERR.BO	-5	Buffer overflow
ERR.NO	-6	Channel not open
ERR.NF	-7	File, device, variable or procedure not found
ERR.EX	-8	File already exists
ERR.IU	-9	File (or device) in use
ERR.EF	-10	End of file
ERR.DF	-11	Drive full
ERR.BN	-12	Bad device or procedure name
ERR.TE	-13	Transmission error
ERR.FF	-14	Format failed
ERR.BP	-15	Bad parameter
ERR.FE	-16	File error
ERR.XP	-17	Expression error
ERR.OV	-18	Arithmetic overflow
ERR.NI	-19	Not implemented (yet)
ERR.RO	-20	Read only
ERR.BL	-21	Bad line syntax (SuperBASIC)

Note that all the error code values are small negative integers. This structure enables standard error codes to be distinguished clearly from pointers to specific device-driver error messages, as the latter are passed as (pointer.to.message - $8000).

Appendix D – EDITOR/ ASSEMBLER QUICK REFERENCE GUIDE

The editor and assembler packages are discussed in Chapters 13 and 14. Given here are quick reference guides for their use.

EDITOR REFERENCE GUIDE

a) Top level commands:

```
^E  -  Execute extended command:
    -  D  -  Delete block (marker to cursor inclusive)
    -  F  -  Find text string
    -  I  -  Include external file (at cursor)
    -  M  -  Move to line absolute
^F  -  Finish - return to SuperBASIC
^H  -  Give help on cursor control and deletion commands
^L  -  Load a file in from Microdrive
^M  -  Set current cursor line as marker line
^S  -  Save editor buffer on to Microdrive
```

b) Cursor control commands:

KEY	NORMAL	SHIFT	ALTMODE
up	line	page	start of text
down	line	page	end of text
left	character	word	start of line
right	character	word	end of line

c) Text deletion commands:

KEY	CTRL
up/down	delete current line
left	delete char/gap left
right	delete cursor char/gap

ASSEMBLER/LOCATOR REFERENCE GUIDE

a) Comments:

Must be preceded by a semi-colon (;)

b) Labels:

Must be followed by a colon (:)

c) Directives:

i)	*EJECT	– Force a new page
ii)	*HEADING	– Create new heading and new page
iii)	*LIST \<on/off>	– Switch listing file on/off
iv)	*NUMBER \<on/off>	– Switch line numbers on/off
v)	*INCLUDE \<file>	– Include external source file

d) Pseudo-operators:

i)	EQU (=)	– Static equate
ii)	QRY	– Dynamic equate
iii)	ORG	– Set program counter
iv)	ALIGN	– Align to word boundary
v)	COND \<expr>	– Conditional assembly
	ELSE	
	ENDC	

e) Expression operators:

+	add	SHR	shift right
–	subtract	SHL	shift left
*	multiply	OR	logical 'or'
/	divide	AND	logical 'and'
		NOT	ones's complement

INDEX

QL
Editor/Assembler